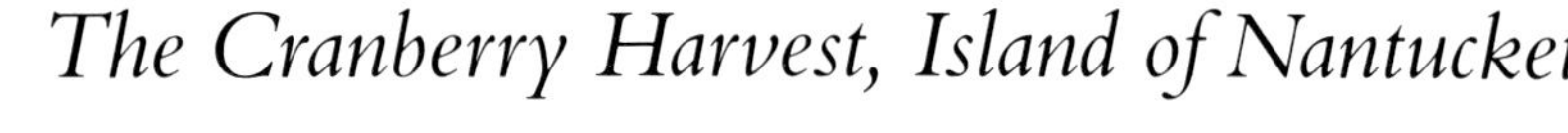

The Cranberry Harvest, Island of Nantucket

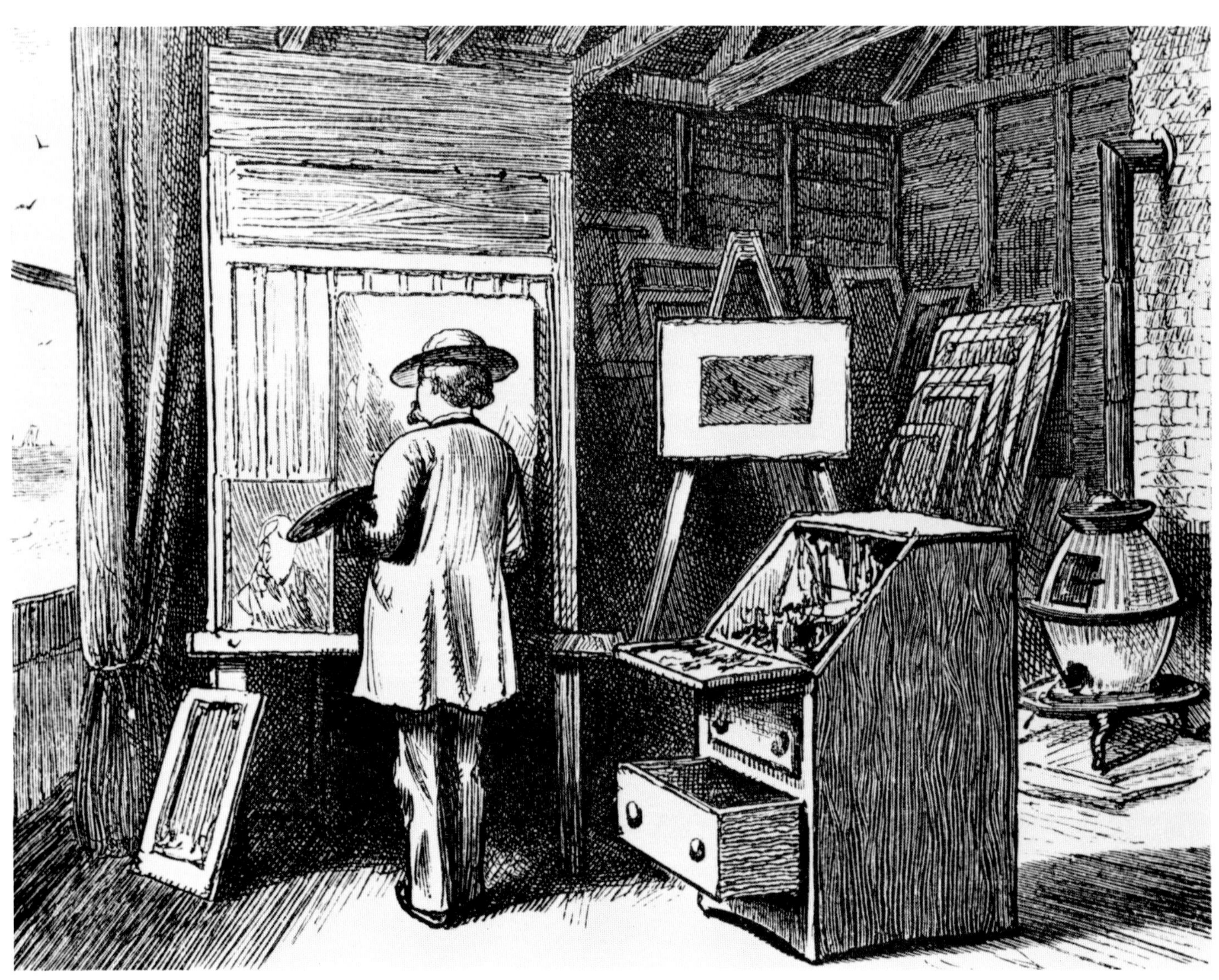

Marc Simpson

Sally Mills

Patricia Hills

Eastman Johnson

The Cranberry Harvest, Island of Nantucket

25th Anniversary Exhibition

Timken Art Gallery

San Diego, California · 1990

This catalogue has been published in conjunction with the exhibition *Eastman Johnson: The Cranberry Harvest, Island of Nantucket*

Timken Art Gallery
April 15–June 24, 1990

The Fine Arts Museums of San Francisco
July 5–September 16, 1990

Yale University Art Gallery
September 29–December 9, 1990

The exhibition has been organized by the Timken Art Gallery.

This project is made possible by a generous grant from the National Endowment for the Arts, a federal agency.

Printed in the United States of America.

ISBN: 0-9610866-9-6

Cover: Eastman Johnson, *The Cranberry Harvest, Island of Nantucket.*
Page 2: *Eastman Johnson's Studio*, ca. 1875. Wood engraving in Charles Nordhoff, "Cape Cod, Nantucket, and the Vineyard," *Harper's New Monthly Magazine* 51, no. 3301 (June 1875): 65.

Publication Coordinator: Hal Fischer
Editor: Fronia Simpson
Designer: Lilli Cristin

Typeset in Bembo by Andresen Typographics, Tucson. 3000 copies were lithographed on Quintessence Book and Cover by Typecraft, Inc., Pasadena.

Contents

Acknowledgments

Eastman Johnson: The Cranberry Harvest, Island of Nantucket is the fourth in a series of exhibitions which has been developed to increase awareness and understanding of significant works in the collection of the Putnam Foundation. The exhibition and accompanying catalogue have benefited from the expertise and skill of many individuals. We are indebted to Marc Simpson, The Ednah Root Curator of American Paintings at The Fine Arts Museums of San Francisco, for the scholarship and knowledge he has brought to this project. For the comprehensiveness and insight of their contributions to the exhibition catalogue, we wish to thank Sally Mills, Associate Curator of American Art at The Fine Arts Museums of San Francisco, and Patricia Hills, Professor and Director of Museum Studies at Boston University.

The authors have asked me to thank a number of institutions and individuals who were invaluable in supplying information and research opportunities: Addison Gallery of American Art—Jock Reynolds, Susan Faxon, Nicki Thiras; Archives of American Art, New England and West Coast Regional Centers, Smithsonian Institution—Robert F. Brown and Paul J. Karlstrom, Jack von Euw, Victoria Ricciarelli; Joan Barnes; Boston Atheneum; Boston Public Library; The Brooklyn Museum—Teresa A. Carbone, Deborah Wythe; Coe Kerr Gallery—Odile Duff; The Fine Arts Museums of San Francisco—Catherine A. Johnson, Joseph McDonald, Jerry Smith, James M. Wright; Frick Art Museum—Alan Fausel; Deborah Gardner; Isabella Stewart Gardner Museum—Karen Haas; Abigail Booth Gerdts; Michael Hall; Inventory of American Paintings, Smithsonian Institution; Kennedy Galleries—Lawrence Fleischman, Lillian Brenwasser; M. Knoedler & Co., Inc.—Melissa De Medeiros; The Library, University of California, Berkeley; Library of Congress; Library of the National Museum of American Art/National Portrait Gallery, Smithsonian Institution; James Maroney; Professor Angela Miller; Nantucket Atheneum Library—Barbara P. Andrews; Nantucket Historical Association—Jacqueline Kolle Haring; Nantucket Registrar of Deeds; Newhouse Galleries—Meg Newhouse; New York Public Library—Robert Rainwater; Kim O'Dell; Meg Perlman;

Nancy Ames Petersen
Director, Timken Art Gallery

Carl H. Pforzheimer, Jr.; Philadelphia Museum of Art—Anne d'Harnoncourt, Darrel Sewell, Ellen Doney; Santa Barbara Museum of Art—Barry Heisler; Fronia W. Simpson; Theodore E. Stebbins, Jr.; D. Dodge Thompson; June Tracy; Mary Crawford Volk; Alan Wallach; and Stephen E. Weil.

Eastman Johnson: The Cranberry Harvest, Island of Nantucket would not have been feasible without the cooperation of the public institutions and private lenders who so graciously made their paintings available for exhibition in San Diego, San Francisco, and New Haven. Also, we wish to acknowledge Harry S. Parker III, Director, The Fine Arts Museums of San Francisco, and Mary Neill, Director, Yale University Art Gallery, for their participation in this project.

For their efforts on behalf of the exhibition, I wish to thank the following individuals: Hal Fischer, who coordinated the exhibition and catalogue with his usual efficiency; Lilli Cristin, who once again brought her consummate skills to bear on a Timken exhibition catalogue; David Bull, whose conservation of *The Cranberry Harvest* has added greatly to our aesthetic enjoyment of this masterwork; and Victoria Harrison, Administrative Assistant, Timken Art Gallery, who consistently attended to a myriad of administrative details. Additional support has been provided by Debra Pughe, Exhibitions Manager, and Paula March, Manager of Corporate Relations, The Fine Arts Museums of San Francisco; Helen A. Cooper, Curator of American Paintings and Sculpture, and Anthony Hirschel, Assistant to the Director, Yale University Art Gallery; Fronia W. Simpson, catalogue editor; and the Balboa Art Conservation Center, San Diego.

Finally, it is with sincere appreciation that we acknowledge the National Endowment for the Arts, a federal agency, for its support of this exhibition.

Lenders to the Exhibition

The Ackland Art Museum, The University of North Carolina at Chapel Hill

Addison Gallery of American Art, Phillips Academy, Andover

Art Museum, Arizona State University, Tempe

Childs Gallery, New York & Boston

Detroit Institute of Arts

Kenneth Lux Gallery, New York

Manoogian Collection

Philadelphia Museum of Art

Private collections

Timken Art Gallery, Putnam Foundation Collection

Washington University Gallery of Art, St. Louis

Yale University Art Gallery, New Haven

The Cranberry Harvest at the Timken Art Gallery

Nancy Ames Petersen

The exhibition *Eastman Johnson: The Cranberry Harvest, Island of Nantucket* marks a milestone in our institutional history: the twenty-fifth anniversary of the Timken Art Gallery. That an exhibition and catalogue celebrating Eastman Johnson's masterwork should constitute the focus of our anniversary celebrations is eminently appropriate. From a purely popular point of view, *The Cranberry Harvest* (PLATE I) is one of the Gallery's most admired paintings. From the standpoint of connoisseurship, *The Cranberry Harvest* typifies the Putnam Foundation's commitment to acquiring and exhibiting paintings that are representative of an artist at the peak of his ability. The decision to focus on *The Cranberry Harvest* for our anniversary exhibition was predicated on the importance of this masterwork to Johnson's oeuvre and on its stature within the history of nineteenth-century American art. However, another, albeit more singular, factor came into play: the relationship of Johnson's masterwork to the Gallery's history and purpose.

The Putnam Foundation's collection of American paintings was initiated in 1964. The decision to acquire American art was unique in two respects. First, it expanded the Putnam Foundation's collecting interests beyond European old master paintings and Russian icons, which had been the concentration of the original benefactors, Misses Anne and Amy R. Putnam. Second, as the Foundation's first American art acquisition occurred just a few months before the Timken Art Gallery opened to the public, the creation of the Timken's American collection was to take place almost totally within the public sphere.

In 1969, in conjunction with San Diego's municipal bicentennial celebration, Walter Ames, founding president of the Putnam Foundation, announced the opening of a new exhibition space at the Gallery for the display of American paintings. While the Foundation's American holdings at this time numbered just three works, Ames was able to secure the long-term loan of twenty-eight American paintings from the collection of Morton C. Bradley. The announcement of this loan and the exhibition gallery at the Timken devoted to American art that appeared in the *San Diego Union* included this statement by Ames: "We are hoping that major art dealers will make us aware of important American works when they become available."[1]

Robert C. Vose, Jr., of Vose Galleries in Boston, must have received word of this announcement, for early in 1972 Vose wrote Ames offering the Putnam Foundation the opportunity to purchase *The Cranberry Harvest.* He went on to state that "this painting is the greatest by an American artist that we have handled in our one hundred thirty years in business."[2] Vose informed Ames that the price of the painting was a firm $400,000, an extraordinarily high figure for an American painting in the early 1970s.

Vose made his offer on 21 January and urged Ames to make his decision quickly, as both The Metropolitan Museum of Art and the National Gallery of Art were interested in the painting. In Chicago, the collector Daniel Terra was trying to decide if he wanted to spend that much money on an Eastman Johnson. On 11 February Ames wired Vose that he would meet the $400,000 price. The painting was acquired by Ames for the Timken Art Gallery just twenty-one days after it had been offered by Vose.

Prior to coming to San Diego, the painting was featured in a major retrospective of Johnson's work organized by Patricia Hills for the Whitney Museum of American Art. At the Whitney exhibition *The Cranberry Harvest* occupied the place of honor in the center of the main wall. Its quality and significance were widely commented on, and critics and scholars alike hailed it as one of the key works of late-nineteenth-century American painting. Interest in *The Cranberry Harvest* was no doubt stimulated by the fact that this was the first major public showing of the work in decades. A catalogue of the artist's works published in 1940 listed the painting as unlocated, suggesting that it had dropped from public view some years earlier.[3]

The circumstances surrounding the painting's twentieth-century provenance remain sketchy at best. Auguste Richard, a wealthy New Yorker, is known to have owned it by 1881. Richard died in January 1908, and in April of that year an illustration of the painting appeared in *International Studio* (FIG. 1).[4] The painting was not published again until 1969, when Bernard Bivall, a London dealer, featured the painting in an advertisement in *Connoisseur* magazine.[5] The facts that the painting resurfaced in England and that its whereabouts were unknown to American scholars for some time suggest, circumstantially, that *The Cranberry Harvest* may have left America not long after Richard's death.

The reemergence of the painting and subsequent analysis by scholars raised a provocative issue—the specter of additions to the painting by another hand. Patricia Hills was the first to point out "a crudely rendered small, background figure to the right of the standing woman." Hills went on to note that this figure was not present in a reproduction of *The Cranberry Harvest* which had appeared in Wilfred Meynell's *The Modern School of Art* of 1883 (FIG. 2).[6]

In preparation for this exhibition, Guest Curator Marc Simpson broached the subject of the painting's condition. He suggested to the Timken that this might indeed be an appropriate time to take corrective measures relative to additions thought to have been made to the painting (FIG. 3). Extremely cognizant of the seriousness of altering a work of this stature, the directors of the Putnam Foundation formed an ad hoc committee of prominent American scholars to recommend what, if any, course of action should be followed.

The committee proposed a conservation program that would address three elements. The most obvious concern was the question of removing the bent-over figure, which was not only awkwardly rendered but a distraction from the key figure of the standing woman. A second area of concern was a light green color that had been added to the middle ground. This addition altered the spatial conception, which, given the size of the figures on the hill, created a problem of scale. Finally, the varnish, which had become moderately discolored (giving the sky a yellowish cast), needed to be removed.

The Timken's advisory committee, which included Patricia Hills; Robert C. Vose; John Wilmerding, Professor of Art, Princeton University; Theodore E. Stebbins, Jr., John Moors Cabot Curator of American Painting, Museum of

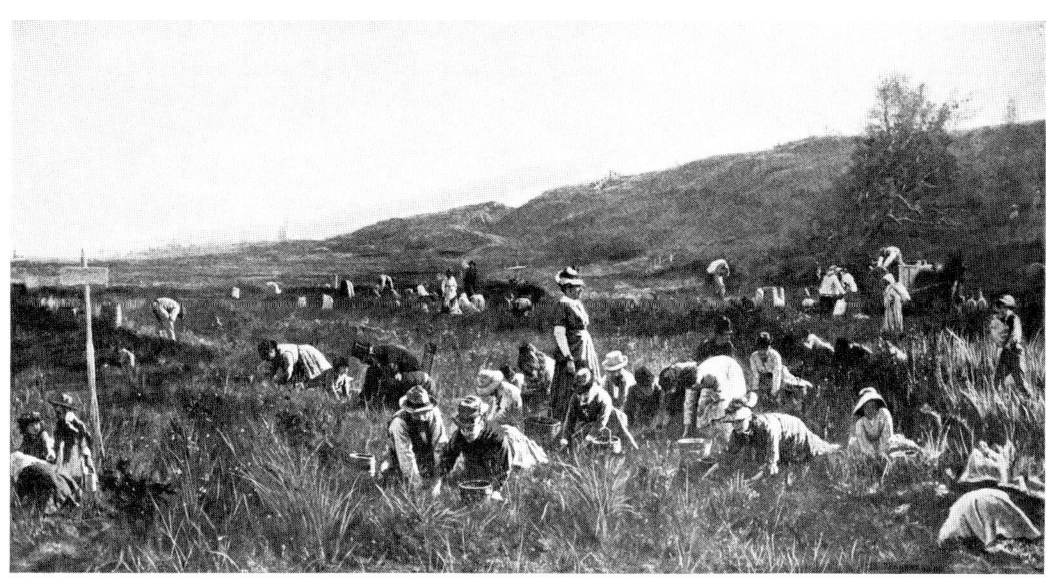

FIG. 1. After Eastman Johnson, *The Cranberry Harvest, Island of Nantucket.* Photogravure in Sadakichi Hartmann, "Eastman Johnson: American *Genre* Painter," in *The International Studio* 34, no. 134 (April 1908): 109.

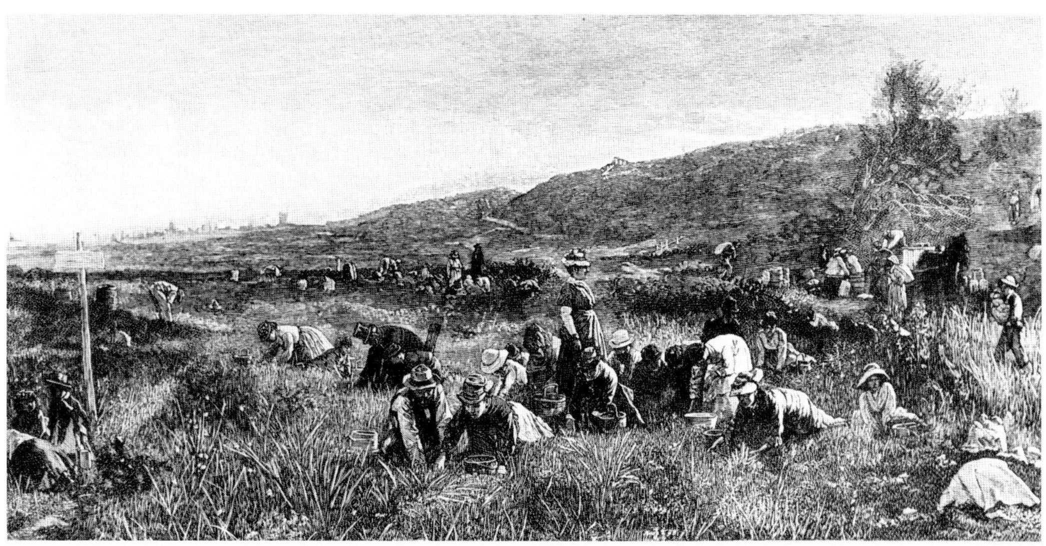

FIG. 2. After Eastman Johnson, *The Cranberry Harvest, Island of Nantucket.* Wood engraving in S. G. W. Benjamin, "A Representative American," *The Magazine of Art* 5 (1882): 489; later reprinted in Wilfred Meynell, ed., *The Modern School of Art* (New York: Cassell & Company, 1883), 227.

Fine Arts, Boston; and Grant Holcomb III, Director of the Memorial Art Gallery, Rochester, were in favor of conservation but cautioned that every effort should be made to ascertain that the additions—particularly the stooping figure—were by another hand.

The Cranberry Harvest was sent to David Bull, the Gallery's Consulting Conservator, for treatment. Bull began by removing the varnish. Under the varnish he found areas of overpainting. The solubility and appearance of this overpaint, which was noticeably different from paint known to be original, provided more evidence that the additions were made by a hand after Johnson's.

The overpaint, when removed, did not reveal damage, which normally might have been disguised in this manner. Instead, now visible were changes of mind by Eastman Johnson himself. For example, Johnson had apparently altered the sky and clump of trees on the right and the formation of the hill on the left. Earlier versions had begun to show through as *pentimenti,* and much of the overpaint probably had been added to cover these elements.

The blue figure in the middle distance appears to have been added for similar reasons. When the overpaint was removed, a ghost form of a stooping figure in exactly the same proportions and shape became visible (FIG. 4). Johnson had painted this figure out, but a ghost had begun to appear and a later hand had "solved" this problem by adding a figure to the composition in Johnson's original but rejected configuration.

Whether *pentimenti* should be retained or suppressed depends on their impact on the composition, and requires a careful assessment of how they function both aesthetically and compositionally. David Bull's treatment of *The Cranberry Harvest* has revealed some of Johnson's compositional changes of mind. The majority of *pentimenti* have been left visible because they do not aesthetically impair the composition. Happily, the removal of discolored varnish and overpaint has brought the painting to greater life. There is an increased sense of light and space, and the composition is measurably strengthened by the open space achieved by the removal of the stooping figure. The conservation reveals the emphasis

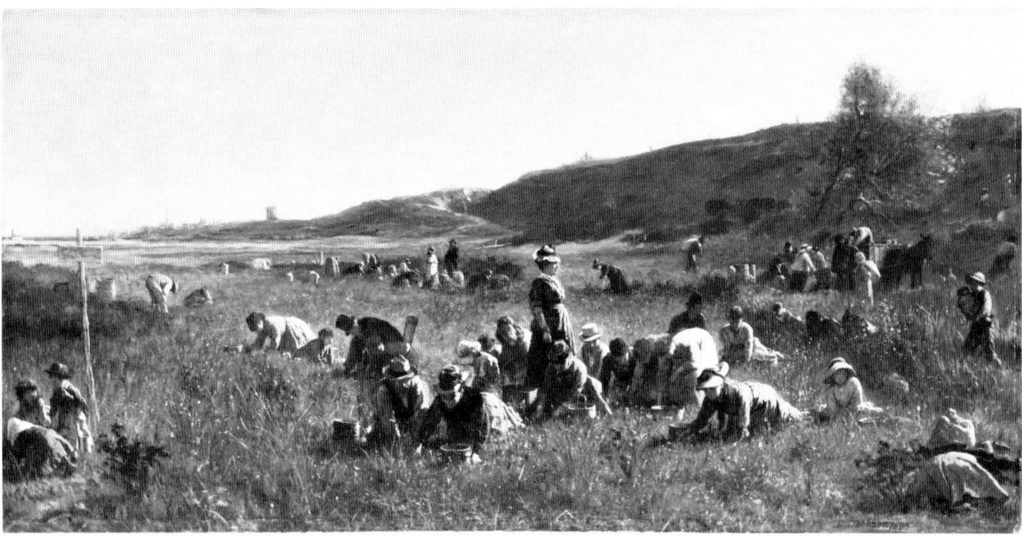

FIG. 3. Eastman Johnson, *The Cranberry Harvest, Island of Nantucket.* Before 1989 conservation treatment.

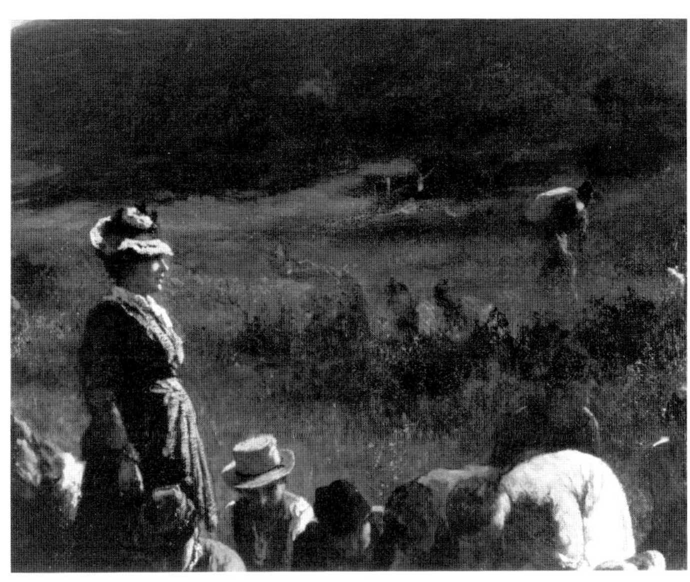

FIG. 4. Detail of Eastman Johnson, *The Cranberry Harvest, Island of Nantucket,* showing *pentimenti* revealed in 1989 conservation treatment.

Johnson put on the main standing figure, and how he reinforced her prominence with a stronger outline.

Subsequent to its showing in San Diego, *Eastman Johnson: The Cranberry Harvest, Island of Nantucket* will be on view at the M. H. de Young Memorial Museum in San Francisco and the Yale University Art Gallery in New Haven. It is worth noting that *The Cranberry Harvest* has not been on loan in over six years. In 1980 the painting was lent to the National Gallery of Art for the exhibition *American Light: The Luminist Movement,* which inaugurated the opening of the National Gallery's East Wing. Sending *The Cranberry Harvest* to the National Gallery altered a fifteen-year-old policy prohibiting the loan of works from the collection of the Putnam Foundation. Then in 1983 the painting was seen in Boston, Washington, D.C., and Paris as part of the exhibition *A New World: Masterpieces of American Painting, 1760–1910.*

We are especially pleased that *The Cranberry Harvest* is the focal point for our twenty-fifth anniversary celebration. Within our institutional history Johnson's masterwork has been a catalyst for change and growth. From the circumstances of its acquisition to the painting's role in altering our loan policy, it has been at the center of issues relating directly to our mission. Although selecting *The Cranberry Harvest* to serve as the basis of our anniversary exhibition was relatively easy, the decision to restore the work was far more difficult. How we arrived at the decision—through the counsel and advice of specialists—is indicative of how we function.

Since its inception the Timken has been fortunate to have had the support and interest of prominent art historians, museum administrators, and art dealers. Our acquisition, education, and conservation programs have benefited from the generosity and expertise of these individuals. Therefore it seems appropriate to conclude this introduction with a special recognition of the many professionals—past and present—who have helped over the last twenty-five years: Thomas Agnew; Morton C. Bradley; Richard Brettell; J. Carter Brown; David Bull; James Byam-Shaw; A. B. de Vries; Lorenz Eitner; Albert Elsen; Everett Fahy; Ernest Fiedler; Cecil Gould; Grant Holcomb III; Evelyn Joll; Al Lank; Harold McCracken; Denis Mahon; Agnes Mongan; Elizabeth Mongan; Sir John Pope-Hennessy; Richard Reilly; John Rewald; John Rorimer; David Rust; Seymour Slive; Theodore E. Stebbins, Jr.; George L. Stout; John Walker; John Walsh; Robert Wark; and John Wilmerding.

Finally, I dedicate this catalogue to Robert C. Vose, Jr. His support, efforts, and friendship have helped to foster the growth and quality of our American collection.

NOTES

[1] *San Diego Union,* 22 December 1968.

[2] Robert C. Vose, Jr., to Walter Ames, 11 February 1972, in Timken curatorial files.

[3] John I. H. Baur, *Eastman Johnson, 1824–1906: An American Genre Painter,* exh. cat. (Brooklyn: Brooklyn Museum, 1940), 57.

[4] Sadakichi Hartmann, "Eastman Johnson: American *Genre* Painter," *The International Studio* 34, no. 134 (April 1908): 109.

[5] *Connoisseur* 172, no. 693 (November 1969): lxxi.

[6] Patricia Hills, *The Genre Painting of Eastman Johnson: The Sources and Development of His Style and Themes* (New York: Garland Publishing, 1977), 153.

Plates

PLATE 1. *The Cranberry Harvest, Island of Nantucket,* 1880. Timken Art Gallery, Putnam Foundation Collection.

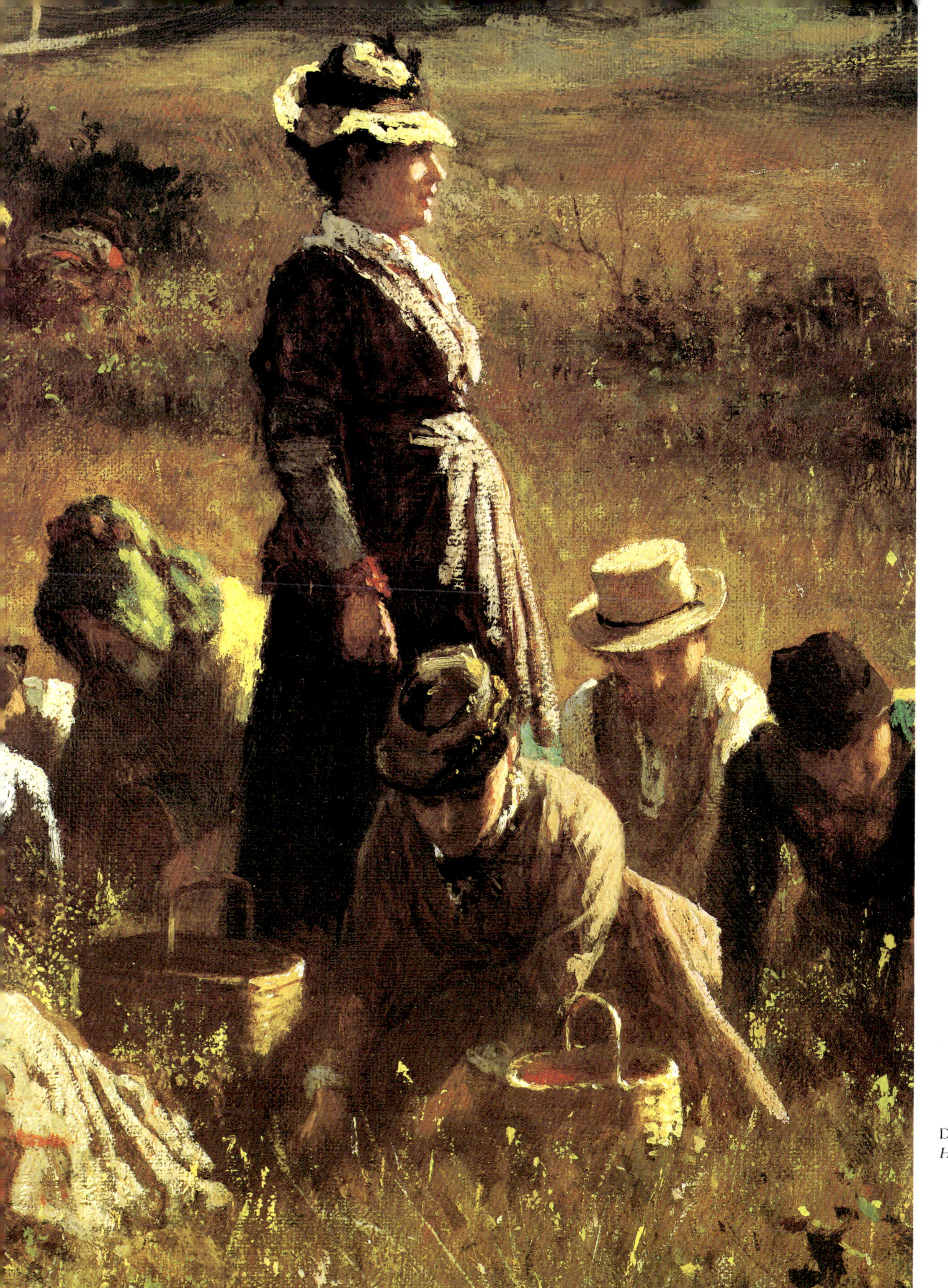

Detail of *The Cranberry Harvest*.

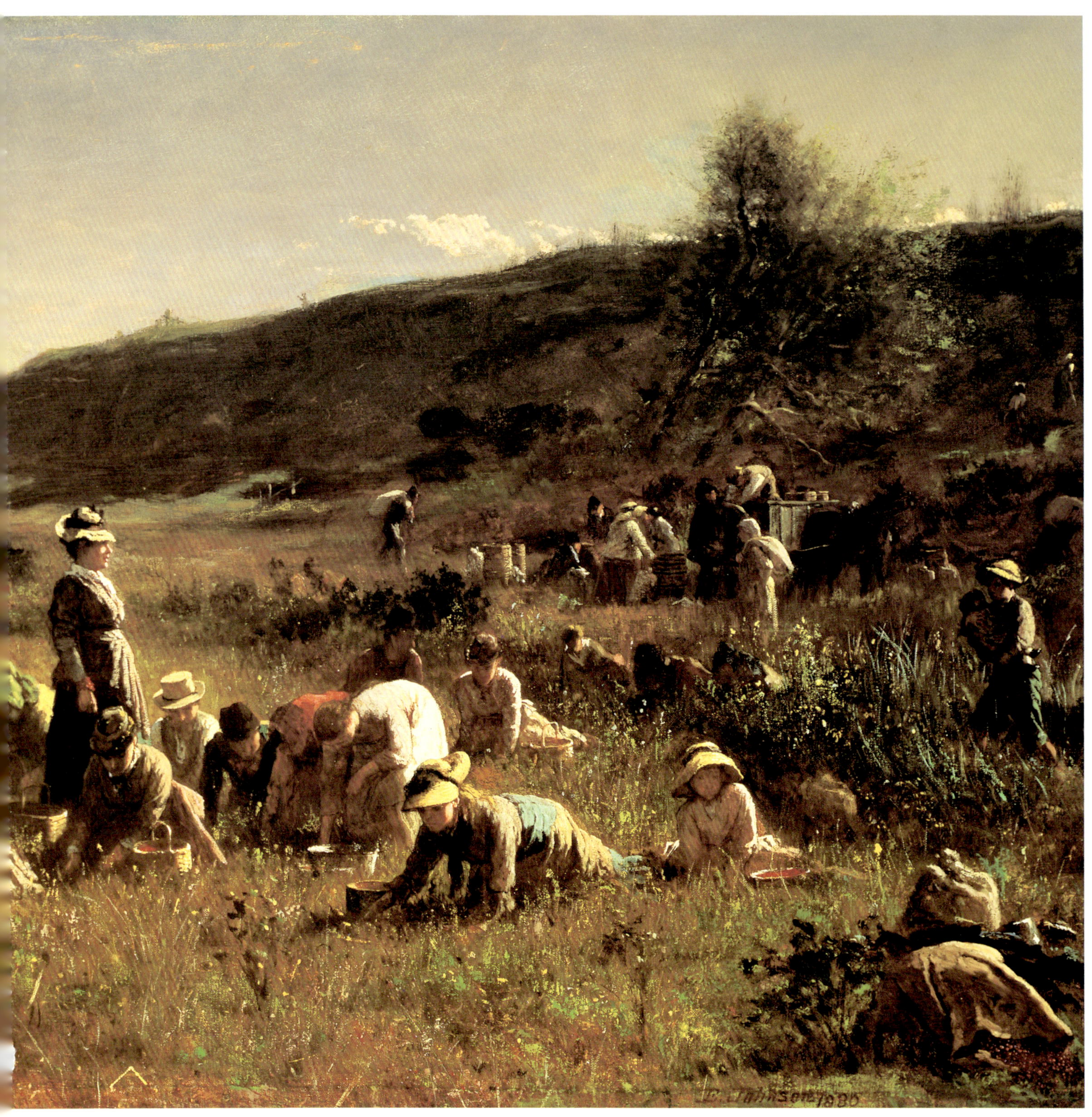

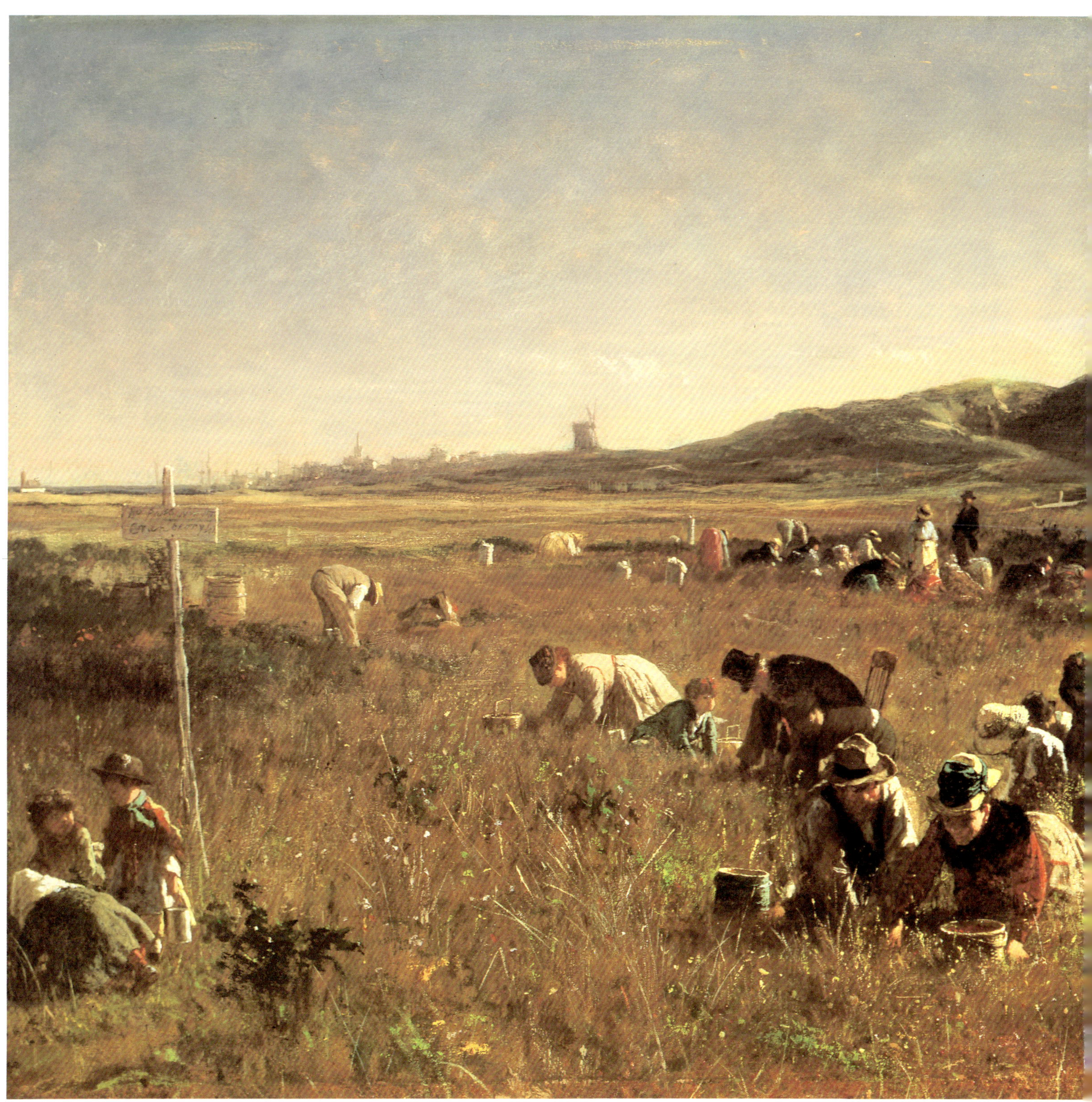

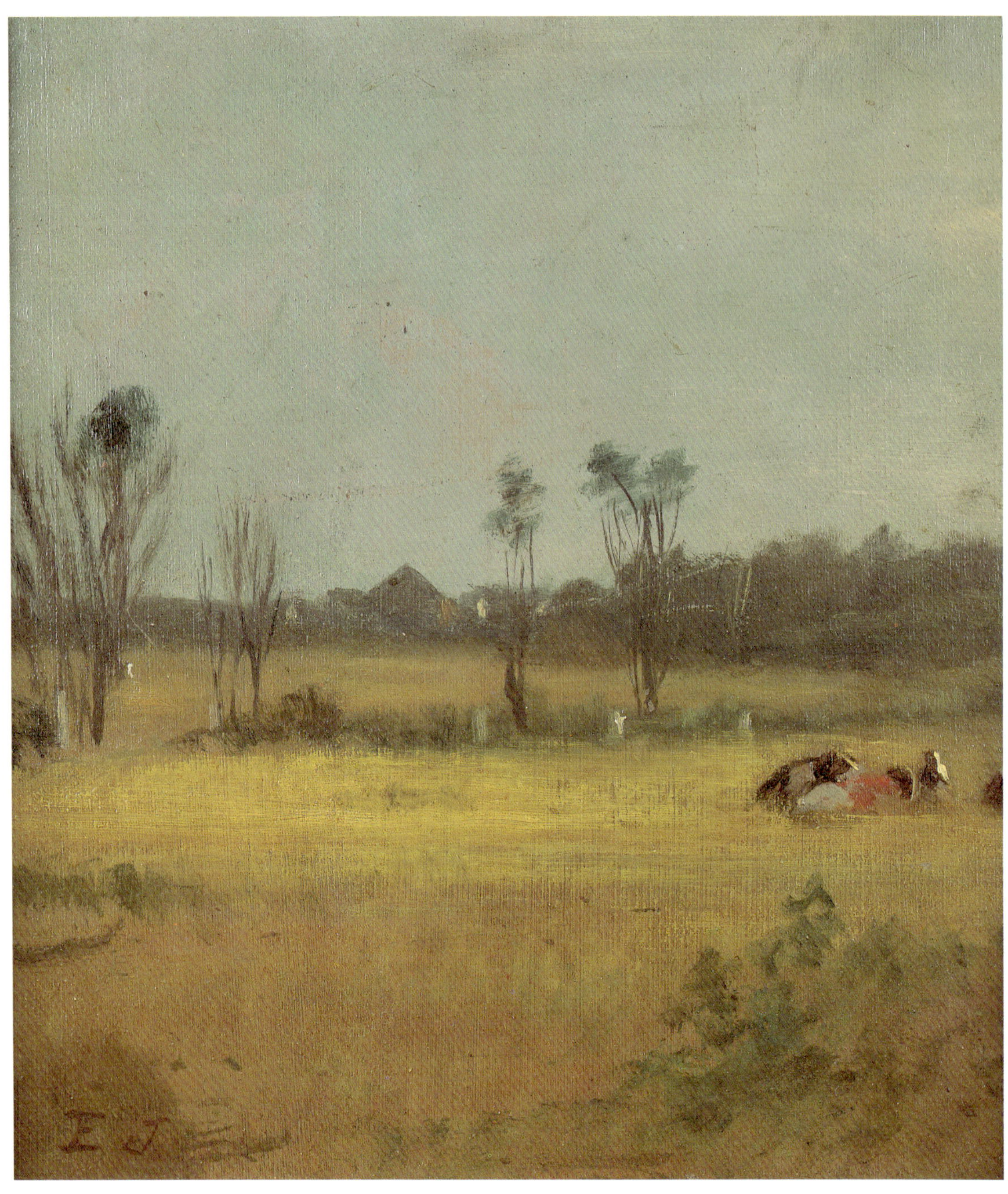

PLATE 2. *Cranberry Harvest.*
Kenneth Lux Gallery.

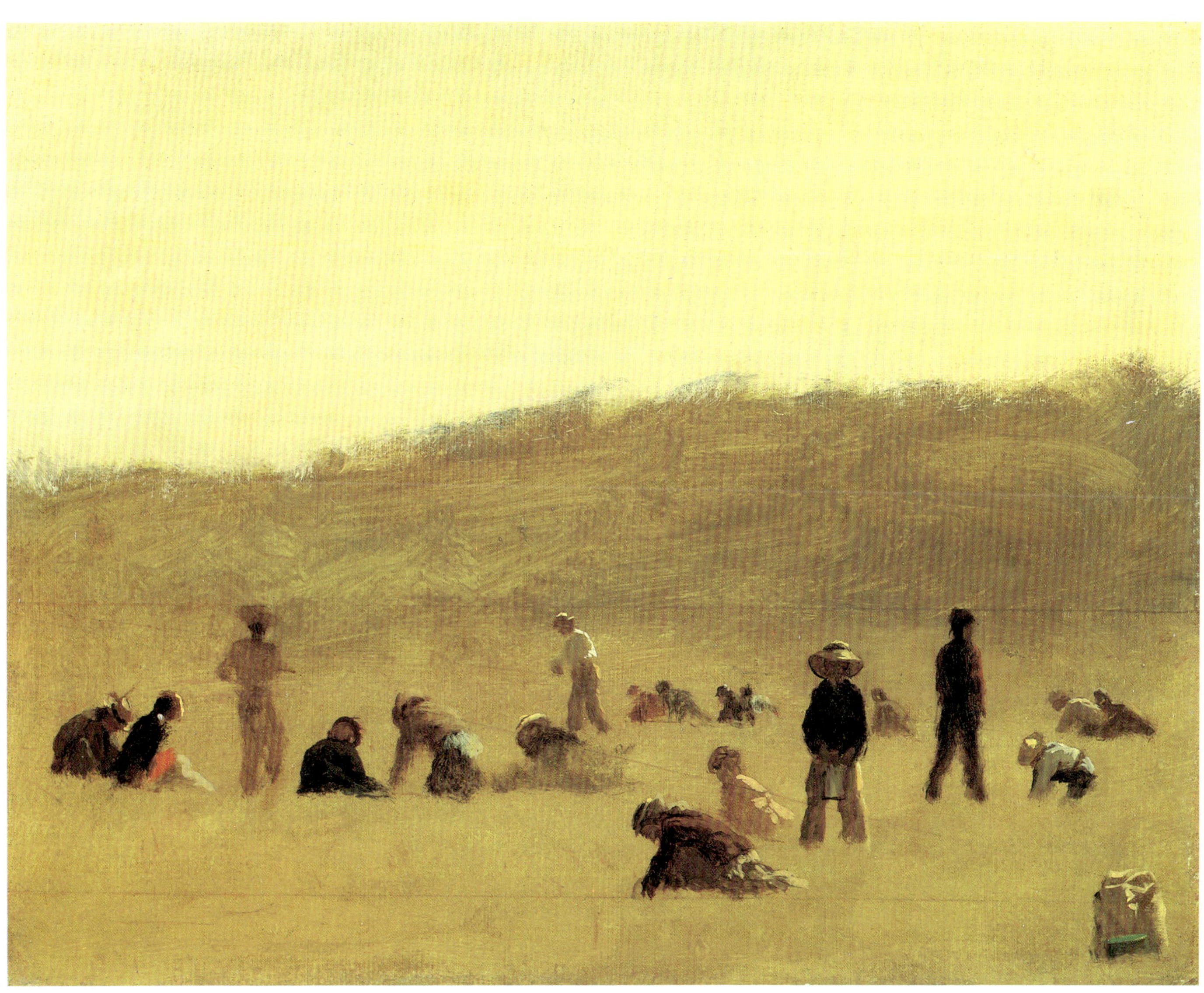

PLATE 3. *The Cranberry Pickers.*
Philadelphia Museum of Art.

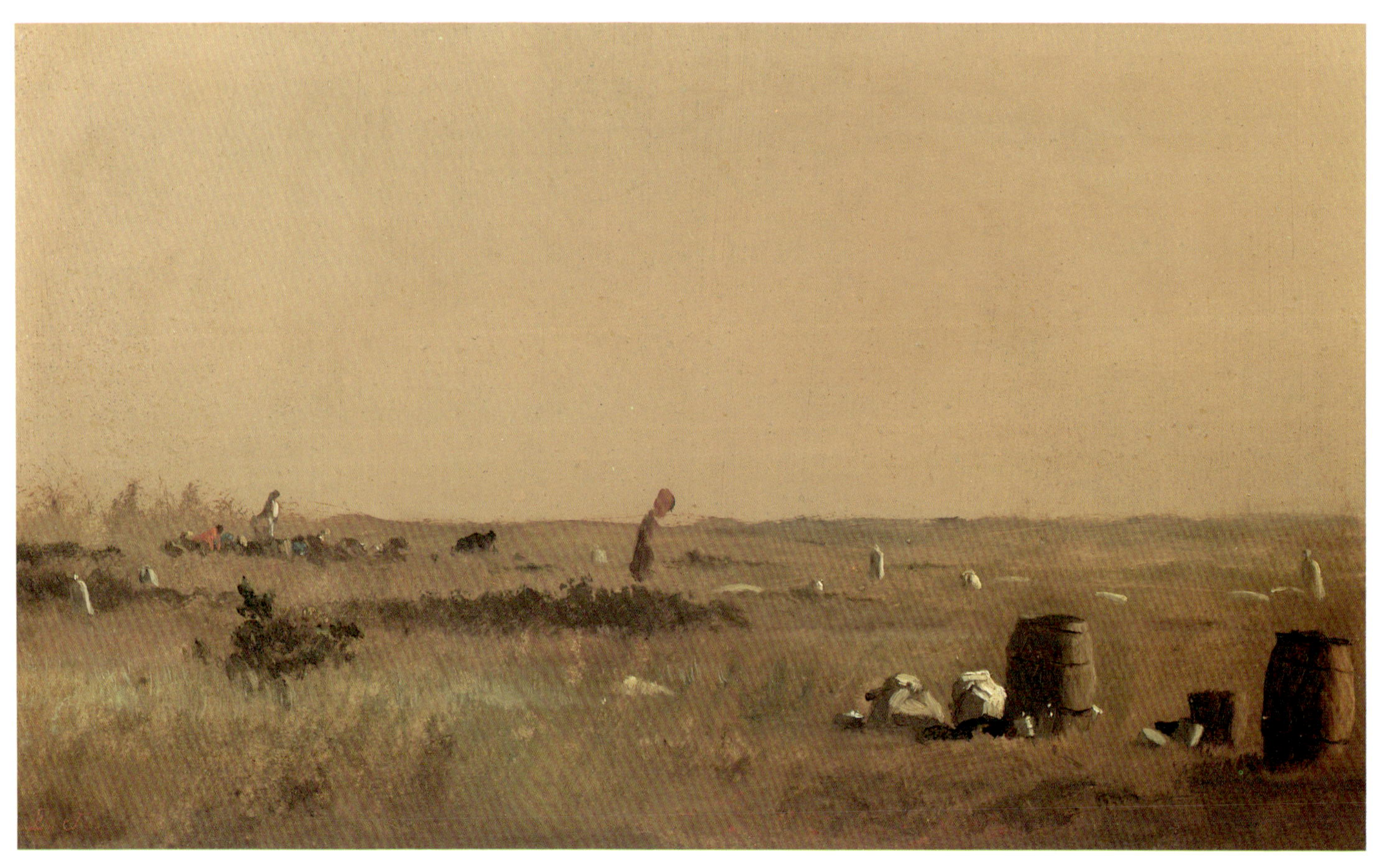

PLATE 4. *Study for "Cranberry Pickers."* Childs Gallery, New York & Boston.

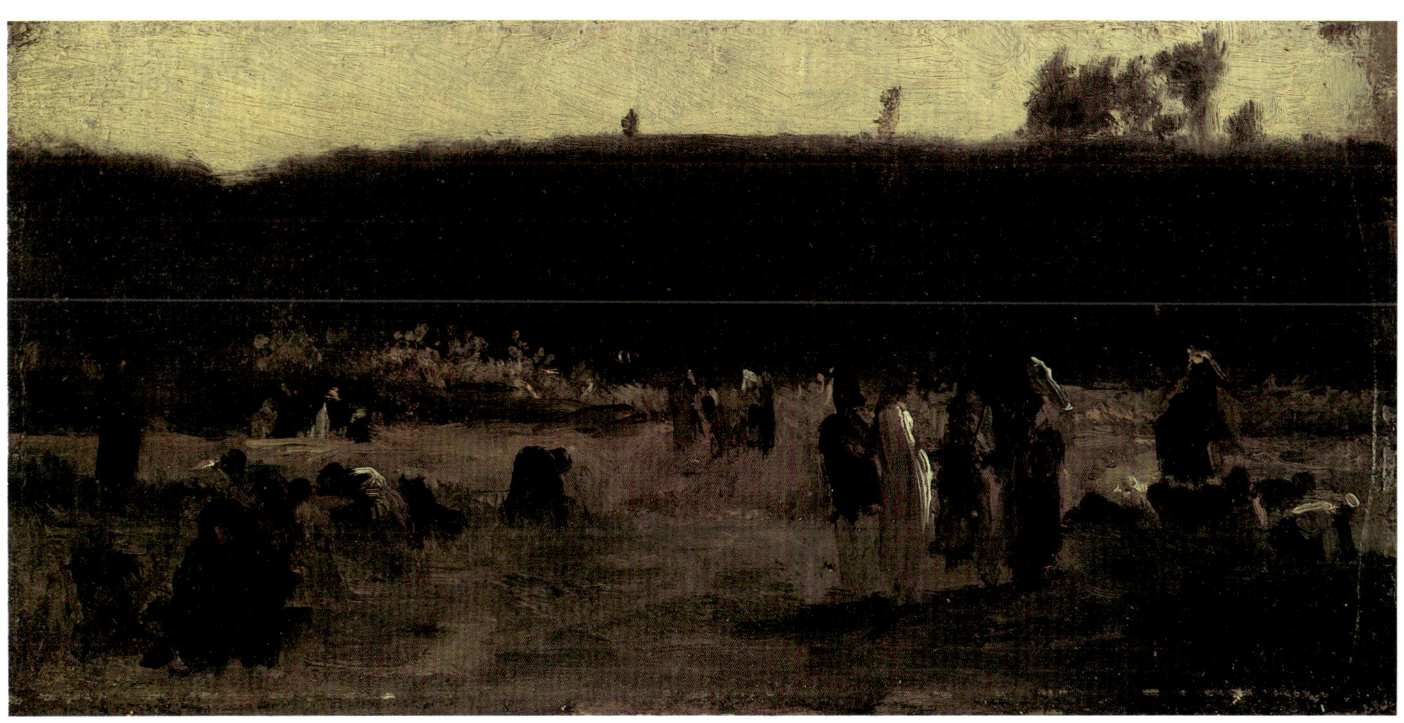

PLATE 5. *Cranberry Pickers.* The Ackland Art Museum, The University of North Carolina at Chapel Hill.

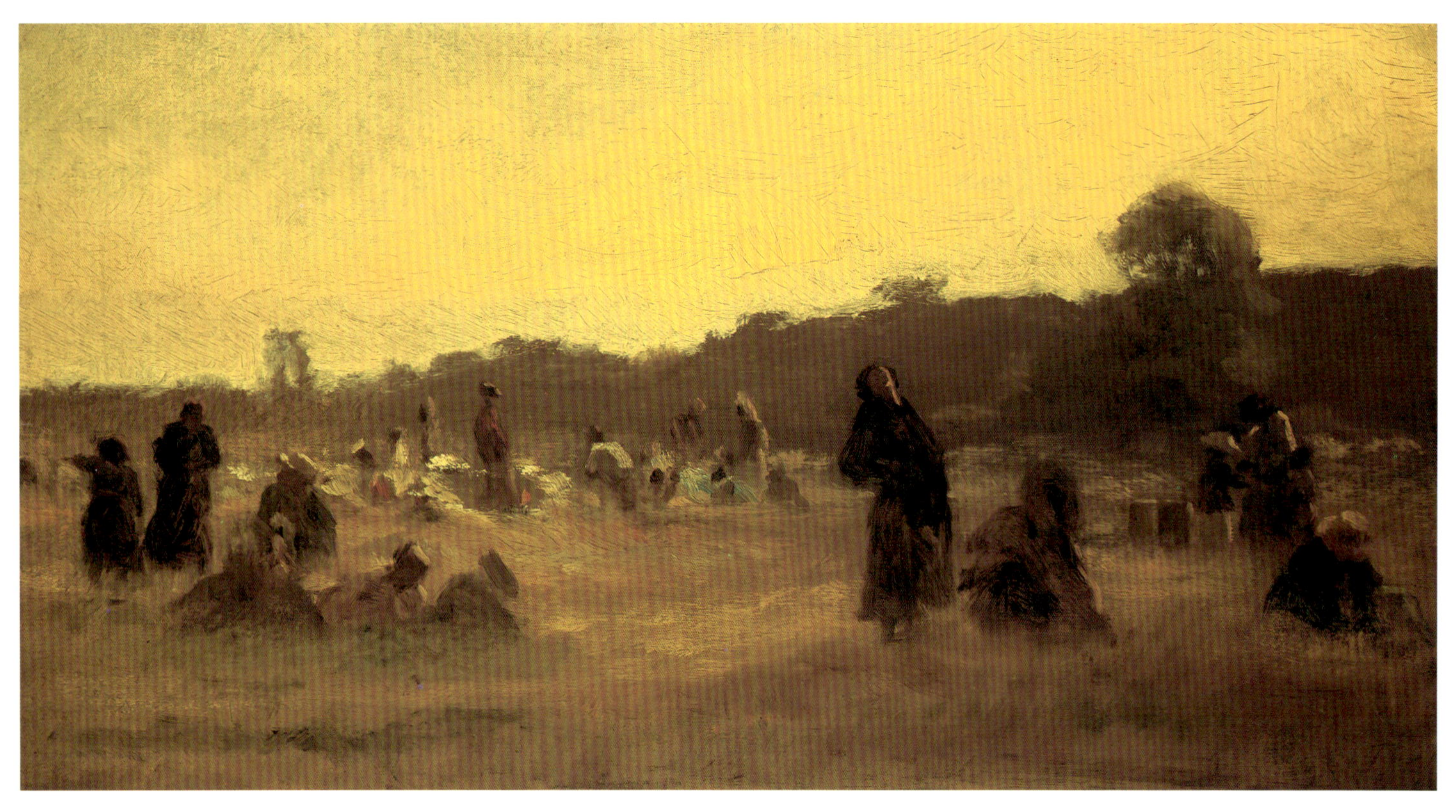

PLATE 6. *Cranberry Pickers—Study.* Washington University Gallery of Art, St. Louis.

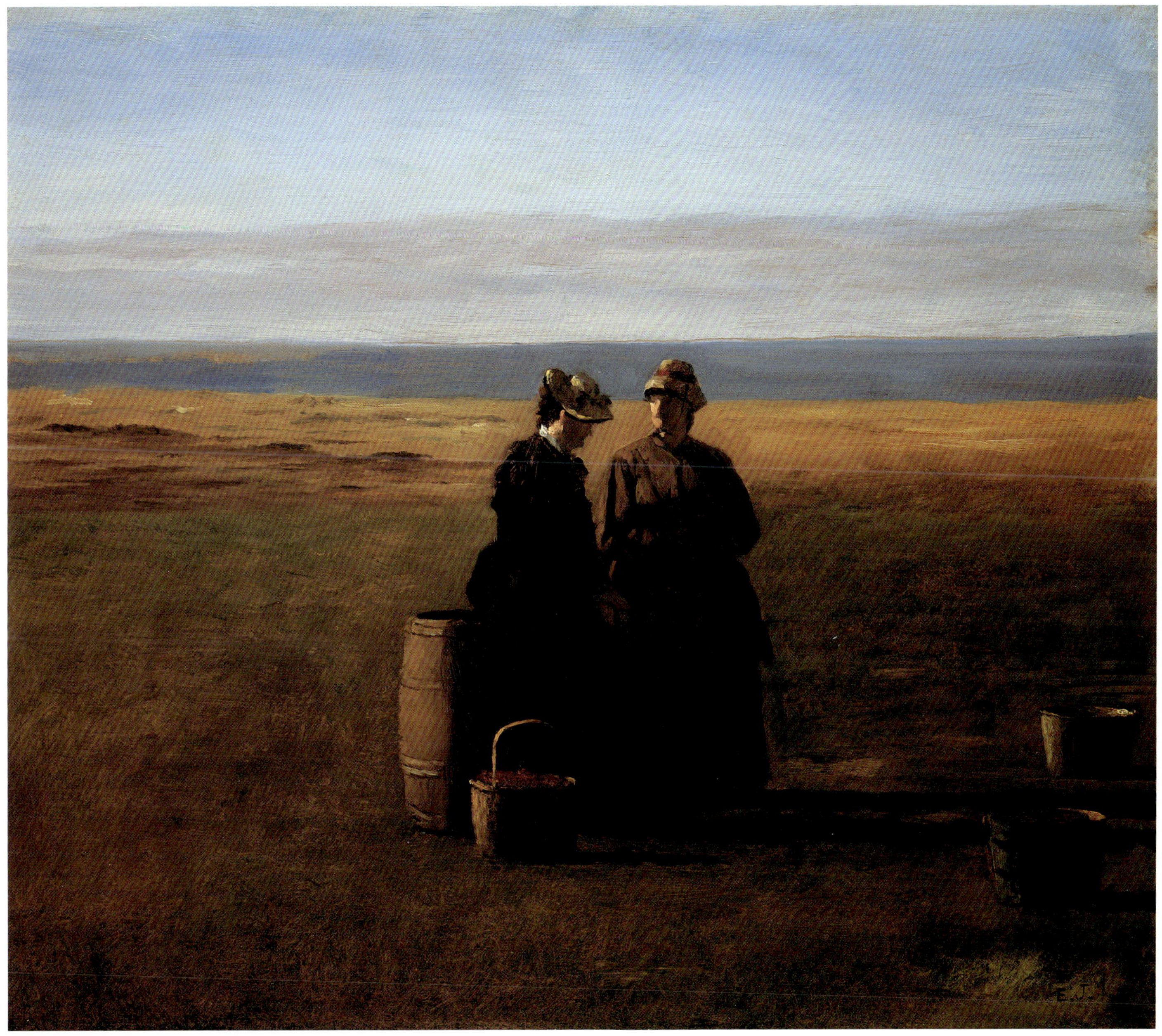

PLATE 7. *The Conversation.* Addison Gallery of American Art, Phillips Academy, Andover.

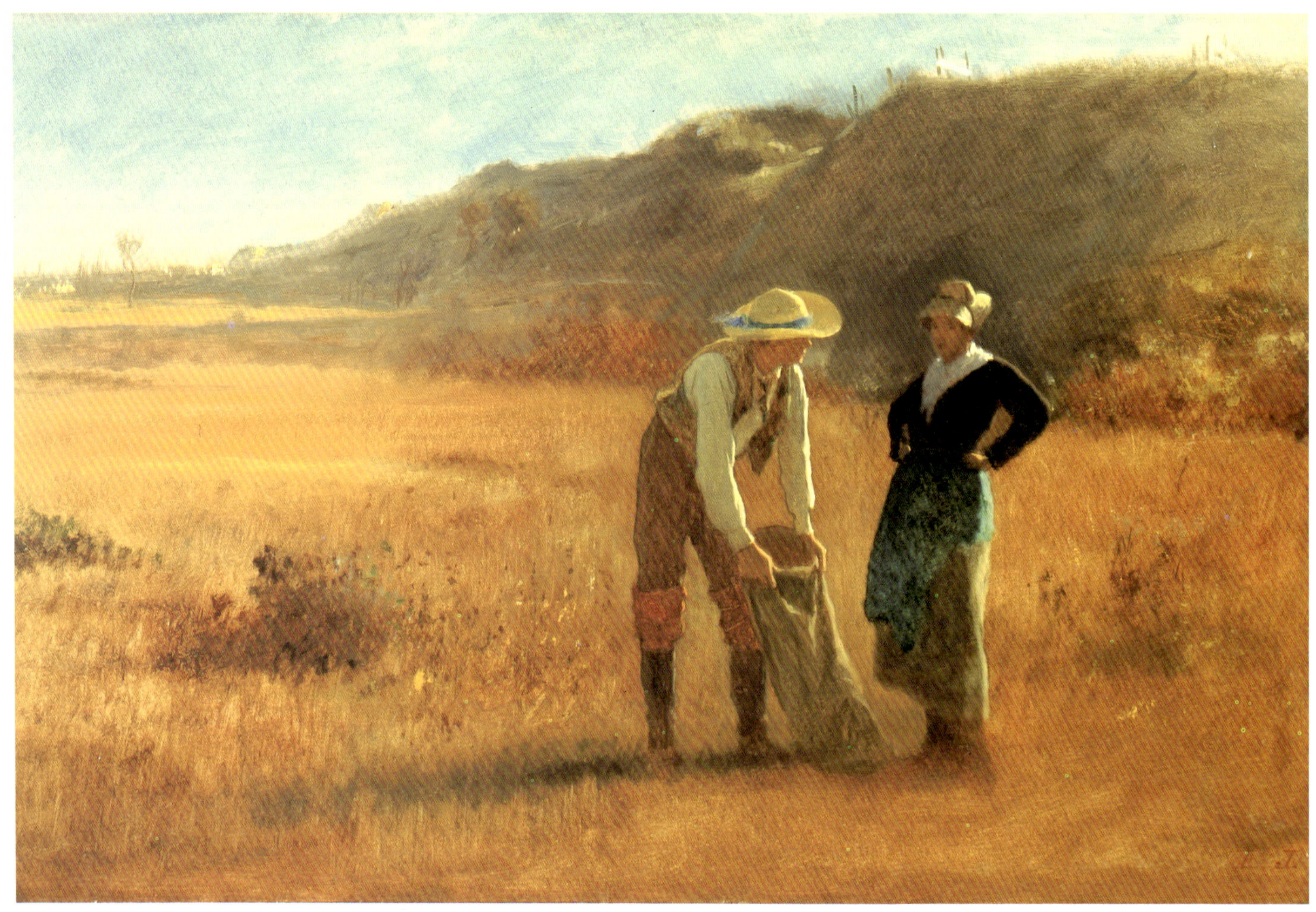

PLATE 8. *Cranberry Pickers.* Private collection.

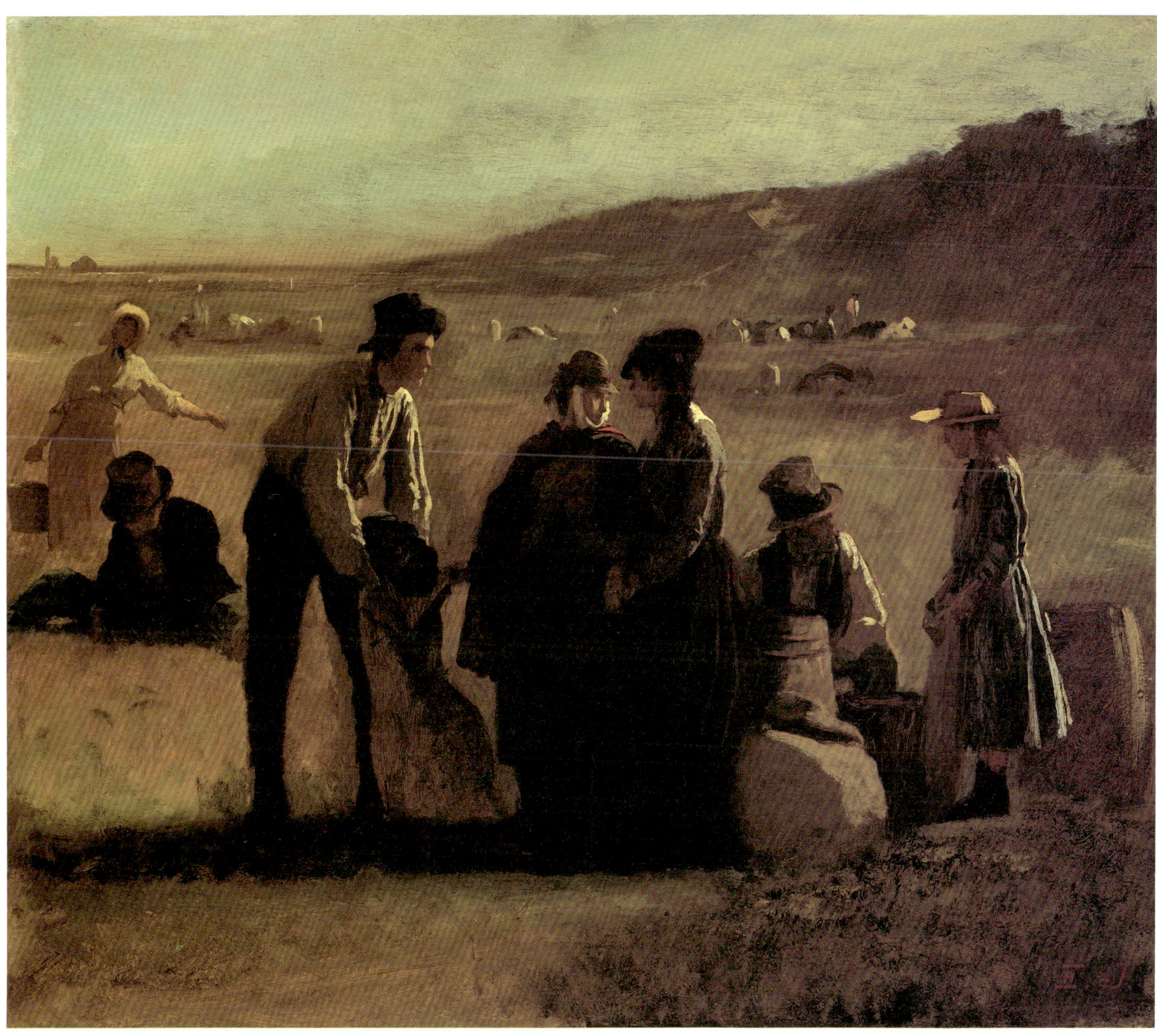

PLATE 9. *Cranberry Pickers.* Private collection.

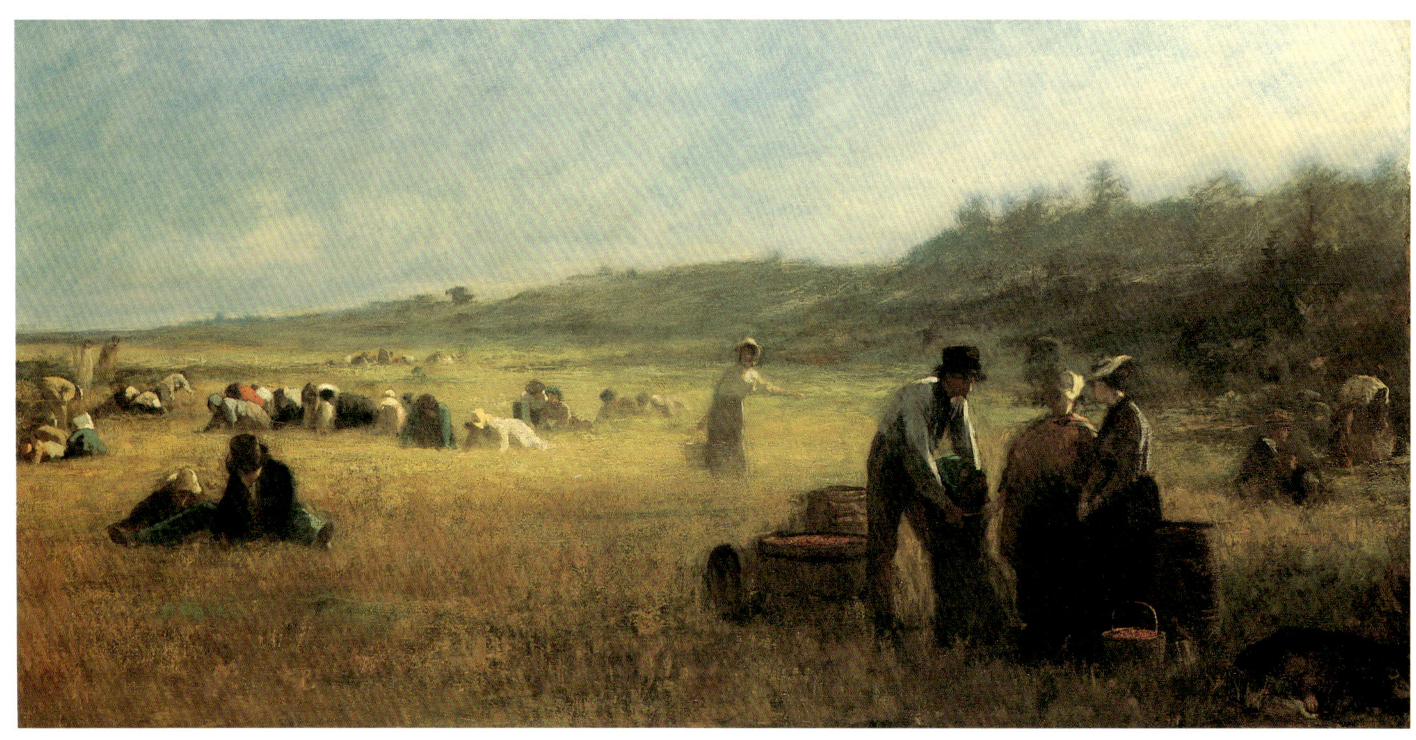

PLATE 10. *Cranberry Pickers.* Yale University Art Gallery, New Haven.

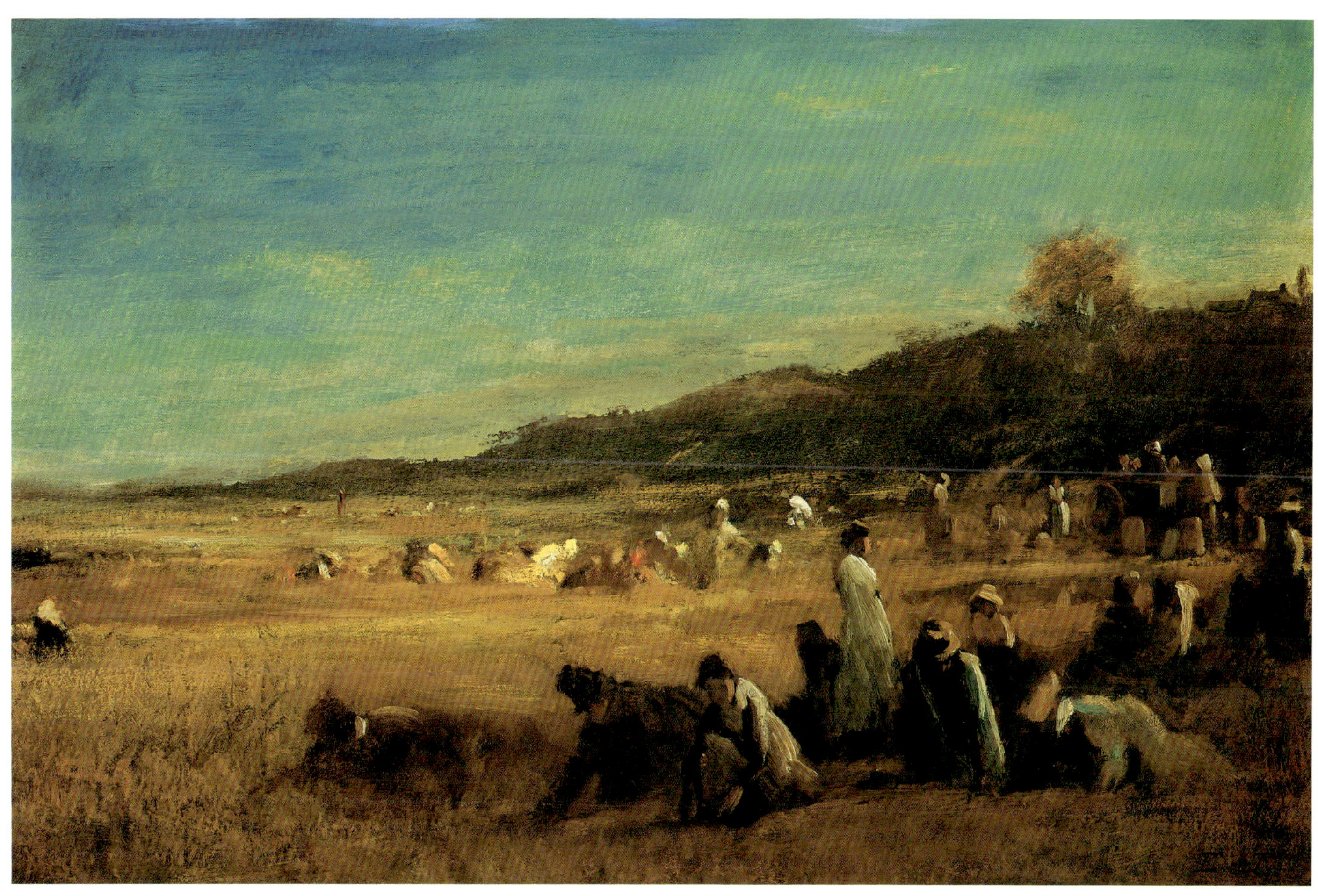

PLATE 11. *Cranberry Pickers.* Private collection.

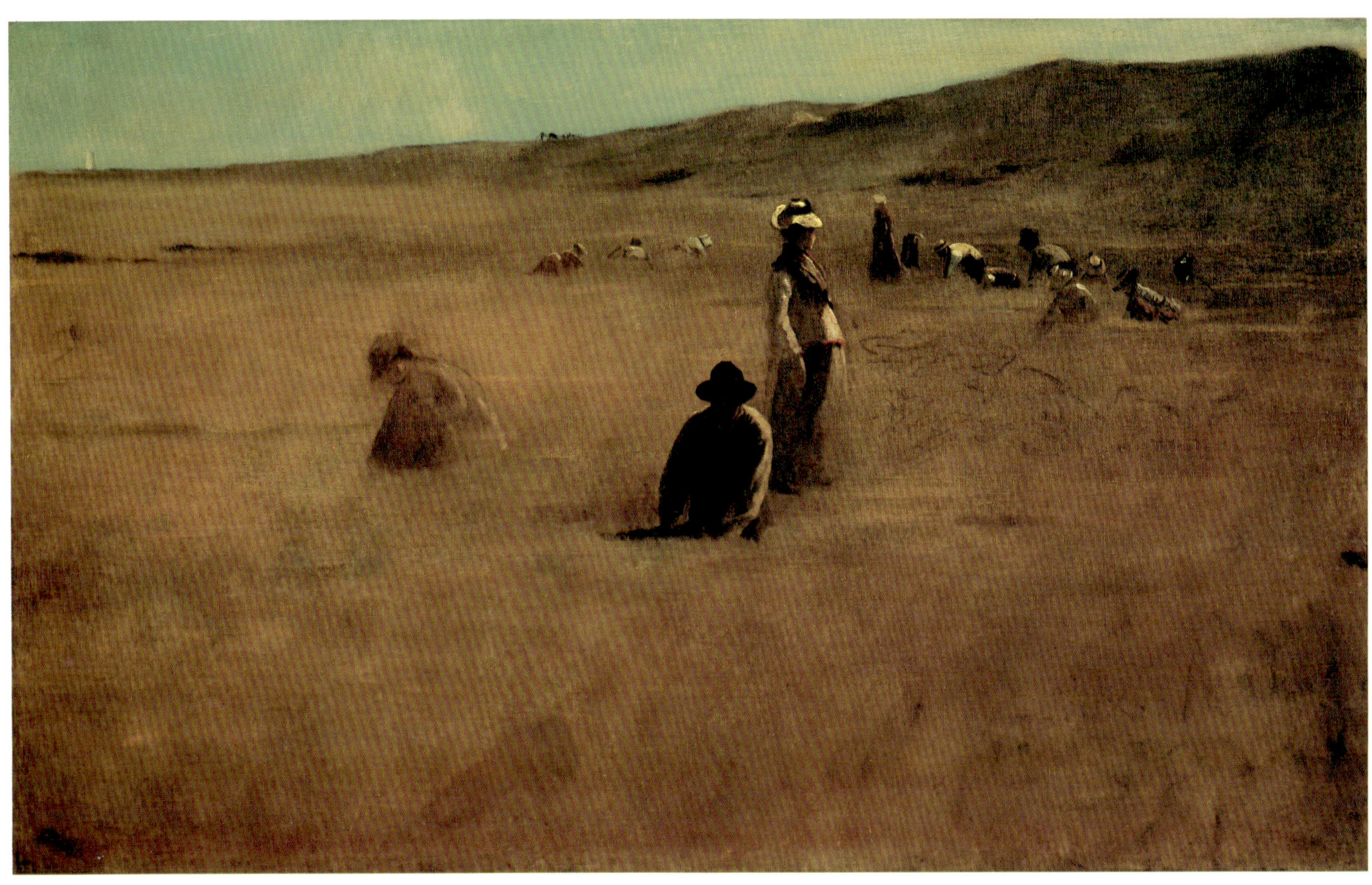

PLATE 12. *Cranberry Pickers in Nantucket.* Art Museum, Arizona State University, Tempe.

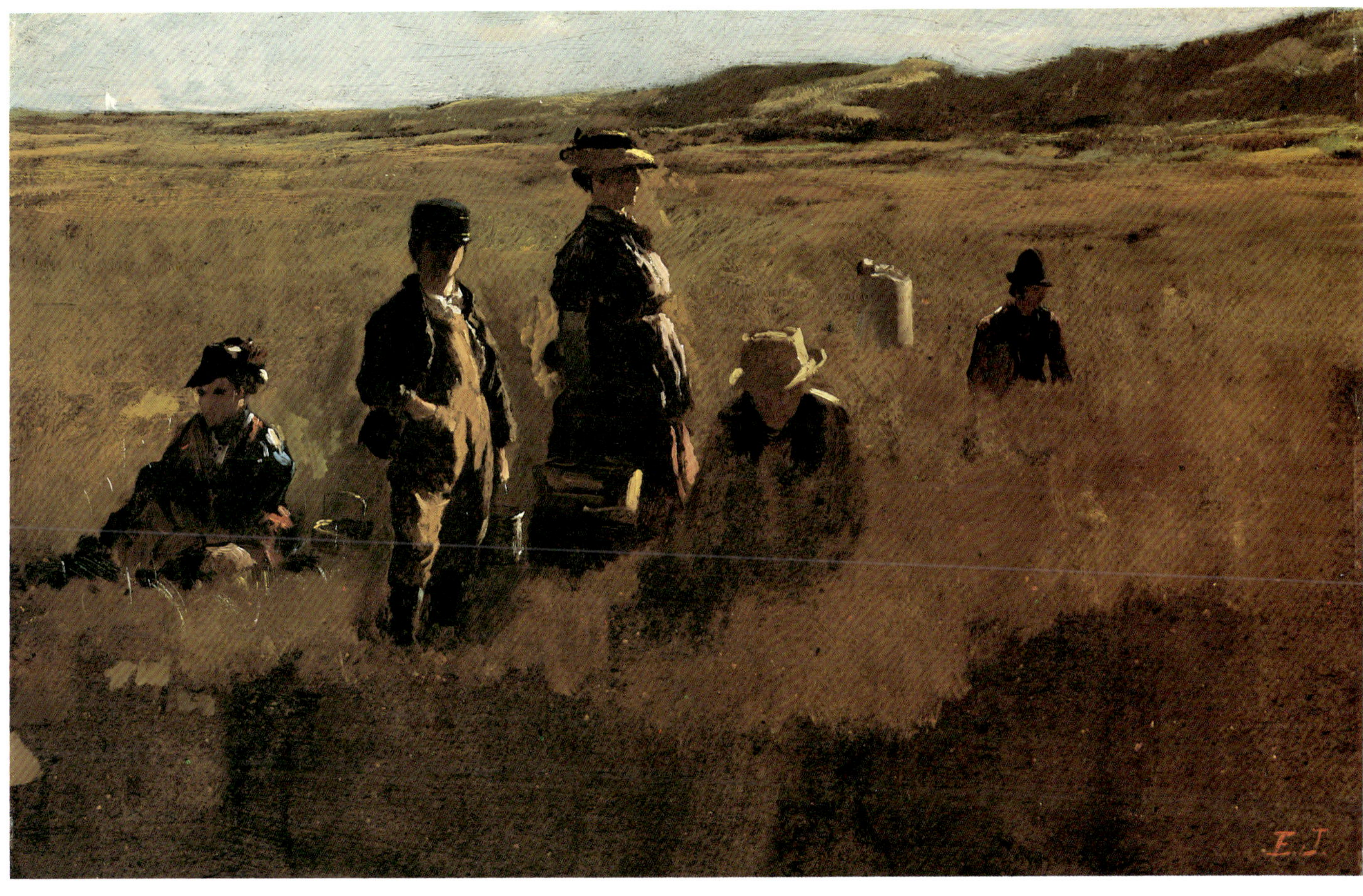

PLATE 13. *In the Fields.* Detroit Institute of Arts.

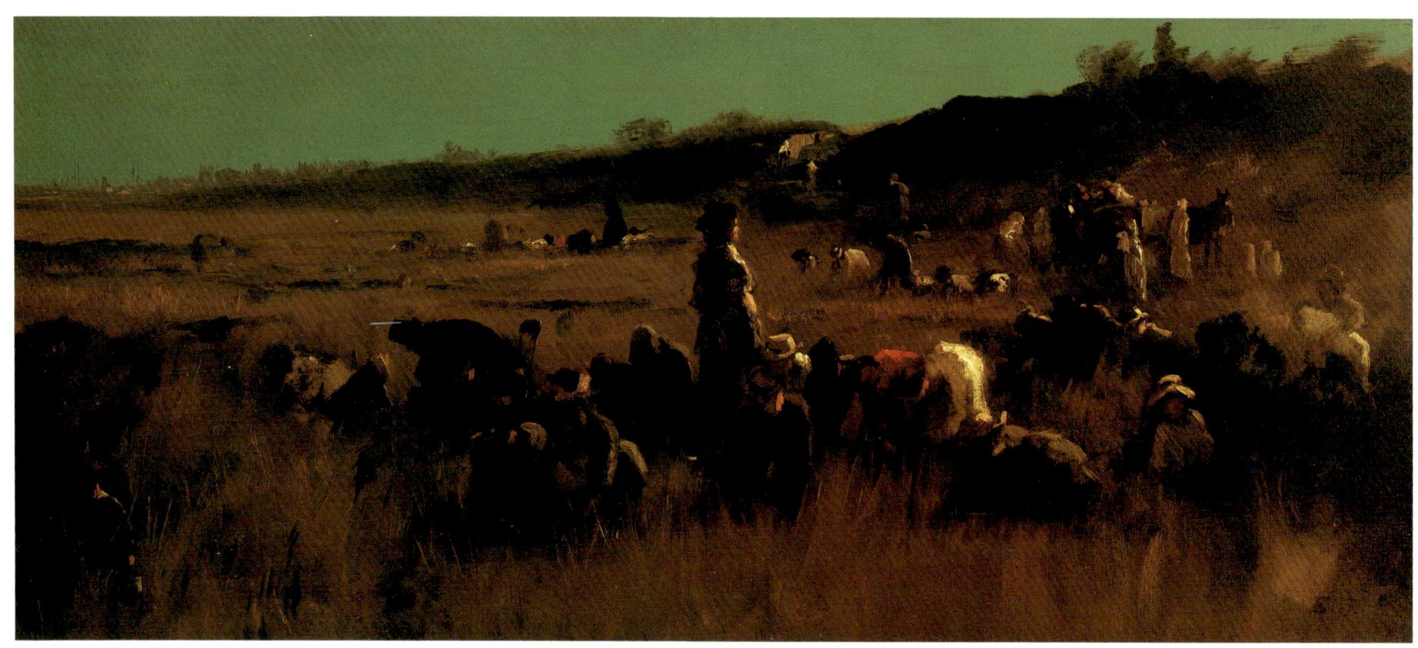

PLATE 14. *Cranberry Pickers, Nantucket.* Manoogian Collection.

Taken with a Cranberry Fit: Eastman Johnson on Nantucket

Marc Simpson

INTRODUCTION

From his island home on Nantucket in late 1879, Eastman Johnson wrote to the artist Jervis McEntee:

> I was taken with my cranberry fit as soon as I arrived (some people have Rose fever yearly—I have the cranberry fever) as they began picking down on the meadow a day or two after we arrived and I have done nothing else since I have been here, *not a thing,* but if I dare to show you it [McEntee was expected to arrive on Nantucket the next week] you may help me maybe, or maybe complete my despair. I have no finished picture at all, maybe further off than ever.[1]

Johnson's "cranberry fit" was a seasonal and site-specific malady. He contracted it only in the autumn when on the island of Nantucket. And in spite of his claim of despair and dissatisfaction, the artist's fit was a highly productive one, leading to one of the most luminous and fully realized paintings of his career—*The Cranberry Harvest, Island of Nantucket* (PLATE 1). Johnson surely recognized the success of the work, for he showed it at the National Academy of Design annual spring exhibition in 1880, where it was centrally placed and widely admired. For the next two years the painting was included in the loan exhibition of pictures at the new uptown location of The Metropolitan Museum of Art. In 1893, *The Cranberry Harvest* again represented him before the public in the prestigious art section of the World's Columbian Exposition in Chicago.[2]

A more telling measure of the work's importance for the artist is this: as far as we know he never again attempted a work even remotely like it. For the previous twenty years Johnson had worked toward a major canvas that would depict closely observed figures reveling in the open air. From his first public success with *Negro Life at the South,* known more commonly as *Old Kentucky Home* (see FIG. 1, Mills essay), through the decade of the 1870s he continually tackled this problem in many guises. During at least five years in the 1860s he attempted to show a maple-sugaring scene at Fryeburg, Maine (see, for example, *A Different Sugaring Off* [see FIG. 3, Mills essay]). With *The Old Stage Coach,* begun in

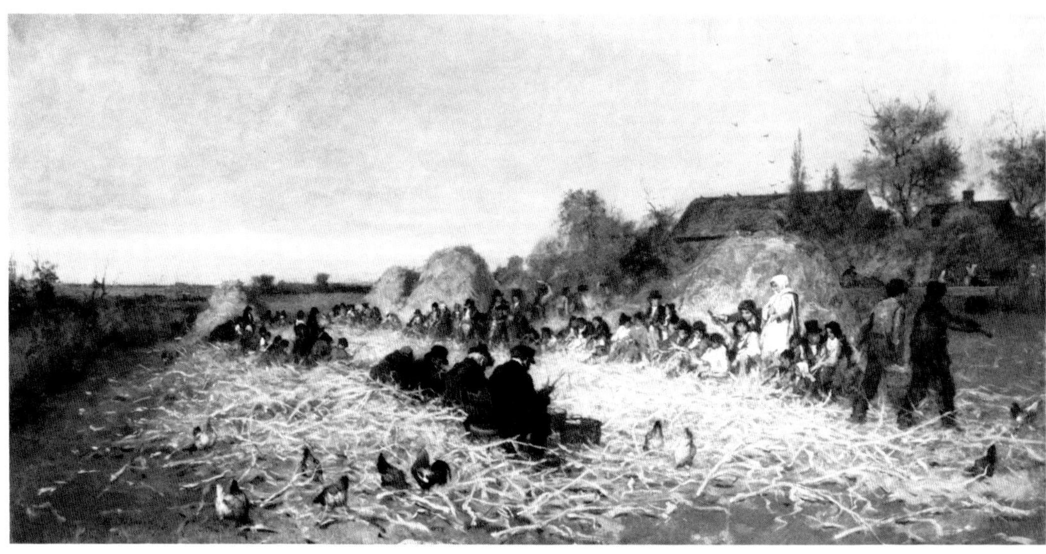

FIG. 1. Eastman Johnson, *Husking Bee, Island of Nantucket,* 1876. Oil on canvas, 27¼ x 54$^{3}/_{16}$ inches.

the Catskills and finished on Nantucket (1871, Layton Art Gallery Collection, Milwaukee Art Museum), *Hollyhocks* (1876, The New Britain Museum of American Art), and his *Husking Bee, Island of Nantucket* (FIG. 1), which brought him immense critical acclaim, he rang changes on the theme. But *The Cranberry Harvest* culminated his quest to depict a multi-figured, outdoor scene. After painting it he turned almost exclusively to portraits and never again looked to open-air genre activity for his subjects.

THE PAINTING

The Cranberry Harvest shows a bog on the north shore of the island of Nantucket, along the region known as the Cliff. The bog (contrary to its name a cranberry bog is a dry, sandy meadow—not swamp-like at all), its largely brown and autumnal surface touched by bright-colored wildflowers, is filled with over forty people—mostly women, children, and old men[3]—bent low to gather the berries. Off to the right men load the berries onto a wagon, while in the distance, singly and in pairs, figures climb the Cliff toward North Road. The pickers are the painting's principal focus. Their multicolored clothes, sparkling under the late afternoon sun, as well as their irregular and seemingly random groupings, provide the canvas with its animation and sense of scale. Near the painting's center a woman stands and pauses. She looks to the right at a boy carrying an infant toward her. While nearly all the other figures in the picture concentrate on their immediate vicinity, combing the ground for berries or speaking with someone in close proximity, this central woman fixes her attention to the far edge of the scene; her expectation becomes the painting's main emotional element and, along with her position and stance, marks her as the work's heroine.

The town of Nantucket, with its identifiable church spires, lies at the horizon to the left of the canvas. Brant Point Light is to the far left. To identify the island clearly for his New York audience the artist painted a windmill on the distant ridge—the island was one of the few sites in New England where windmills were still intact at the end of the nineteenth century[4]—although in fact the structure was located on the far east side of the town and could not have been seen from this section of the north shore. The artistic license in its placement is limited but purposeful; through it, even without the painting's full title, Johnson establishes the site and calls the viewer's attention to both the island's colonial heritage (manifest in the windmill and architecture) and its maritime legacy (by means of the lighthouse and the masts of the ships in the harbor). Johnson's view of the cranberry harvest, a contemporary activity that many of his urban audience would have found exotic, thus encapsulates much of the island's history. Through this allusiveness, which works in tandem with the large scale and elegant spareness of the canvas, *The Cranberry Harvest, Island of Nantucket* attains an imposing dignity.[5]

The true magic of the painting, however, lies in the effectiveness of Johnson's summary technique in evoking air and light. Brightly colored highlights play across the lower two-thirds of the canvas, defining the edges of forms and suggesting the roundness of human bodies set amid the dried grasses of the bog. Over all stretches an almost clear blue sky, shot through with enough pink near the horizon to make the colors shimmer. As do the most exciting paintings of his time, Johnson's treads between skilled illusion and a vigorous appreciation of freely applied paint.[6] The impression is of an outdoor scene freshly observed and recorded in the out-of-doors, with glaring lights and deep, form-hiding shadows, as if Johnson shared with the younger Winslow Homer (1836–1910), to whose works his Nantucket scenes have often been compared,[7] the belief in the rightness of painting *en plein air:*

> I prefer every time a picture composed and painted outdoors. The thing is done without your knowing it. Very much of the work now done in studios should be done in the open air. This making studies and then taking them home to use them is only half right. You get composition, but you lose freshness; you miss the subtile and, to the artist, the finer characteristics of the scene itself. I tell you it is impossible to paint an outdoor figure in studio-light with any degree of certainty. . . . I can tell in a second if an out-door picture with figures has been painted in a studio. When there is any sunlight in it, the shadows are not sharp enough.[8]

The design of the large canvas (it numbers among Johnson's larger paintings) seems inevitable in the rightness of its components. And yet Johnson's nearly twenty studies relating to the theme of the cranberry harvest testify to a calculated painting campaign that entertained many compositional options before arriving at this poised resolution.[9] The length of the artist's work on the subject is not known, since none but the large *Cranberry Harvest, Island of Nantucket* itself is dated.[10] It seems likely, however, given the single-mindedness with which the hardworking Johnson claimed to have concentrated on the cranberry subject during the fall of 1879,[11] that the majority of the studies date to that year.

THE ISLAND AND THE ARTIST

Johnson first visited the island of Nantucket (FIG. 2) in the summer of 1869 or 1870.[12] A friend, Dr. Gaillard Thomas, had recommended the place to meet Johnson's "desire for a quiet and incurious locality."[13] The forty-six-year-old painter, just recently married, evidently found there much to his liking. He returned throughout the next several decades on an annual basis and eventually owned (along with his wife, Elizabeth) large tracts of island property. What, besides quiet and incuriosity, did he find there?

First, of course, he must have noted Nantucket's separateness. Herman Melville wrote in *Moby Dick* of the island's geographic isolation:

> Nantucket! Take out your map and look at it. See what a real corner of the world it occupies; how it stands there, away off shore, more lonely than the Eddystone lighthouse. Look at it—a mere hillock, and elbow of sand; all beach, without a background.[14]

But while set apart from the continent, Melville's Nantucket was a bustling and busy seaport, the center of America's whaling and whale-oil industry. Throughout the early nineteenth century the harvest of whales brought great fame and prosperity to the island.

> Were you ever at Nantucket? Who speaks of a whale without mentally associating with that huge monster this little sandy spot that has sent forth so many brave men to catch the big fish, and thereby literally give light to the entire world.[15]

Sea captains and merchants, many raised within the strong Quaker tradition of the island, brought enormous wealth to the community and displayed it, decorously, through the solid, square houses and buildings that even now line the town's streets.

But by the middle of the century the industry and the island it supported had fallen into decline.[16] Harbors better equipped to handle large ships and linked to railroad transportation successfully competed for the whale oil trade. In July 1846 a fire broke out on Main Street and swept through the business district; in less than ten hours nearly one-third of the town center was destroyed. Increasingly less successful returns of the whaling fleet, coupled with the rise of alternative lighting sources, further weakened Nantucket's economic base. Many of the island's men traveled to the mainland for work (several hundred to California in search of gold in 1849 alone).[17] The cumulative effect of these events was economic disaster for the once prosperous island. In 1860 a visitor wrote:

> On entering the harbor of Nantucket one is impressed on every hand by the signs of decadence. A few battered and dismantled hulks of whale ships sleep alongside the lethargic old wharves; quiet, listless seeming people saunter about with an aimless air very uncommon in New England; grass-grown streets and dingy warehouses all combine to complete the picture of departed glory.[18]

"In 1870," notes the island's chief nineteenth-century historical text, "Nantucket had not a ship, bark, brig, or vessel of any kind, suggestive of the vast amount of business done in the past."[19] As the whaling industry dissolved, so did the island's population. From a thriving 9,700 in 1840, Nantucket was home to just over 3,200 in 1875.[20]

In retrospect, the depletion of human and economic resources had its beneficial side. As there was no industrial prosperity in the late nineteenth century, so no industrial slums developed around the town. Nor, for the most part, was there money to raze or dramatically remodel the buildings of the seventeenth, eighteenth, and early nineteenth centuries, as happened in other urban areas. So the history of the town, at least as it was written in its buildings, stood revealed

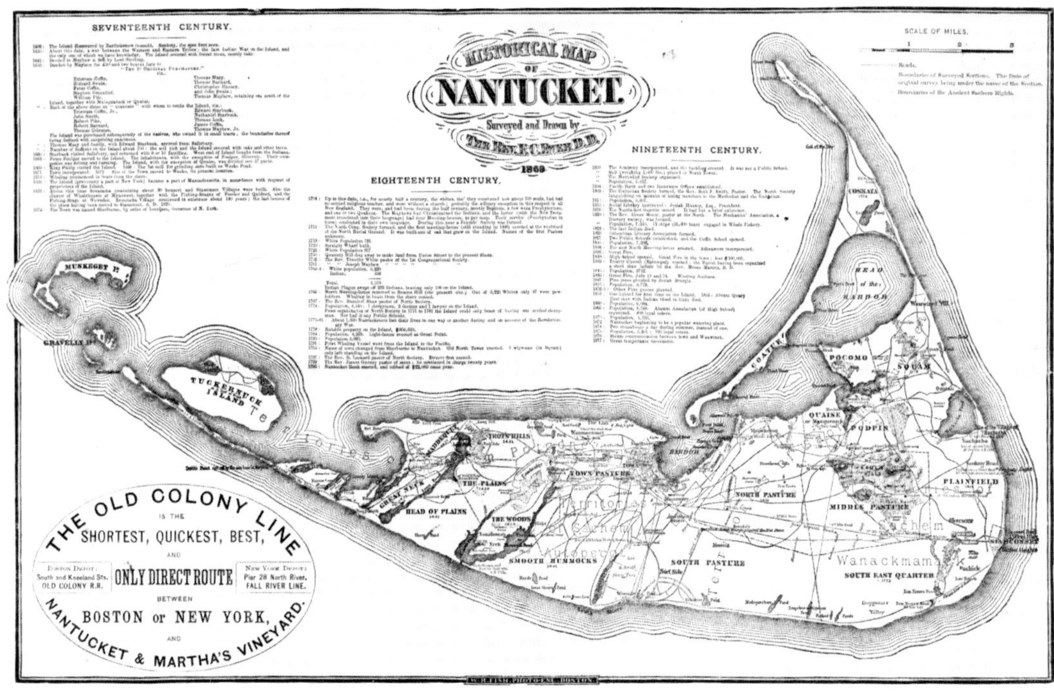

FIG. 2. Rev. F. C. Ewer, *Historical Map of Nantucket*, 1869 (reissue ca. 1877). Library of Congress, Map Division.

as a finished subject. One writer in 1868 felt this strongly:

> Nantucket now has a "body-o'-death" appearance such as few New England towns possess. The houses stand around in faded gentility style—the inhabitants have a dreamy look, as though they live in the memories of the past. To him who has traveled in the Old World a visit to Nantucket forcibly recalls reminiscences of Continental towns. There is that same mossy quiet, the same irregularity of highways and byways, the same quaint forms of architecture.[21]

Instead of accepting the apparently inexorable decline of population and wealth, the leading citizens of the town turned to the mainland for salvation. The island had sea breezes that cooled in the summer and warmed in the autumn, a large remnant of its colonial and early federal past, a significant percentage of its population who would welcome boarders to its homes, and virtually no distractions other than leisurely walks and rides, sails, fishing expeditions, and squantums (a local variant of clambake). Tourism was the community's best hope.[22] As early as January 1855 public meetings were held to urge "placing the island in a proper light before the country, as a desirable place for a summer resort."[23] Working with the Old Colony Railroad and the Island Home ferry service,[24] the islanders promoted the spot with considerable vigor through advertisements and feature articles that appeared on the mainland. In the summer of 1870, just as Johnson began his annual stays, the qualities of the island as a resort were summarized by a correspondent for a Rhode Island paper (and reprinted in the island's own weekly):

> People who love the ocean and hospitality must love Nantucket, for here we find both at their best. We who are enjoying them, often turn our faces continent-ward and compassionately try (through some friendly JOURNAL) to signal to our heated fellow-townsmen, that here are rest and coolness.
>
> . . . We are living for a week in the Atlantic Ocean, we remind you,—on a sand-reef that it has forgotten to cover—a great sand-reef with sheltered coves like this—with quiet, lapping waves on its north shore,—with grand, desolate lines of surf on its south shore,—with pungent, salt air sweeping over it,—with cheery, keen-witted human beings living on it,—with the accumulated traditions of two hundred years clustering around its picturesque town.[25]

The "accumulated traditions" became increasingly important in the tourist literature of the island. As an island writer phrased it at the end of the 1871 summer season:

> The correspondent of the Worcester *Spy* writes to that paper some very interesting and amusing sketches of Nantucket. All our peculiar institutions, as the town-crier, meat-auctions, "cent schools," strange figure-heads of ships doing duty in gardens or on barns, &c., are touched with a skilful and delicate hand.
>
> . . . [A]s we can no longer plume ourselves as formerly, upon our business enterprise, we may be excused for a feeling of pride in our eccentricities. We begin really to think that there is something quaint and picturesque about our own personal and local characteristics as a people, as well as about our island and our town.[26]

During the next decade, when Johnson devoted himself and much of his art to the island,[27] tourism swiftly developed. There were increased lodging facilities, an improved transportation service to the island, guidebooks, the development of leisure industries (especially services to support recreational fishing and day sailing), and a concerted pride in the islanders' eccentricities.[28]

Johnson's role on the island during this period is a complex one. He was initially a visitor. Like others of the summer flock, his annual comings and goings throughout the 1870s were regularly chronicled in the local press (see Appendix 1). On 13 August 1870, for example, the *Inquirer and Mirror* reported:

> There is this to be said in favor of Nantucket as a resort for strangers, that those who have one season's ex-

perience of its attractions, are very apt to come again. Among the familiar and welcome faces now to be seen on our streets are . . . Eastman Johnson, the artist forever famous as the author of Abraham Lincoln, the log cabin boy. William S. Tiffany, of Binghamton, N.Y. and E. W. Perry, M. Morse, and Virgil Williams, of New York, are also here on their second visit, in search of subject, inspiration and life for new contributions to American art.[29]

Although the island press apparently did not report on Johnson's visit of 1871, it seems likely that he was on Nantucket sometime during that year, too. For in April, paying $450.00, he purchased a house and land along the Cliff at the west end of the town.[30] Within a week, for $250.00, he bought an adjacent lot with buildings (including the premises formerly known as the "Jethro Coffin estate") for use as a studio.[31]

His next reported visit was in August 1872. And rather than including Johnson in a mere catalogue of visitors, the writer for the *Inquirer and Mirror* noted the artist's past activity and offered favorable critical comment:

> Among the noted visitors to be met here every Summer is the clever artist, Eastman Johnson. His spirited, and really fine painting, so much admired at one of the Brooklyn Art Receptions in the Winter of '70 and '71, "The Old Stage Coach," was finished here. He told me that the boys' faces and forms in and around the old coach are from life—Nantucket life. The boys were captured and imprisoned in his studio on the "Bluffs" here long enough to paint them. Mr. Johnson's best work is done here.[32]

At the end of the season, on 23 November, the paper reported:

> The distinguished artist, Eastman Johnson, with his family, left us this week for New York, having prolonged his stay with us through all the summer and fall. We have not had the pleasure of visiting Mr. Johnson's studio, but we learn that he has executed some very fine paintings which will doubtless be heard from in due time.[33]

Brief notices of the artist's movements recur throughout the 1870s, revealing (among other facts) that whereas Johnson initially came to Nantucket for the summer, the fall season increasingly appealed to him—in 1878 and 1879 he did not even arrive on the island until September.[34]

But Johnson was not simply a visitor. Over the decade his name was used as a lure to attract more vacationers from the mainland—he and his home became in some sense one of the features of the island promoted for the tourist trade:

> Boating, fishing, and comfortable living among a pleasant population and in a very pleasant old town are the amusements of Nantucket. . . . Of late auctions have furnished recreation also to summer visitors, where they purchased curious old furniture, old china, old table gear; and I was even offered a magnificent brass warming-pan. There is also a public library, an interesting museum, and very pleasant, intelligent society. Eastman Johnson, the artist, has a studio here.[35]

Notices and illustrations of his house and studio appeared in the national press (FIG. 3). Local writers seemed most impressed by the ambition of Johnson's landscaping:

> Mr. Johnson has a fine studio on his grounds that he works in incessantly. This gentleman is always doing some queer thing, or carrying out some quaint conceit, and now he is going to erect a miniature water mill, and build a tank of toward an hundred barrels capacity, that he may have little fountains and also irrigate his land by wind. It will look novel, but pretty, to see such things in operation.[36]

By the early 1880s his property along the Cliff, which has since been dismantled, was eulogized as "almost Italian in its soft summer garniture; our somewhat classic cliff luminous with sunlight . . . all so dreamy and tremulous,—strangers tell us it is a poem."[37]

FIG. 3 *Residence and Studio of Eastman Johnson,* ca. 1873. Wood engraving from Henry M. Baird, "Nantucket," *Scribner's Monthly* 6, no. 4 (August 1873): 390.

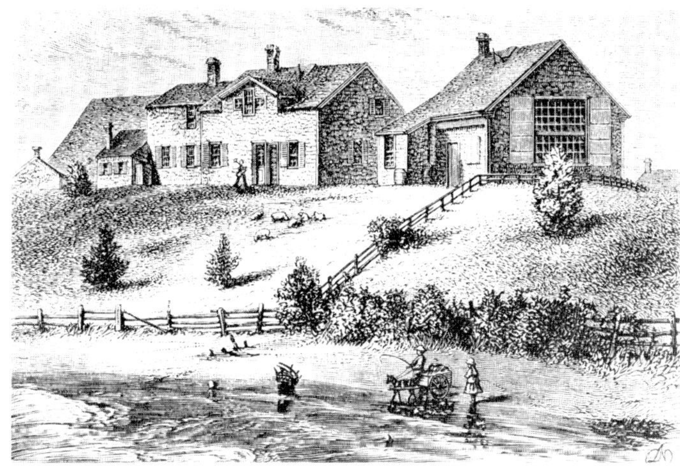

Some of the writing was blatantly commercial. Johnson was praised for choosing Nantucket's Cliff area for his summer home at precisely the same time as the area was being promoted for development. The message to the reader, both in news reports and fictionalized memoirs, was the wisdom of following Johnson's lead:

> In fact, the high ground just above this beach, and commanding a magnificent sweep of the ocean, is the spot which ought to be occupied by cottages and hotels. The artist, Eastman Johnson, has shown his usual fine taste in taking up his summer residence here.

> While Miss Ray was thus struggling with the ocean, and Bessie, and Tom were sporting like two fish—for both were at home in the water—Mr. Gordon was looking around the Cliff with his business eye wide open. As he walked along the road back from the shore, and saw the fine views which it afforded him, he admired the judgment of Eastman Johnson, the artist, in building his summer house and studio there. . . . So the value of the Cliff or Bluffs was jotted down in his note-book for future use.[38]

It is not clear to what extent the artist encouraged these notices.[39] It was attention that would surely disturb the quiet and incuriosity that had first attracted him to the place. Johnson and his wife, however, eventually determined to take advantage of this flurry of publicity surrounding the island and himself. In 1881 they began to invest heavily in Nantucket real estate.[40] Between 1881 and the artist's death in 1906 the Johnsons were involved in nearly sixty transactions recorded by Nantucket's Registrar of Deeds. Varying in size and complexity, nearly all of these purchases were speculative, several involving large tracts intended for subdivision and development (see Appendix 3). Sadly for the Johnsons, as for most of the island's speculators of the time, these ventures appear to have been unsuccessful.[41] In fact, by 1898 the artist claimed a great weariness of his island home:

> Just a line to tell you we are alive and working miserably every day, fussing, straightening, plastering, mending, puttying, painting, puttying, white-washing, sodding, just to keep this *shebang* so as *to rent,* or if not, to *live in* when we have no other place. I wish to the Lord I could *sell* it for even *much less* than it has cost me, and that I would never have to come to this island again. I am done with it, but I cannot *throw it away,* and that is what keeps us here now. We are doing our best to get off, and hope to in three days, or it may be four. I am getting very *tired* and *hate* work, would never do another stroke if I could help it.[42]

We must not take this letter too literally; tone is everything, and rhetorical hyperbole was not unknown to the artist. He was, after all, described as "not so far removed in type from some of the retired captains that he painted so well"—and sea captains are proverbial for their ability to exaggerate and spin yarns.[43]

THE ARTIST ON NANTUCKET IN 1879

If there is an element of truth in Johnson's wish that he "would never have to come to this island again," twenty years earlier, in 1879 when he was engaged in the principal work on *The Cranberry Harvest* and its associated paintings and drawings, his mood was much different. Three letters written by Johnson to his friend McEntee (1828–1891) reveal his pleasure with Nantucket and, in spite of protestations to the contrary, his work there. These are crucial documents that merit quotation at length:

> You will find us here and expecting you and I hope you will not fail to come. The Giffords [Sanford R. Gifford and his wife, Mary Cecilia] came to see us and passed two nights and we had a good time. The weather was lovely and I think they enjoyed it. It has been the same almost uninterruptedly ever since and I hope it may continue for you. But the two last days have been lowering and threatening and a break cannot be far off and you may come in the midst of a storm, but that can't be helped and dont mind it if it so happens. Today is lovely and perfectly calm but hazy. I am glad you had better weather at your camp at the last and finished off with everything pleasant in that respect. Mrs. Gifford gave us graphic accounts of your life in the camp and the pursuit of pleasure under some difficulties of weather, snug stowage &c. and we expect you to finish the tale. I shall have precious little to show you tho. I have been industrious enough since here. I was taken with my cranberry fit as soon as I arrived. . . . [44]

McEntee did not arrive—having miscalculated the ferry departures, he missed his connection and went instead to New York[45]—so Johnson followed him with another letter:

> You probably wonder what keeps me here. I am trying to get some work done. The harder I try the more I cant. Pulling up is a great interruption and for a considerable time and I dread it. The weather is lovely. We dont have fires all the time—a little wood fire in the evening. The house is comfortable and there is less bother than anywhere else and less occasion and need to spend money. But we must be moving now very soon. It is the middle of November. I would very well like to try it here a whole winter, but I dare say it would not be good for me. Oh no, we must keep in the whirl or be left behind, but I foresee a time coming when I shall be glad to be left behind.[46]

But by the middle of December Johnson was still on Nantucket:

> I am staying here to get through with things begun, not much, you will be surprised to see how little I can dawdle over so long a time, but then the models are here and whatever materials I require, and that is all there is of the pictures, so of course I cant do them elsewhere. I sent a little picture to the last Century meeting. Dont know whether it got there or not, as I have not heard. I shall be there myself before the next one, if I am alive. In fact I expect to get off this coming week. It will no doubt be at the end of it. I want to see New York and I want to see you, and some others. . . . You are all in full season there. It must seem strange to you that anybody can still remain in the country and on a desert island. . . . The weather is lovely here, or I couldn't stay. I wish you could come here in a minutes' time and just see how you like it. There is something very peaceful and satisfactory in our life here, tho. It might take a different color if we were never to go to New York again. But I find I am thinking a good deal about some such final retreat. Oh what a working world, no day and no time for sweet quiet leisure, to do what you wish to do.[47]

Johnson sounds several themes in these letters. Most moving is the dialogue between the urban and the rural life. On the island, removed from the pressures of his city existence, Johnson praises the pastoral ideal—simple living without excess bother or extravagance. He notes with regret the need to "keep in the whirl" of his city-based life and career. He clearly does not shun New York—he is curious about friends and art-world activities, and he is wise enough to know that the pastoral vision benefits from an urban perspective. In the end, however, the island tempts him to dream of a final retreat.

From the letters it is also clear that hospitality to visitors was important. The Giffords' visit was noteworthy, and McEntee's was keenly awaited. The young artist Will Low

(1853–1932), looking back twenty years to the months that he spent on Nantucket during 1879 and 1880, provided a warm and glowing account of being one of Johnson's guests:

> I had met Johnson in the meetings of the S. A. A. [Society of American Artists]. . . . He had a handsome summer home upon the sand dunes fronting the water, that are dignified as the Cliffs in Nantucket parlance. . . .
>
> The long evenings of the autumn and the early winter, for he lingered late upon the island, remain memorable; for Eastman Johnson had a store of anecdote which pictured his earlier days as an art student in Germany, Belgium, and Holland; and his later experiences of men and conditions in Washington and New York. . . . An ideal host in his pleasant home, we had merry gatherings around the dinner table, and the ladies of the two families vied in friendly rivalry, with the opposing cook-books of two nations, to furnish a material complement to our spiritual refreshment.[48]

Sadly, Low does not comment on Johnson's current project, the cranberry harvest scenes.

Johnson's own letters to McEntee, however, provide clues that allow us to speculate on the painting's progress. Johnson testifies in early October that he is hard at work exclusively on the cranberry harvest theme: "I have been industrious enough since here.[49] I was taken with my cranberry fit as soon as I arrived . . . and I have done nothing else." The number of extant preliminary studies, and his refining in those closely related works, supports his statement.[50] His frustration at the enterprise is evident a month later: "I am trying to get some work done. The harder I try the more I cant." In retrospect we can trace this frustration in the series of works leading up to and including Yale University's large, unfinished *The Cranberry Harvest* (PLATES 4–10)—in which we see Johnson pushing a composition through blocking-in and complex figure studies, advancing to the final large canvas, and then holding back, wary of some barely discernible lacking or dissatisfaction. By the middle of December, though, far later than either he or his friends probably expected him to remain "in the country and on a desert island," he had apparently reached a resolution. He is still at work on the cranberry harvest—"I am staying here to get through with things begun, not much"—and yet finds "something very peaceful and satisfactory in our life here." Perhaps this contentment signals his break from the Yale composition and, reconfiguring the elements of the picture, the development of the Timken painting.

CONTEMPORARY RESPONSES TO THE PAINTING

When Johnson did eventually return to New York, presumably in late December, he found himself "in the whirl" during the ensuing months. At the Artists' Fund Sale on 12 and 13 February, his *Glass with the Squire* (1880, Annmary Brown Memorial, Brown University), a Nantucket scene featuring two older men in an old-fashioned interior, brought a noteworthy $1,120.00. Also in February he showed another Nantucket interior at the Union League Club, *The Reprimand* (see FIG. 1, Hills essay)—an interior genre scene showing an emotional conflict between an old man and an evidently high-spirited young woman. Together these works drew "much attention to the artist who for the past year or two has not sustained his reputation until now."[51] In early April the Art Students' League featured "an interesting exhibition of studies, sketches and pictures by Eastman Johnson, and H. Humphrey Moore."[52] Johnson was again in the news later that month when his *Pension Claim Agent* (1867, The Fine Arts Museums of San Francisco) was among the works on display at Madison Square Garden when the building collapsed during the evening of the twenty-first.[53]

But the major New York art events of the spring of 1880 were the openings in March, within weeks of one another, of the annual exhibition of the Society of American Artists,[54] the annual spring exhibition of the National Academy of Design, and, at the end of the month, the opening at its new site in Central Park of The Metropolitan Museum of Art. Three of Johnson's Nantucket paintings were conspicuous at both the National Academy of Design and The Metropolitan Museum of Art.

At the National Academy Johnson had two paintings on display, *The Reprimand* and *The Cranberry Harvest.* The latter was hung opposite the doorway to the south gallery—the most prominent position in the exhibition. Critics consistently responded to it, most of them with great favor.[55]

> Among the over seven hundred works hung one of the very best and most creditable to American art is Eastman Johnson's scene on a cranberry patch, which has deservedly been given the position of honor in the centre of the southern wall of the south gallery. A fine effect of sunlight strikes on about fifty remarkably well posed, painted and individualized figures hard at work in a cranberry field, on the stretch between a low cliff line and the seashore by which are seen the buildings of a quiet little town. It is an excellent work and a credit to American art.

> There is no mystery and no pathos in the works of Mr. Eastman Johnson. But as a delineator of the cheerful or picturesque aspects of American genre, he not only stands near the head of our art, but continues to improve in his later works both in genre and portraiture. *The Cranberry Harvest in Nantucket,* representing the lasses and laddies of that seafaring isle stealing a few delightful hours from maritime and domestic pursuits to cull the scarlet berries from the moist meadow-lands, is an ambitious composition of a very meritorious character. The grouping is cleverly arranged, interestingly suggestive, and harmoniously introduced into the well-painted landscape.

> A large class of pictures in the Academy are *genre* subjects, many of which nearly approach the character of landscapes. Foremost among them are Eastman Johnson's two of 'The Cranberry-Harvest' and 'The Reprimand.' In the former, which is on a large scale, country people, men in their homely blue trousers and straw hats, and the women in sunbonnets, are diligently hunting about in a low meadow for cranberries. The out-door look of this picture is very agreeable, while the low-toned landscape is lighted by the artist's consideration of "values," by the real sunshine in the sky, and its bright touches on the clothes of the cranberry-pickers.[56]

Even those who were the advocates of the younger men at the Society of American Artists—and there was a real partisanship visible in critical circles between the new and the old generation[57]—found words of moderated praise for the work: "There were but few interesting figure or *genre* subjects in the exhibition apart from the portraits properly so called. . . . Mr. Eastman Johnson's Cranberry Harvest was to be praised for everything except composition."[58]

At the end of the month, Johnson's *Husking Bee, Island of Nantucket* (see FIG. 1) joined the works on view in The Metropolitan Museum of Art's inaugural exhibition of contemporary European and American painting. *Husking Bee, Island of Nantucket* was one of Johnson's most acclaimed works, having received much praise at the National Academy of Design spring exhibition of 1876[59] and in later years being mentioned as one of the high points of Johnson's career. At the Universal Exposition in Paris of 1878 it was singled out by at least one foreign critic as a "characteristic American scene," along with the works of Winslow Homer.[60] At The Metropolitan Museum the painting was again installed amid contemporary American and European works, the national schools this time hanging intermixed, as *The New-York Times* reported, "cheek by jowl." The painting blossomed in this context and was a source of proud comment on the part of critics: "Eastman Johnson's 'Corn-shucking' is here, and well does it hold its own, whether for its tone of color or the truth and simplicity of the scene."[61]

So for the spring art season in New York, Johnson could count on one of his past triumphs—*Husking Bee, Island of Nantucket*—and his most recent achievement—*The Cranberry Harvest, Island of Nantucket*—being seen by the public. It seems likely, in fact, that Johnson considered the two outdoor scenes as companions to one another. They share a rural, outdoor subject matter based on Nantucket life, comparable size and scale (27 1/4 x 54 3/16 in. for the *Husking Bee* as opposed to $27^{3}/_{8}$ x $54^{1}/_{2}$ in. for *The Cranberry Harvest*), and even an echoing, two-part title. Certainly a number of contemporary critics linked the two:

> Mr. Eastman Johnson's "Cranberry Harvest—Island of Nantucket" is a cheerful companion piece to his "Corn Husking," now in the Art Gallery of the Metropolitan Museum, and shows the same qualities. There is here abundance of incident, much sparkling play of sunshine, and real people working in a real scene. As a picture it is, however, ineffective seen a few feet off; nor, indeed, was there any room here for the art of composition. The landscape is too monotonous and the groups too scattered for any possibility of pictorial effect, and we must content ourselves with a picture to be seen at close hand on a drawing-room wall. Mr. Johnson has a curious inability to maintain a quiet chord of color, or of tone, we must rather say, for colorist he is none. Here he refuses to let the eye rest anywhere, much less does he compel it by strong or gentle means, to rest in one spot: he scatters his colors, as he does his glints of sunlight, all over the canvas, and as we can make out nothing at a distance, so when we come near we enjoy most the imaginary parcelling out of the picture into a number of smaller ones, each a clever study in its way.[62]

The sentiment that *The Cranberry Harvest,* as good as it was, did not quite equal the mark of the *Husking Bee* was often repeated through the rest of the century, either explicitly or through the prominence given to the earlier painting in commentaries.[63] *The Cranberry Harvest*'s most frequently noted "failing," as in the passage above, was its subversion of "the art of composition," its lack of a unified arrangement. In fact, however, the work's apparently random arrangement of figures is a deliberate and calculated whole constructed from a series of carefully observed studies.[64] The cranberry harvest, lacking the rigid parallel-lines structure of a cornhusking bee,[65] did not provide a clear, grid-like frame for the action. Johnson has used this lack of restraining reality to impose, very effectively, an air of spontaneity on the scene. At least for some critics, he was too successful in the art of hiding his art.

CONCLUSION: JOHNSON'S SUBJECT MATTER—TRUTH OR NOSTALGIA?

One of the principal questions asked of Johnson's Nantucket scenes concerns their relationship to reality: do they portray contemporary truth or are they scenes constructed to evoke a nostalgic, sentimentalized response to rural myths? By and large recent scholars have favored the latter view, asserting that, for example, Johnson's image of the cranberry harvest "expresses the sentimental idealization of agrarian life" and "makes light of work that was actually difficult and wearying."[66] The correlative of this is the opinion that the artist censored reality: "No poor people inhabit Johnson's America; figures are classless, rural Yankees working gaily and effortlessly, joking and flirting as they move from bog to bog in the autumn afternoon sun."[67]

Writers of Johnson's time on occasion took a different point of view. Some critics in 1880, for example, in writing of *The Cranberry Harvest,* noted "individualized figures hard at work" in "a rather uninviting swamp," and spoke of "real people working in a real scene."[68] Another, associating Johnson with two other genre painters, said that he "has striven to paint what he saw with his own eyes—to interest the spectator with the simplest annals of the poor."[69] A later author observed that the "absence of affectation, the utter truthfulness, in the pictures of Nantucket life, are very impressive. The painter has made you see the scenes as they are."[70]

The explanation of these diverse points of view would involve a discussion of shifting perspectives toward a given subject, differing criteria for the judging of truth, and the cultural blinders necessarily worn by writers from two different periods.[71] These are factors in any attempt to understand disagreements between two ages. One element specific to reconciling these varying opinions concerning *The Cranberry Harvest,* however, is the island of Nantucket itself, and its peculiar ability to remain outside the flow of time.

As early as 1885 some writers tended to confuse Johnson's predilection for Nantucket's quaint (to use the word the islanders often turned upon themselves) subject matter with an urge toward historical re-creation:

> Nantucket [is] one of the rare spots which preserve the flavor and atmosphere of the olden time. The island, with its types of old men and women that are fading out elsewhere, even in other remote nooks of Massachusetts, its queer houses and windmills, its antique furniture and costume—has long been the artistic "property" of Mr. Eastman Johnson. The man and the place have a natural sympathy for each other. He is a chronicler of a phase of our national life which is fast passing away, and which cannot be made up with old fashion-plates and the lay figure of the studio. He lives in a fascinating "house of seven gables," filled with curiosities. . . . Mr. Johnson's studio is stored with antique furniture, spinning-wheels, and costumes. A row of battered hats suggest the antiquated squires, Quakers, and gentlemen of the olden time that have made their bow to us in his pictures [FIG. 4].[72]

The writer of this passage has erroneously conflated the out-of-date with the passed away. For, of course, the "gentlemen of the olden time" who bowed from Johnson's paintings were a living part of the island, and the artist portrayed them as such. Nantucket's visible past, revealed not only in its people but in the town's stately architecture and plentiful antiques, was a fact of commercial as well as aesthetic value to the promoters of the island as a summer resort.[73] The sensitive visitor to the island might, by a stretch of imagination, momentarily believe that he or she had gone, when stepping onto the island, backward in time. But those who live in such a place do not often make this imaginative leap. Nor did Johnson. In spite of his "natural sympathy" for olden days, he did not use Nantucket as a setting for historical genre scenes.[74] What he painted there were scenes of daily life as it was lived—always limited, of course, by the island's special character and Johnson's own definitions of art and decorum.

With *Husking Bee, Island of Nantucket* Johnson was depicting a scene that many of his urban viewers might have considered old-fashioned, since for much of the country by the 1870s the husking had become largely a commercial rather

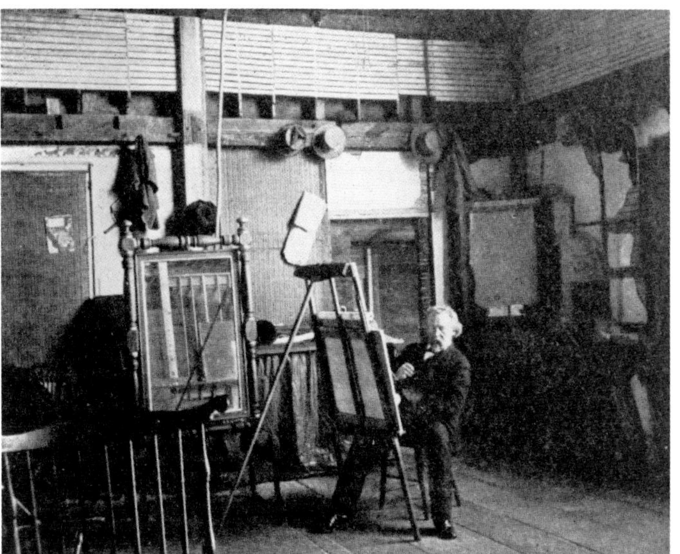

FIG. 4. *Studio of Eastman Johnson, Nantucket,* ca. 1885. Photograph from Everett U. Crosby, *Eastman Johnson at Nantucket* (Nantucket, Mass.: Privately printed, 1944), 10. This photograph apparently served as the basis for a wood engraving reproduced in Lizzie W. Champney, "The Summer Haunts of American Artists," *The Century Magazine* 30, no. 6 (October 1885): 852.

than social activity.[75] On the island, however, such events did still take place:

> The husking at the farm of Mr. Charles W. Gardner, which was postponed Wednesday on account of the rain, came off on Thursday afternoon. The day was fine, and a merry party of about seventy-five persons assembled. Three or four hundred bushels of ears were husked out, and then the party sat down to a bountiful repast—such a one as Mrs. G. knows so well how to get up—to which they did ample justice.[76]

Johnson's widow later wrote that the composition of *Husking Bee* grew from such an observed event; regarding the version of the work now at The Metropolitan Museum of Art she noted that in late November 1875, on a "day of dark skies and wind he came upon the scene," and described the old sea captains in their chairs and even the chickens in the foreground as if they were in fact transcriptions of reality.[77]

With *The Cranberry Harvest,* the result of his "cranberry fever," Johnson again celebrated a rural task seen on the island. And again, as in the earlier work, Johnson depicted the scene in a manner that emphasized the pleasurable, social side of the labor. But here the artist was not dealing with an outmoded technology. Quite to the contrary he shows an activity, one barely twenty years old on Nantucket and only recently of economic importance, being practiced in the standard manner for the time—hand picking.[78] This was an image of current concern: articles describing the mode and method of cultivating the berry appeared in periodicals during the 1870s, and the facts of the harvest—predictions, warnings, and comparisons with past years—were featured in the island's newspapers.[79] In 1876 a form of industrial crime was even reported:

> Cranberry thieves are now making raids. Folger & Bunker, who own around Cupaam Pond and Trots Hills have had a barrel or more of the tart berries stolen within a few days. The thieves can expect no leniency if they are detected in their predatory visits.[80]

Within the island context, *The Cranberry Harvest, Island of Nantucket* is a view of modern life.

Nonetheless, Johnson accentuates the scene's festival air by placing a laughing couple in the foreground and children at the corners of the composition. These provide emotional access into the painting and attempt to persuade the viewer that the harvest was more play than work. His contemporaries accepted this characterization and praised him for capturing it:

> Among the many subjects which he has painted at Nantucket none is more characteristic or agreeable than his "Cranberry-Picking." . . . [T]he time of gathering it is in autumn, and, like hop-picking in England, the business is made the occasion of much mirth and love-making.[81]

Literary accounts of cranberry harvesting from the time, while discussing fiscal realities, stress a comparably festive point of view:

> As for the Cape girls, it's a pretty sight to see them picking cranberries [FIG. 5]. With rosy cheeks and rippling laughter and bursts of song; with a shout for the baby girl who proudly carries up her tiny cupful to be measured and written down to her credit; with pleasant jokes over the sorting and barreling; with kindly emulation and neighborly helpfulness—the picking goes on.
> . . . [T]he cranberry culture has done much to enrich the people of Cape Cod, and to afford pleasant and profitable employment to women and girls during the picking season.[82]

For Johnson's harvesters, work is play and good spirits abound. This may be a fiction—although it seems a pervasive one concerning cranberry harvesters—for we do not now know the pickers' attitudes toward their days in the bogs of Nantucket in 1879. Before attributing to the artist a nostalgicizing viewpoint, however, we ought at least to consider that what Johnson put on canvas he actually saw—town residents only irregularly recruited for agricultural labor, enjoying themselves as they earn extra money on a warm autumn afternoon.

In several other fundamental ways, Eastman Johnson was seeking after truth in his painting of the cranberry harvest. This is apparent from his testimony to McEntee ("the models are here and whatever materials I require, and that is all there is of the pictures, so of course I cant do them elsewhere"). Johnson's cranberry pickers are his neighbors on the island, and he portrays them without anachronistic props or activities.[83] Moreover, Johnson approached the art-making process as honestly and sincerely as possible, working at least some of the time in the outdoors[84] and transferring the freshness of his observations to the finished work. That is why he had to see the figures out in the bogs, why simply transporting the costumes and his sketches to his New York studio to re-create the scene was not sufficient. In *The Cranberry Harvest, Island of Nantucket*—although he arranged the figures arbitrarily and positioned a windmill along the Cliff where one had never stood—Johnson sought to evoke the truly magical atmosphere of the desert island on which he made his summer home. In this he was splendidly successful. He has managed to impart to this painting of labor the impression of "sweet quiet leisure," the quality, as he wrote to McEntee, of "something very peaceful and satisfactory in our life here."

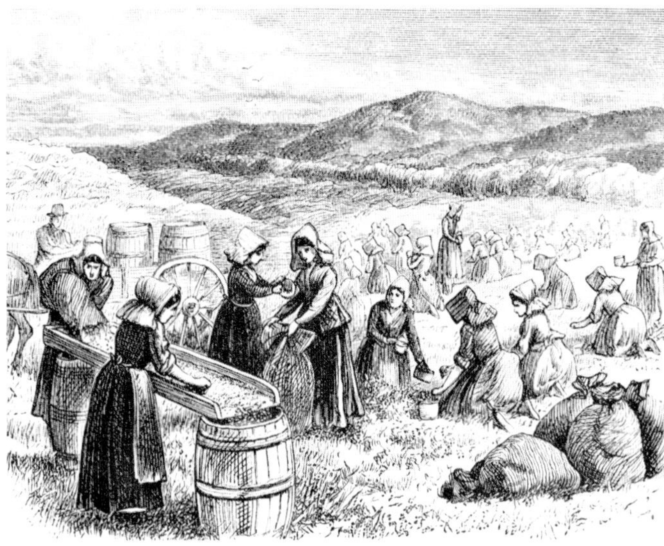

FIG. 5. *Picking and Sorting Cranberries,* ca. 1875. Wood engraving in Charles Nordhoff, "Cape Cod, Nantucket, and the Vineyard," *Harper's New Monthly Magazine* 51, no. 3301 (June 1875): 59.

NOTES

[1] Eastman Johnson to Jervis McEntee, 12 October 1879; Archives of American Art, Smithsonian Institution, Misc. MSS: Jervis McEntee, Gift of Charles E. Feinberg, roll D30, frame 517.

[2] The recognition of the painting's importance has continued. After being hidden from public view for nearly eighty years, the painting reappeared at a commercial English gallery in 1969. Since then it was one of the most acclaimed works in the artist's retrospective of 1972 (organized by Patricia Hills for the Whitney Museum of American Art) and was included in the exhibitions *American Light: The Luminist Movement* (organized by the National Gallery of Art in 1980) and *A New World: Masterpieces of American Painting, 1760–1910* (organized by the Museum of Fine Arts, Boston, in 1983).

[3] "Of her ancient mariners, indeed, we saw few; but their wives and children seemed numerous enough. One can not but remark the great preponderance of women and children in the visible population of the place; and this circumstance gives to the streets and thoroughfares in the interior of the town a more cheerful and home-like air. Inquiring for the cause of this disparity in the sexes, your response is found in the old song of The Sea:

'The sea has one and all,
Fathers, brothers, sons, and lovers.'

In addition, a few years since, the California fever swept the island with a virulence more fatal than war and pestilence combined. It is estimated that Nantucket lost some six or eight hundred men by that epidemic. At night there was music in the Public Place, and observing the crowd collected to hear it, I judged that at least four-fifths were women" (D.H. Strother, "A Summer in New England [Third Paper]," *Harper's New Monthly Magazine* 21, no. 126 [November 1860]: 746).

[4] "In the course of my ramblings I came across what one so seldom sees now, even in the East, a wind-mill, in 'sailing order.' There are two of them on the Island, and the date at which one of them was built was cut in the stone door-step—1765" (R.R. Minturn, "Nantucket," *The Lakeside Monthly* 10, no. 56 [August 1873]: 142).

[5] Although Johnson uses the diagonals of the composition—real (in the boundary between light sky and rising hillside) and illusory (in the groupings of the harvesters)—to relieve any tendency toward static monumentality.

[6] The artist Carroll Beckwith wrote an appreciation of the artist that early made this point: "The art conveyed to the canvas always prevailed over the simple story. The work of the *painter* was dominant" (in Will H. Low, Carroll Beckwith, Samuel Isham, and Frank Fowler, "The Field of Art: Eastman Johnson—His Life and Works," *Scribner's Magazine* 40, no. 2 [August 1906]: 254).

[7] For brief discussions of the two artists, see John I. H. Baur, *Eastman Johnson, 1824–1906: An American Genre Painter,* exh. cat. (Brooklyn: Brooklyn Museum, 1940), 22; and Patricia Hills, *The Genre Painting of Eastman Johnson: The Sources and Development of His Style and Themes* (New York: Garland Publishing, 1977), 99–101, 137–39. The critic Mark Selby was one of the earliest twentieth-century commentators to remark on the similarities between the two artists: "Hardly any of [Johnson's Nantucket works] were marines, however; perhaps only that one of the couple on the cliff, looking seaward, 'Flying the Kite,' which was also in the final exhibition and seemed to so many, in its directness and its rejection of the unessential, a precursor of Winslow Homer. Maine or Nantucket, the painter all his life remained an unmistakable 'Down Easter,' in his outward ways and modes of speech, as well as in his ways of thinking and in his shrewd and humorous outlook on life. 'A very vernacular man,' as was said of Daniel Webster" (Mark Selby, "An American Painter: Eastman Johnson," *Putnam's Monthly* 2, no. 5 [August 1907]: 533).

At least two of Johnson's Nantucket works—*Lambs, Nantucket* (1874, Collection of Mr. and Mrs. Paul Mellon, Upperville, Va.) and *Woman Reading* (ca. 1875, San Diego Museum of Art)—were long attributed to Homer (see Robert A. diCurcio, *Art on Nantucket: The History of Painting on Nantucket Island* [Nantucket, Mass.: Nantucket Historical Association in cooperation with the Nantucket Historical Trust, 1982], 141).

[8] Winslow Homer, quoted in G. W. Sheldon, *Hours with Art and Artists* (New York: D. Appleton, 1882), 138.

[9] For a discussion of these studies, see Sally Mills, " 'Right Feeling and Sound Technique': French Art and the Development of Eastman Johnson's Outdoor Genre Paintings," in this volume.

[10] Hills has posited that the cranberry harvest series dates from sometime between 1875 and 1880 (*Genre Painting of Eastman Johnson,* xvii, 149). *Girl with Glass* (see FIG. 5, Mills essay), bears the inscription of 22 September 1875, but that date apparently refers only to the main figure. The drawing of the cranberry harvesters at the side appears to have been added later, as if Johnson reached for a handy surface on which to jot down this sketchy notation of pickers. Johnson would have had little compunction in using the drawing in this fashion: "Most of the preparatory drawings have since disappeared; Johnson probably thought of them as notations with little independent value" (Hills, *Genre Painting of Eastman Johnson,* 157–58).

[11] The artist's contemporaries remarked often on his industry. William Walton, who wrote one of the fullest accounts of the artist's life and works at the time of Johnson's death, noted: "All the talent that a man may have is required to make him an artist, Mr. Johnson was in the habit of declaring, 'and *all* his time.' . . . In the early summer, when the household arrangements were being made for the annual removal to Nantucket, Mr. Johnson would work till the last day and begin again immediately when in his island studio" (William Walton, "Eastman Johnson, Painter," *Scribner's Magazine* 40, no. 3 [September 1906]: 263).

[12] Scholars, following Walton, have cited the first visit as occurring in 1870 (Baur, *Eastman Johnson,* 21; Patricia Hills, *Eastman Johnson,* exh. cat. [New York: Clarkson N. Potter in association with the Whitney Museum of American Art, 1972], 71; Hills, *Genre Painting of Eastman Johnson,* 127). The artist's chronology, however, is by no means complete and an article in Nantucket's weekly paper on 31 August 1870 clearly implies that Johnson had been on the island at least once before. See below, note 29.

[13] Walton, "Eastman Johnson, Painter," 272.

[14] Herman Melville, *Moby Dick: or, the Whale* (1851; New York: The Modern Library, 1950),

61–62. In 1868 one author wrote simply: "It is entirely safe to say that Nantucket is the most eccentric and anomolous of all the geographical eccentricities and anomolies in America" (W. B. Drake, "Nantucket," *Lippincott's Magazine* 2, no. 15 [September 1868]: 283).

[15]P., "Country Correspondence," *The Crayon* 5, no. 9 (September 1858): 269–70.

Writing in the late eighteenth century, when the whaling industry was still young, J. Hector St. John de Crèvecoeur wrote of the contrast between the island's natural resources and the accomplishments of a people living in a democracy:

> Would you believe that a sandy spot of about twenty-three thousand acres, affording neither stones nor timber, meadows nor arable, yet can boast of a handsome town consisting of more than 500 houses, should possess above 200 sail of vessels; constantly employ upwards of 2,000 seamen; feed more than 15,000 sheep, 500 cows, 200 horses; and has several citizens worth £20,000 sterling! Yet all these facts are uncontroverted. Who would have imagined that any people should have abandoned a fruitful and extensive continent filled with the riches which the most ample vegetation affords . . . to come and inhabit a little sandbank to which nature had refused those advantages.
>
> . . . When their fleets have been successful, the bustle and hurry of business on this spot for some days after their arrival would make you imagine Sherborn [the original name of the town, Nantucket] is the capital of a very opulent and large province.

Letters from an American Farmer, in *Letters from an American Farmer and Sketches of Eighteenth-Century America,* ed. Albert E. Stone (New York: Penguin Books, 1981), 109, 112.

[16]There are numerous books and articles on the history of Nantucket dating from the end of the nineteenth century onward. Many of these are cited in Marie M. Coffin, *The History of Nantucket Island: A Bibliography of Source Material* (Nantucket, Mass.: Nantucket Historical Trust, 1970). Two of the fuller overviews of Nantucket and its industries are R. A. Douglas-Lithgow, *Nantucket: A History* (New York: G. P. Putnam's Sons, 1914) and Alexander Starbuck, *The History of Nantucket, County, Island, and Town* (1924; reprint, Rutland, Vt.: Charles E. Tuttle, 1969).

[17]For Nantucket's nineteenth-century development, see: Obed Macy, *The History of Nantucket with a Concise Statement of Prominent Events from 1835 to 1880, by William C. Macy,* 2d ed. (1880; reprint, Ellinwood, Kans.: Macys of Ellinwood, 1985), 285–313; [Isaac H. Folger], *Handbook of Nantucket, containing a Brief Historical sketch of the Island, with Notes of Interest to summer visitors* (Nantucket, Mass.: Island Review, 1875), 43; John W. McCalley, *Nantucket: Yesterday and Today* (New York: Dover, 1981), 6–7.

[18]Strother, "A Summer in New England," 745.

The mention of "listless seeming people" stands in direct contrast to Crèvecoeur's observation that "idleness is the most heinous sin that can be committed in Nantucket: an idle man would soon be pointed out as an object of compassion, for idleness is considered as another word for want and hunger" *(Letters from an American Farmer,* 156).

[19]Macy, *History of Nantucket,* 301.

[20]Census figures cited in Macy, *History of Nantucket,* 312.

[21]Drake, "Nantucket," 284. Another wrote, "Returning from my stroll early in the afternoon, I was surprised at the almost death-like stillness of the town. As I turned into the main street, but a single person was in sight; every one seemed to be asleep, and I imagined that the houses blinked drowsily as I passed" (Minturn, "Nantucket," 142).

[22]For a thorough discussion of the development of tourism on the island, see Edwin P. Hoyt, *Nantucket: The Life of an Island* (Brattleboro, Vt.: Stephen Greene Press, 1978), 147–74.

[23]Macy, *History of Nantucket,* 299.

Given the island's reputation for industry, the pursuit of a position as a leisure center is ironic. Crèvecoeur had earlier observed: "Such an island, inhabited as I have described, is not the place where gay travellers should resort in order to enjoy that variety of pleasures the more splendid towns of this continent afford" *(Letters from an American Farmer,* 161*)*.

[24]The trip between Nantucket and New York was straightforward: "The round trip from Pier 28, foot of Murray Street [New York], to Nantucket and back, by way of the Fall River boats, Old Colony Railroad to New Bedford, and thence by 'Island Home' steamboat to Nantucket,—say eighteen hours,—costs exactly $8; and the expenses there at the best hotels vary from $1.50 to $3 per day" (Barry Gray, quoted in Edward K. Godfrey, *The Island*

of Nantucket, what it was and what it is; being a complete index and guide to this noted resort [Boston: Lee and Shepard, 1882], 2).

[25] "Correspondence of the *Providence Journal*," quoted in *Inquirer and Mirror,* 27 August 1870.

[26] "Summer Is Over," *Inquirer and Mirror,* 23 September 1871.

[27] Of the twenty-three genre paintings Johnson exhibited at the National Academy of Design spring exhibitions after 1870, eight of the more important either were done on or demonstrably depict Nantucket: *The Old Stage Coach* (NAD 1871); *Bo Peep* (NAD 1874); *Husking Bee, Island of Nantucket, The New Bonnet* (NAD 1876); *The Reprimand, The Cranberry Harvest, Island of Nantucket* (NAD 1880); *Old Whalers of Nantucket* (NAD 1887); *Embers* (NAD 1899). Others could well have been located there, such as *Catching the Bee* (NAD 1873), *The Peddler* (NAD 1875), *"Dropping Off," City People in Country Quarters, The Tramp* (NAD 1877); *The New England Pedler* [*sic*] (NAD 1879).

[28] In July 1871 R. H. Cook published a text specifically for the island visitor—*Historical Notes of the Island of Nantucket and Tourist's Guide*—one of the first of a long line of guides that continues to the present.

[29] "Visitors at Nantucket," *Inquirer and Mirror,* 13 August 1870. The text is interesting, for not only does it demonstrate that artists besides Johnson visited Nantucket early in the decade, but it also implies that 1870 was, contrary to most published sources on the artist, Johnson's second visit to the island.

[30] Nantucket Registry of Deeds, book 61, page 248.

[31] Nantucket Registry of Deeds, book 61, page 252. In May the property was transferred to Elizabeth (book 61, pages 292–94) who, along with her husband, in the 1880s and 1890s would play an active role in land speculation along the north shore. They added approximately 40 rods of land to the property the next year, paying $50.00 to Henry Coleman (book 62, page 160). See Appendix 3.

[32] *Liberal Christian,* quoted in *Inquirer and Mirror,* 31 August 1872.

[33] *Inquirer and Mirror,* 23 November 1872.

[34] "Personal," *Inquirer and Mirror,* 14 September 1878 and 13 September 1879.

[35] Charles Nordhoff, "Cape Cod, Nantucket, and the Vineyard," *Harper's New Monthly Magazine* 51, no. 301 (June 1875): 65. By the early 1880s the painter is included in the island's professional directory: "Eastman Johnson (summer resident)./Studio, Centre St." (Godfrey, *The Island of Nantucket,* 262).

[36] "Personal," *The Island Review,* 29 July 1875. Johnson tackled a great challenge. As a later writer acidly noted: "But in the new order of things dawning upon the shores of Nantucket, the Cliff has been seized upon by 'strangers,' who are putting up the regulation seaside villa in great numbers. . . . Another little eccentricity of the breezes sweeping these cliff estates is the blowing away of the gardens attempted by the proprietors; the only way to keep a cuticle of soil upon the sand composing this eminence is to plant it with beach-grass; and however appropriate to the environs of a villa, beds of gladioli, pelargonium, and begonias may be, they do not answer the purpose, or in any sense hold their own before the piping winds which tear the poor things up by the roots, bury them in sand, and shriek exultingly upon their way" (Jane G. Austin, *Nantucket Scraps* [Boston: James R. Osgood, 1883], 119–20).

[37] Dr. A. E. Jenks, quoted in Godfrey, *The Island of Nantucket,* 17.

[38] Henry M. Baird, "Nantucket," *Scribner's Monthly* 6, no. 4 (August 1873): 390; "Ten Days in Nantucket," *The Granite Monthly* 8, nos. 7 and 8 (July–August 1885): 217. See also, "Ho! for the Cliff Shore!" *Inquirer and Mirror,* 17 August 1872, and J. S. Doyle, "The Nantucket" [hotel promotional brochure] (Nantucket, Mass.: Privately printed, ca. 1885).

[39] "On our drive to town again [from the Cliff], we passed the fine large cottage of the artist, Eastman Johnson, who doubtless was then painting his picture, 'The Nantucket Sea-Captain.'. . .

Another day in comes, like a breeze from the mountains, with a hearty greeting, another friend, bringing with him, as he says in his introduction, 'the King of Nantucket, Mr. Sanford [the President of the Pacific National Bank, whose portrait Johnson painted in 1878]!' and the artist, Eastman Johnson. We show them the simple wonders of our mansion, but modestly assure them that while our cottage is small, yet the boundless ocean, just back of the cottage, is ours!" (A. Judd Northrup, *'Sconset Cottage Life: A Summer on Nantucket Island* [New York: Baker, Pratt & Co., 1881], 92, 150).

There is a wonderful irony here, given Johnson's impression of the tourist traps he encountered abroad: "One must live amongst them for a time and learn to divest himself of the multitude of annoyances that are mixed up with all sight-seeing in these lands before one can enjoy the fine things to a reasonable extent" (Johnson to Charlotte Child, March 1851; quoted in Baur, *Eastman Johnson,* 11).

[40] In this link between subject matter and financial interest Johnson anticipates the tie that later existed between Winslow Homer and his landscapes of Prout's Neck, Maine. See the work of Patricia Junker, "Expressions of Art and Life in *The Artist's Studio in an Afternoon Fog,"* in *Winslow Homer in the 1890s: Prout's Neck Observed,* exh. cat. (New York: Hudson Hills Press, for Memorial Art Gallery, University of Rochester, forthcoming).

[41] As one recent historian has noted, "land speculators descended like vultures to 'develop' the island through the subdivision of the land. . . . Fortunately for Nantucket, all of these ventures by land despoilers failed" (McCalley, *Nantucket,* 11). For a more detailed account, see Henry Barnard Worth, *Nantucket Lands and Land Owners* (Nantucket, Mass.: Nantucket Historical Association, 1906), 213–16.

[42] Letter of ca. 1898 to his nephew Philip J. Wilson, quoted in Baur, *Eastman Johnson,* 26.

[43] Will H. Low, *A Chronicle of Friendships, 1873–1900* (New York: Charles Scribner's Sons, 1908), 266–67.

[44] Eastman Johnson to Jervis McEntee, 12 October 1879; Archives of American Art, Smithsonian Institution, Misc. MSS: Jervis McEntee, Gift of Charles E. Feinberg, roll D30, frames 516–17.

[45] As McEntee recorded in his journal entry for 26 October 1879: "On Thursday I started for Nantucket to visit Eastman who was expecting me but misled by an advertisement in the paper I was too late for the boat and as no boat went again until Saturday I got off at New Bedford and came to N.Y. by the Fall River boat arriving there on Friday morning" (Archives of American Art, Smithsonian Institution, Jervis McEntee diary, roll D180, frame 300).

[46] Eastman Johnson to Jervis McEntee, 17 November 1879; Archives of American Art, Smithsonian Institution, Misc. MSS: Jervis McEntee, Gift of Charles E. Feinberg, roll D30, frame 457.

[47] Eastman Johnson to Jervis McEntee, 13 December 1879; Archives of American Art, Smithsonian Institution, Misc. MSS: Jervis McEntee, Gift of Charles E. Feinberg, roll D30, frames 460–62.

[48] Low, *Chronicle of Friendships,* 266–68.

[49] "Eastman Johnson, the artist, arrived in town last week, accompanied by his family" ("Personal," *Inquirer and Mirror,* 13 September 1879).

[50] See Mills, " 'Right Feeling and Sound Technique,' " in this volume.

[51] "American Art News," *The Art Interchange* 4, no. 4 (18 February 1880): 31. See also "My Note Book," *The Art Amateur* 2, no. 4 (March 1880): 68.

[52] "American Art News," *The Art Interchange* 4, no. 8 (14 April 1880): 63.

[53] "A Disaster at the Fair," *The World* [New York], 22 April 1880.

[54] Johnson, despite the fact that he was a generation older than most of its members, attended meetings of the Society of American Artists—an exhibition society that promoted the work of young men, many just returned from European training.

[55] Very few writers were as neutral as the critic for *The Evening Post,* who simply reported: "Enter the south room from the corridor and you are confronted by a large Eastman Johnson 'Picking Cranberries.' There are many pickers in a broad field. . . . The exhibition is unusually bright and interesting" ("The Academy Exhibition," 26 March 1880).

[56] "Fifty-Fifth Annual Exhibition of the National Academy of Design—Private View Day—First Article," *New York Herald,* 27 March 1880; S. G. W. Benjamin, "The Exhibitions. V.—National Academy of De sign," *The American Art Review* 1 (1879–1880): 309; and "The New York Spring Exhibitions. I. The National Academy Exhibition," *The Art Journal* 6, no. 5 (May 1880): 154.

[57] The critical split doubled the one perceived among the artists. Mariana Griswold van Rensselaer wrote simply: "In view of this year's exhibitions it does not seem incorrect or premature to speak of an elder and a younger school in American art" ("Spring Exhibitions and Picture-Sales in New York.—I," *The American Architect and Building News* 7, no. 227 [1 May 1880]: 190).

[58] M[ariana] G[riswold] van Rensselaer, "Spring Exhibitions and Picture-Sales in New York.—II," *The American Architect and Building News* 7, no. 228 (8 May 1880): 201.

[59] See, for example, the review in *The Art Journal:* "For breadth of handling, depth of perspective and general effect as an outdoor composition of figures in a landscape, praise is due to Mr. Eastman Johnson's 'Husking Bee, Island of Nantucket.' The opposing companies have been formed, the old people on one side and the young men and girls on the other, and the work, it is apparent, is going on with spirit. In the left foreground there is a group of old men who are working to win, but, in the company on the right of the field, there is considerable flirtation going on among the girls and boys. The ground between the opposing sides is covered with corn-husks, and in the middle-ground is a long table spread with rich country delicacies for the entertainment of the company. The picture is of large size and will take a high rank among the earnest works in the Exhibition" ("The National Academy of Design. First Notice," *The Art Journal* n.s. 2, no. 5 [May 1876]: 159).

[60] Quoted in G. W. Sheldon, *American Painters* (New York: D. Appleton, 1881), 168.

[61] "A Metropolitan Museum," *The New-York Times,* 30 March 1880.

[62] "National Academy of Design. Fifty-Fifth Annual Exhibition. (Third Article)," *The New-York Daily Tribune,* 18 April 1880. A portion of this review was reprinted on 24 April 1880 in the Nantucket *Inquirer and Mirror.*

[63] See, for example, William A. Coffin: " 'Corn Husking,' one of the most important of his pictures, and one that completely realizes what we are wont to speak of as 'American genre,' is owned by Mr. Potter Palmer of Chicago. 'The Cranberry Harvest,' 'The Pedlar,' 'Fiddling his Way,' 'The Old Stage-Coach,' 'What the Shell Says,' 'Two Men,' and 'The Pension Agent,' are some of the pictures that made his fame as a painter, and have given him popularity" (William A. Coffin, "Eastman Johnson: The Century's American Artist Series," *The Century Magazine* 48, no. 6 [October 1894]: 958).

[64] See Mills, " 'Right Feeling and Sound Technique,' " in this volume, for a discussion of Johnson's European training and the roots of this working method.

[65] At least as Johnson portrayed it, there was no rigid structure. In many accounts of the time describing the cranberry harvest on Cape Cod or Long Island, patches were set off by white cords, and individuals were responsible for the thorough picking of their zone. See, for example, an account of 1885: "They pick with their backs to the sun, in rows divided by strings, to insure 'clean picking,' each one being kept in the prescribed place till the vines are well picked" ("Making a Cranberry Bog," *Harper's Weekly* 29, no. 1503 [10 October 1885]: 670).

We cannot know whether the small bog Johnson shows would have been subject to this more professional method of gathering, although one of his studies—the verso of *At the Closing of the Day* (see FIG. 7, Mills essay)—seems to show white strings stretched over the ground.

[66] Carol Troyen, "Eastman Johnson, *The Cranberry Harvest, Nantucket Island,*" in Theodore E. Stebbins, Jr., Carol Troyen, and Trevor J. Fairbrother, *A New World: Masterpieces of American Painting, 1760–1910,* exh. cat. (Boston: Museum of Fine Arts, 1983), 270–71.

[67] Patricia Hills, "Images of Rural America in the Works of Eastman Johnson, Winslow Homer, and Their Contemporaries: A Survey and Critique," in *The Rural Vision: France and America in the Late Nineteenth Century,* ed. Hollister Sturges (Omaha, Nebr.: Joslyn Art Museum, 1987), 77.

[68] "Fifth-Fifth Annual Exhibition," *New York Herald,* 27 March 1880; "National Academy of Design," *New York Commercial Advertiser,* 27 March 1880; "National Academy of Design. Fifth-Fifth Annual Exhibition. (Third Article)," *The New-York Daily Tribune,* 18 April 1880.

[69] George William Sheldon, *Recent Ideals of American Art* (New York: D. Appleton and Co., 1888), 20.

[70] Edward King, "The Value of Nationalism in Art," *The Monthly Illustrator* 4, no. 14 (June 1895): 267–68. Referring specifically to *Husking Bee,* King wrote: "In the 'Husking Bee' how easy to have composed a group which should tell a sentimental story in connection with his rustic island-gathering of industrious folk! Yet that would have been to intrude the theatre upon a thing as remote from it, as foreign to it, as are the Egyptian Pyramids. . . . No story is lugged in. We are allowed to look in upon real beings, untouched by self-consciousness."

[71] I wonder if the disposition to read the image as nostalgic is reinforced by our own perspective. Look, for example, at the graphics of Celestial Seasonings "Cranberry Cove" Herb Tea (FIG. 6). There are strong echoes here of *The Cranberry*

Harvest: the single standing woman looking to the side (left rather than right) surrounded by kneeling women wearing beribboned straw hats, and the lighthouse to the left. The modern fantasy of "Cranberry Cove"—clearly nostalgic in purpose—highlights how easily the elements of Johnson's work can be reassembled into evocative symbols. Does the aspect in our collective imagination that made "Cranberry Cove" a successful packaging image affect our response to the work from 1880?

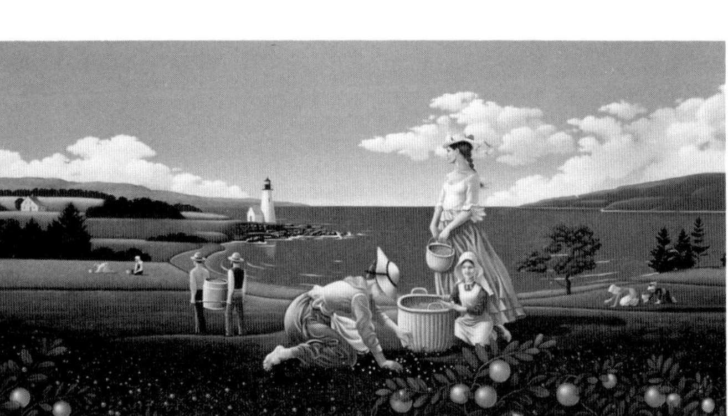

FIG. 6. Bob Giusti, *Cranberry Cove® Herb Tea Art,* ca. 1985. Acrylic on canvas, 10 1/8 x 22 1/2 inches. Used with permission of Celestial Seasonings, Inc. © 1985.

[72] Lizzie W. Champney, "The Summer Haunts of American Artists," *The Century Magazine* 30, no. 6 (October 1885): 854.

[73] "But if Nantucket has few attractions to offer such as arise from present prosperity, there is scarcely a seaboard town in America so quaint and so interesting on account of the reminiscences of the past which one constantly meets in every ramble" (Baird, "Nantucket," 385).

[74] Johnson did on occasion attempt historical themes, as with his *Prisoner of State* (1874, unlocated) and *John Milton Dictating "Paradise Lost" to His Daughters* (1876, Blanden Memorial Art Gallery, Fort Dodge, Iowa). But he did not use Nantucket as a background for colonial-revival images of the type that his younger colleagues, artists as diverse as Thomas Eakins, Frank Millet, and Thomas Wilmer Dewing, were doing during precisely these years.

[75] "The husking-bees, in which girls took a part, when a red ear was a coveted treasure, are remembered only by the old" (Rowland E. Robinson, "Glimpses of New England Farm Life [1878]; quoted in Sarah Burns, *Pastoral Inventions: Rural Life in Nineteenth-Century American Art and Culture* [Philadelphia: Temple University Press, 1989], 36).

[76] The notice ends: "After spending a pleasant evening, the party separated and arrived in town at an early hour. We regret that our engagements were such that it was impossible for us to be present" ("Husking," *Inquirer and Mirror,* 4 November 1871). See also "Husking," *Inquirer and Mirror,* 11 October 1879, for notice of Abner Fish's social husking in which "stalks were soon stripped of their ears by the many and willing hands," and "the edibles vanished like a dream. During the evening the time was pleasantly passed in singing, dancing, and social games."

To be sure, other notices in the local press throughout the decade mention the activity as tinged with nostalgia: "An old-fashioned husking is in progress at the farm of Mr. Charles Burgess this afternoon" ("Local Items," *Nantucket Journal,* 10 October 1878).

[77] Mrs. Eastman Johnson to Metropolitan Museum, 28 January 1913; quoted in Natalie Spassky, *American Paintings in The Metropolitan Museum of Art* (New York: The Metropolitan Museum of Art in association with Princeton University Press, 1985), vol. 2, p. 227. Certainly the known drawings for the painting (Free Library of Philadelphia; Karolik Collection, Museum of Fine Arts, Boston) have the air of being made from an observed scene rather than studio poses.

[78] "Cranberries were first cultivated on Nantucket in the middle of the 19th Century. . . . Small plots were started on several places on the Island, including two five-acre tracts in Polpis cultivated by Henry Swain and Captain J. Gardner in 1857" (Nantucket Conservation Foundation, *A Handbook for Visitors to the Windswept Cranberry Bog;* quoted in *Nantucket Guide 1989* [Nantucket, Mass.: Deborah M. Anderson, 1989], 60). See also "Cranberry Growing on Nantucket," broadside prepared by the Nantucket Conservation Foundation, Inc., ca. 1988.

As late as 1906 one writer could note, "[M]ost of the picking is done by hand, although where the berries are thickest they are taken by raking the vines with long toothed 'pickers' " (Frank Overton, "Three Hundred Dollars an Acre from Cranberries," *Country Life in America* 11 [November 1906]: 71).

[79] "Our cranberry growers have now commenced gathering in their crop, which we have heard was generally good, although it received much injury from the frost of two or three weeks ago" ("Cranberries," *Inquirer and Mirror,* 26 September 1874); "The cranberry pickers are getting out their camphire antidotes for running ivy poison" ("Review Scraps," *Island Review,* 16 September 1876).

[80] "Review Scraps," *Island Review,* 27 September 1876. The post and sign to the left of Johnson's work, with the terse notice "No pass over Cranberry bog" may respond to this threat, as well as to the damage more inadvertently perpetrated by idle trespassers. For the latter problem, see C. S. Reinhart, "A Warning to City Visitors," *Harper's Weekly* 21, no. 1079 (1 September 1877): 685, 690.

[81] S. G. W. Benjamin, "A Representative American," *The Magazine of Art* 5 (1882): 489. Or, as another early writer put it: "[H]is conception of this rendering of 'the life of the poor,' of 'the tillers of the soil' (and the ex-toilers of the sea), preaches no ugly gospel of discontent, as does so much of the contemporary French and Flemish art of this genre; his Nantucket neighbors know nothing of the *'protestation douloureuse de la race asservie à la glèbe'*; there is no *'cri de la terre'* arising from his cranberry marshes or his hay-stuffed barns" (Walton, "Eastman Johnson," 270–71).

[82] Nordhoff, "Cape Cod, Nantucket, and the Vineyard," 59–60. See also G. E. Adams and L. H. Bailey, who wrote in 1902: "Perhaps the reader has picked the cherry-red berries when the frost has loosed the maple leaves and the haze was in the sky of the early Indian summer. Merry days these may have been, when the whole family, and the neighbors' boys and girls, ran away to the ripening swamps for cranberries and a holiday" ("Turkeys and Cranberries," *Country Life in America* 3 [November 1902]: 8).

The accompanying wood engraving and other written accounts of the cranberry harvest emphasize a uniform apparel for the women—as reported in 1885, "The picking is a picturesque sight, the common costume for the women being a calico dress and a sun bonnet (in shape the same as the Shakers wear)" ("Making a Cranberry Bog," 670). The more fashionable dress of Johnson's women, straw hats and clothes that seem less than wholly utilitarian, perhaps indicates that these are not habitual farm laborers.

[83] Indeed, one later writer looked on the works as so accurate that they could bear historical witness, citing them as "careful studies of characteristic types, costumes and interiors which have since disappeared entirely. . . . [H]is studies are now of great historic value" (*The Works of the Late Eastman Johnson, N.A.,* sale cat. [New York: American Art Galleries, 1907], "Note").

The artist's aim in this regard is best suggested not simply by what he chose to include in his Nantucket outdoor scenes but also by what he omitted. Throughout the eighteenth and early nineteenth century, the principal outdoor festival on the island was the annual sheep-shearing (William F. Macy, *The Story of Old Nantucket: A Brief History of the Island and its People from its Discovery down to the Present Day* [2d ed., 1928; reprint, Ellinwood, Kans.: Macys of Ellinwood, 1983], 74–76). The art critic and chronicler Henry T. Tuckerman wrote an account of the event that was quoted in Drake ("Nantucket," 283–92). By Johnson's arrival, however, the flocks had been sold and the grazing land began to be subdivided. Johnson did not try to reconstruct on canvas the past tradition of the sheep-shearing, honoring a memory of old-time Nantucket. He instead looked about him and recorded the events that he saw.

[84] Many years after the fact one of the models, Peter Hussey, on looking at an unspecified Johnson work, "discovered himself as a small boy. He remembers the time he posed for the artist, standing in the cranberry bog which existed at that time near Cliff Road" ("The Kenneth Taylor Galleries Offers Unusual Exhibits," *Inquirer and Mirror,* 28 July 1945).

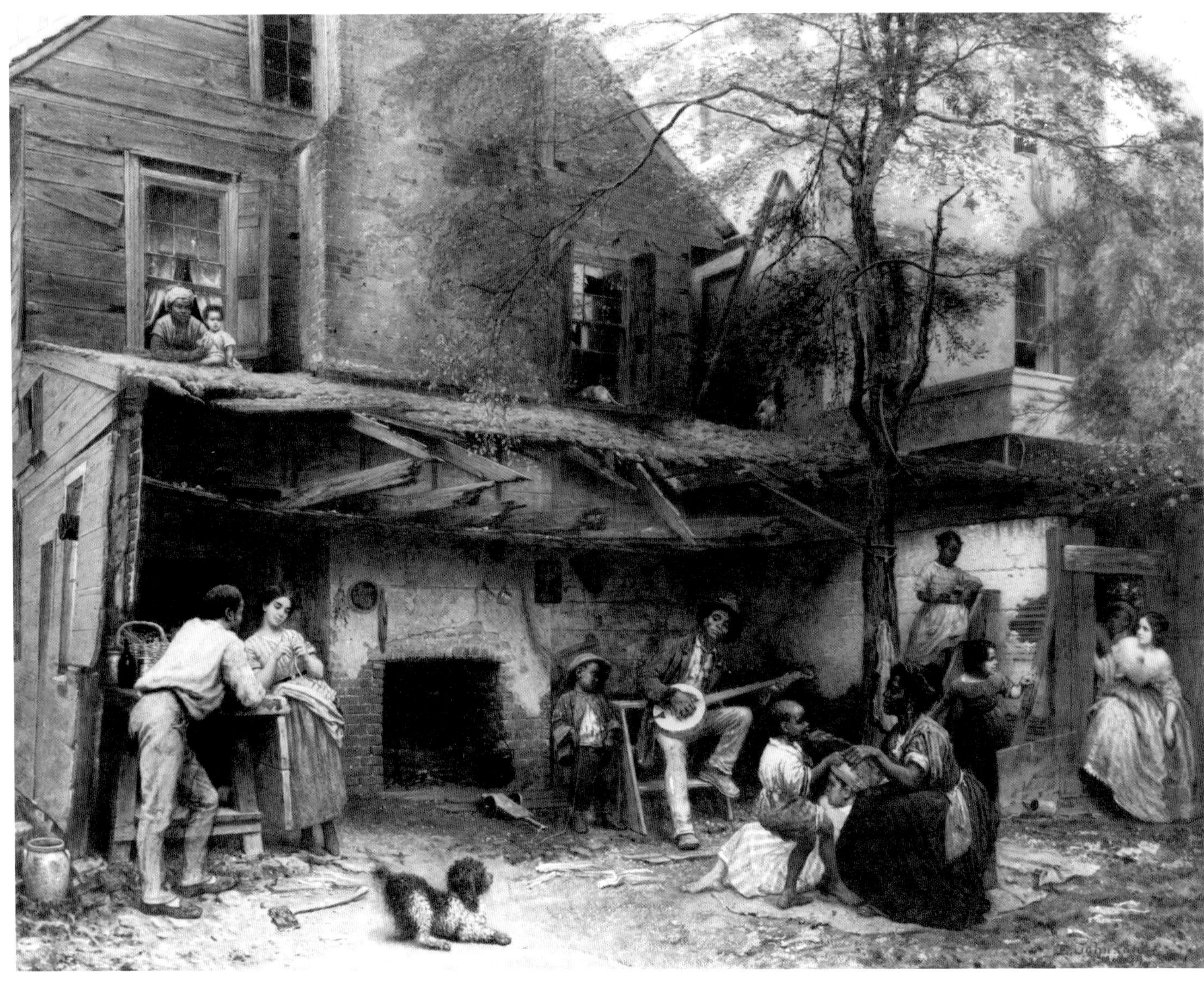

FIG. 1. Eastman Johnson, *Negro Life at the South,* 1859. Oil on canvas, 36 x 45 1/4 inches. Courtesy of The New-York Historical Society, New York City, the Robert L. Stuart Collection, on permanent loan from The New York Public Library.

"Right Feeling and Sound Technique": French Art and the Development of Eastman Johnson's Outdoor Genre Paintings

Sally Mills

Eastman Johnson was well established as a genre painter in America by the time he painted *The Cranberry Harvest, Island of Nantucket* (PLATE 1). In the nearly twenty-five years that had passed between Johnson's return from European study (October 1855) and the exhibition of this painting (March 1880), the artist had won critical acclaim and substantial patronage on the basis of portraits and genre scenes, most of which featured domestic interiors and focused on individual incidents or anecdotes. Yet with the 1859 exhibition of *Negro Life at the South,* now more commonly known as *Old Kentucky Home* (FIG. 1), Johnson announced the kind of art that would characterize the major efforts of his career: a large-scale genre scene, of demonstrably American subject matter, set outdoors, combining several vignettes within a well-integrated composition. Looking back over Johnson's career, one finds ample evidence that the artist sought to alternate and augment his smaller-scaled genre paintings with this type of composite, outdoor scene. If the first indication of this goal is *Negro Life at the South,* the last is *The Cranberry Harvest, Island of Nantucket.* The ambitions seemingly fulfilled in *The Cranberry Harvest*—for Johnson never again painted an outdoor genre scene on this scale, although he continued to paint for twenty years after 1880—justify a review of his career, giving special consideration to the formation of those ambitions and the acquisition of skills to accomplish them.

When he left for Europe in 1849, Johnson was a proficient and apparently successful portrait draftsman in America. His decision to turn from portraiture to genre painting was influenced (if not actually prompted) by the American Art-Union in New York, an organization that promoted American art in general and genre art in particular.[1] Following the recommended course of the Art-Union, Johnson traveled to Düsseldorf; but soon tiring of the academy there, he moved on—first to the Düsseldorf studio of Emanuel Leutze (1816–1868), then to The Hague, and finally to Paris, before returning home in 1855. Thus Johnson had many sources and different examples available to him when he embarked on the creation of his own genre paintings.

Johnson's first genre works, such as *The Peasants of the Rhine* (ca. 1850, unlocated), exhibited at the American Art-Union in 1852, or *The Savoyard Boy* (1853, The Brooklyn Museum), exhibited at the National Academy of Design in 1856, were painted in Germany and Holland; they are European both in subject and in style. But even as Johnson searched for and developed a repertoire of American subjects,[2] his art continued to reveal an awareness of European developments. Throughout the 1860s his smaller domestic scenes recalled to critics the work of the Frenchman Edouard Frère or the Englishman David Wilkie, even as those critics proclaimed the truthful "American-ness" of the subject portrayed.[3] After the exhibition of Johnson's larger outdoor compositions of the 1870s, a new comparison was invoked: in 1882, the critic S. G. W. Benjamin proclaimed that "In tone and colour and in the acute perception of rural human nature," Johnson's *Husking Bee, Island of Nantucket* (see FIG. 1, Simpson essay) "loses nothing by comparison with the work of Jules Breton."[4]

That Johnson's work could so readily—and (in general) favorably—bear comparison with those European artists, especially the French ones, deserves attention. It demonstrates that critics saw in Johnson's work parallels with the most popular European art of the time, even as they took pains to delineate the differences. It reveals that Johnson's art could, for the most part, stand up to the European example. And, of course, it suggests how thoroughly Johnson had assimilated his European training and put it to the service of American subjects.

Johnson seems to have had in mind a composite genre work almost as soon as he returned to America. In the summers of 1856 and 1857, he traveled to Superior, Wisconsin, the home of his sister and her family, where he eventually painted several studies of Chippewa Indians. When Henry Wadsworth Longfellow, of whose family and friends Johnson had drawn crayon portraits in 1846, invited Johnson around May 1857 to return to Boston and paint portraits of his youngest daughters, Johnson kindly refused the offer: " 'I should take the greatest pleasure in painting the three little subjects you designate,' [he wrote,] but explained that it would be impossible because of his intention of, 'making sketches of Frontier life.' "[5]

While most of his 1857 "sketches of Frontier life" seem to be portrait and figure drawings (many of them exceptionally beautiful),[6] Johnson also painted a small oil sketch of a townscape, *Grand Portage* (FIG. 2) and a larger *Canoe of Indians* (17¾ x 38¾ in., St. Louis County Historical Society, Duluth, Minn.). Whether these works represent Johnson's first ideas toward a major work one has no way of knowing. But his collecting of data seems purposeful, even if no final painting resulted from the expedition.

That Johnson was seeking subjects to match his ambition can be seen in a letter to one of his earliest patrons, John F. Coyle of Washington, D.C. In a letter of 1864 Johnson underscores the importance of a subject that would involve his full range of powers as a figure painter, as well as one that would describe a happy occasion, ripe with pleasant associations:

> I am getting on well enough so far as commissions & plenty to do goes, but getting wealth is a hard matter, & will take bigger prices than I have been getting. . . . I hope in the next year to do something more considerable than I have yet done, to paint two or three larger and more *pretentious* pictures. . . . In furtherance of one of these I am about starting for the country to make studies for a month or six weeks. This will be my fourth annual trip for the same purpose to the wilds of the State of Maine— The scene is a Down-east *Sugaring,* a picturesque & to me very interesting one, partly perhaps on account of its being associated with my pleasantest early recollections. . . . There will be forty figures or more, the occasion an entirely social one, even jolly, & very well adapted as I think to exhibit character & picturesque combination of form color &c. At all events I am very much interested in the subject, have spent a good deal of time on it already & not yet begun the picture nor indeed got nearly all the materials. But this spring will do me, I hope, in that respect.[7]

Johnson never completed such a scene, but at least thirty studies testify to his earnest attempts (see, for example, FIG. 3).[8]

In addition to demonstrating progress toward a compositional and narrative goal, these maple-sugaring studies also display a distinctive working method, one not seen in Johnson's work until that time. In his first attempt at a "more *pretentious*" picture, Johnson employed a French working method, and in doing so, moved away from the tight description and local color—hallmarks of the Düsseldorf style—that characterized both his *Savoyard Boy* and *Negro Life at the South.*[9] It is this method, exercised but never brought to a finish in a sugaring-off picture, that Johnson developed and improved over the next ten to fifteen years, and finally brought to bear on *The Cranberry Harvest.*

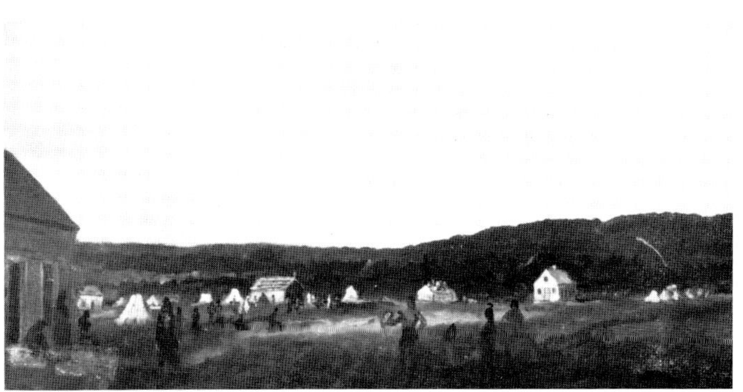

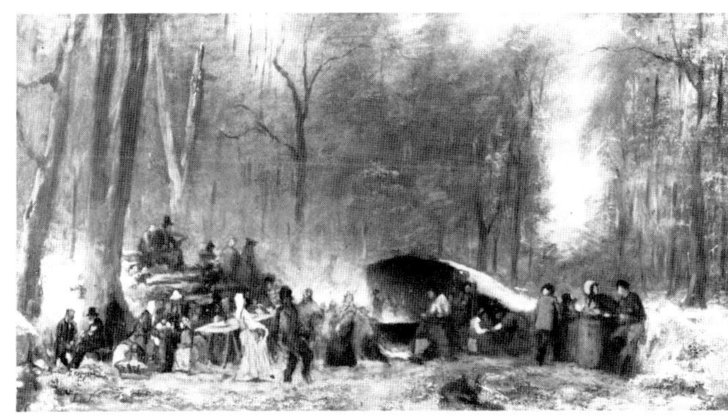

FIG. 2. Eastman Johnson, *Grand Portage,* 1857. Oil on canvas, 9 x 19½ inches. St. Louis County Historical Society, Duluth, Minn.

FIG. 3. Eastman Johnson, *A Different Sugaring Off,* ca. 1861–1866. Oil on canvas, 17¼ x 32¼ inches. The Fine Arts Museums of San Francisco, Gift of Mr. and Mrs. John D. Rockefeller 3rd.

"SOUND TECHNIQUE": EASTMAN JOHNSON AND THOMAS COUTURE

Johnson was first exposed to the French academic system in Paris while studying under Thomas Couture (1815–1879), a period that constituted the shortest segment of his long European sojourn. In August 1849 Johnson had sailed for Düsseldorf in the company of his friend George H. Hall (1825–1913), persuaded by the American Art-Union to study in Germany rather than Italy.[10] Johnson spent about a year and a half at the Düsseldorf Academy before entering the studio of Emanuel Leutze, expressing to the Art-Union in a letter of January 1851 "regret now that I had not been with [Leutze] during my entire stay in Düsseldorf."[11] But in July 1851 Johnson left Germany altogether, traveling via London (probably in order to see the Crystal Palace Exposition) to The Hague, where he spent the next four years. In Holland, as the art critic Henry Tuckerman described it, Johnson "struck upon a congenial vein of work, found unexpected opportunities for study, and met with flattering success in portraiture."[12] He copied works by Rembrandt and Van Dyck; secured several portrait commissions with the help of the American ambassador to The Hague, August Belmont; became known as "The American Rembrandt"; and was eventually offered the position of court painter, which he refused.[13]

Despite his success in Holland (or perhaps because of it, for that success seems to have been built largely upon the portrait trade that he was studying to move away from), Johnson left that environment as well; "he had not yet seen Paris."[14] He had been thinking of visiting Paris as early as 1851;[15] he was finally there by May 1855.[16] It was a good time to be in the city. From May to November 1855 Paris hosted a Universal Exposition, which incorporated the annual Salon and provided unparalleled opportunities for art viewing.[17] In Paris Johnson was surrounded by friends both American and German: George P. A. Healy (1813–1894), with whom he had painted a portrait of Daniel Webster in 1845; Ludwig Knaus (1829–1910), one of his friends from the Düsseldorf Academy; and others. Following the pattern of several German and American students before him who had left the academy at Düsseldorf for improved opportunities in Paris,[18] Johnson entered the studio of Thomas Couture. In doing so, he was no doubt encouraged by Healy, Couture's closest American friend, as well as by Knaus or any number of the other Couture students whom Johnson could have known.[19]

In The Hague Johnson had worked unsupervised, copying paintings and proceeding on his own. Now in Paris he would be studying directly under an acknowledged master, one whose atelier drew students from nearly every European country as well as from America. Johnson would be learning a prescribed studio technique, very different from his training in Düsseldorf, but in fact well suited to capture the warm undertones and control of light that he seems to have admired in Rembrandt.

Couture's actual instruction resembled that of the traditional French Academy he so abhorred: he insisted that drawing was the foundation of painting; his pupils studied anatomy and classical art; and he encouraged their appreciation of select masters, both old and modern.[20] Yet Couture's atelier differed from the academy in its emphasis on spontaneity and immediacy, even in final, so-called finished works. Couture elevated the *ébauche,* or painted sketch, to a central position within the art-making process, not only using it as a separate aid to achieve the proper light, color, and composition in a more finished work but also using the physical sketch itself as an integral element of the finished work painted on top of it. Couture allowed the layers of underpainting as well as the outlines of the composition to remain visible in his final works, using the warm tones of the *ébauche* itself to define areas of shade or texture, and dragging lighter hues across the underpainting to give greater depth and transparency to his shadows. Couture's method gave primacy to both the creation and the aesthetic of the sketch, although he still believed in the "finished" work and did not carry his own aesthetic as far as did his pupil Edouard Manet (1832–1883) or the impressionists of the later nineteenth century.

Like his method, Couture's atelier itself offered the student a measure of disciplined freedom and supervised experiment unavailable in other systems. Tuckerman described this appeal in 1867 when he wrote:

> Nothing can present a greater contrast than one of the large, dreary studios of Rome, where a solitary artist works slowly and fondly over some favorite conception, and the life-school wherein the student of painting at Paris learns to draw. Coiture's [*sic*] studio, where several American artists acquired their facility as draughtsmen, and their aptitude for *genre* art, is situated far away from the fashionable centre of Paris. In a vast hall, a crowd of young men from every quarter of the globe may be seen and heard, yielding unconcernedly to a vivacious mood that is quite the reverse of that earnest, contemplative atmosphere which we associate with art-studies. They whistle and smoke and sing and argue, sometimes blaspheme, and sometimes narrate or dramatize, as the humor suggests; but all the while they observe, practice, think, and, if endowed with the least skill or ambition, *learn.* Excellent models, valuable hints, the example, encouragement, or criticism of the master, emulation, sympathy, and a certain social ardor, quicken perception; and it is rare that a practical facility and felicity of execution, and in the choice of the *naive,* picturesque, or dramatic, in life and nature, do not result from the curious combination of discipline and *abandon* thus realized.[21]

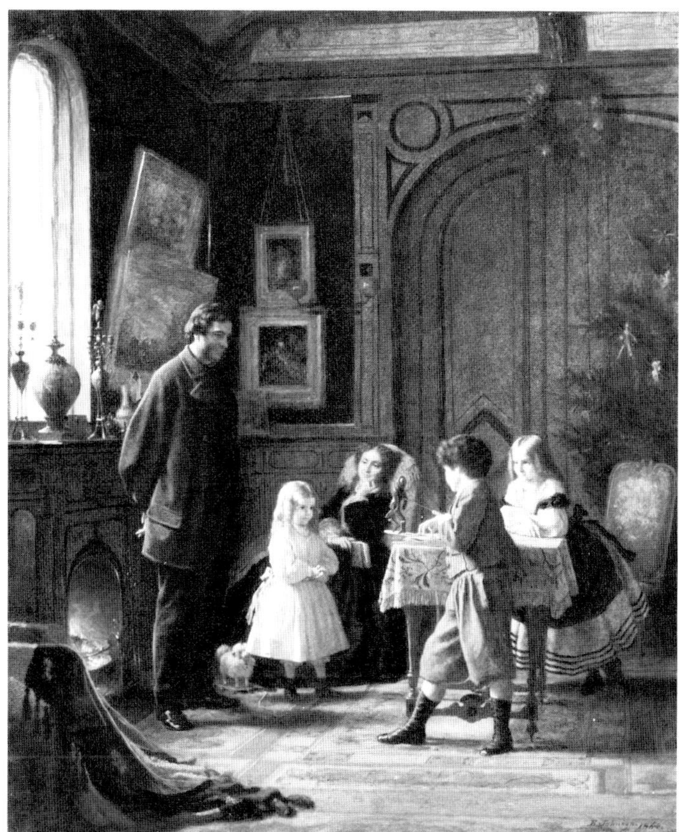

FIG. 4. Eastman Johnson, *Christmas Time (The Blodgett Family)*, 1864. Oil on canvas, 30 x 25 inches. The Metropolitan Museum of Art, New York, Gift of Mr. and Mrs. Stephen Whitney Blodgett, 1983 (1983.486).

Couture advocated that his students find subjects in the modern life around them, insisting that "when we have a picturesque vocabulary we ought to use it for the purpose of describing our own times," and further urging his pupils to "be Parisians, as they of Athens were Athenians."[22] Was Johnson remembering this call when he returned to America and traded in his Rhineland peasants and Savoyard boys for American Indians and Negro slaves?

During the summer and early fall of 1855, while Johnson was in Couture's atelier, the French artist was busy with a mural commission for the church of Saint-Eustache. The fame of his *Romans of the Decadence* (1847, Musée d'Orsay, Paris) had been renewed with its exhibition at the Universal Exposition;[23] Sadakichi Hartmann, describing in 1908 Johnson's European study, specifically mentioned "Orgie Romaine" when saying that "it was [Couture's] work to which Eastman Johnson felt himself irresistibly drawn."[24] As well, Couture's unfinished opus, *The Enrollment of the Volunteers of 1792* (1848 *et seq.*; Musée départemental de l'Oise, Beauvais) begun in 1847, was still in his studio, as no doubt were many of the "no less than twenty-seven separate studies" for that one painting.[25] In Leutze's studio, Johnson had witnessed the creation of *Washington Crossing the Delaware* (1851, The Metropolitan Museum of Art, New York), even painting a reduced copy of Leutze's work that was sent to the engravers Goupil, Vibert, et Cie.[26] In Couture's studio he would have seen evidence of even larger commissions and more complicated compositions. Thus, in addition to technical instruction—and we have evidence only that Johnson made "a copy of the head of a sleeping soldier by Couture"[27]—it seems likely that Johnson would have observed Couture's success, heard his admonitions, and witnessed his method for constructing a large, multifigure composition.[28]

According to his biographer William Walton, Johnson was thriving in his new Parisian environment:

> Comfortably installed at No. 14, Boulevard Poissonière, [Johnson] soon found himself so content that, as he said in later life, nothing less than the news of the death of his mother, he thought, would have brought him back to his native shore.[29]

But with that very news, Johnson sailed for America in late October 1855.

Though his Parisian study was cut short, Johnson had several opportunities in America to develop his knowledge of Couture's method and works. The 1867 publication of Couture's *Méthode et entretiens d'atelier* provided Johnson with one such opportunity to refresh his memory.[30] Another likely source was Couture's friend Healy, who, like Johnson, had returned to America from France in 1855; Healy brought with him Couture's *The Prodigal Son* (which, sadly, was destroyed in the Chicago fire of 1871).[31] Although Healy settled in Chicago, he received several portrait commissions that took him to Washington, D.C., from the late 1850s to the mid-1860s; it seems that he and Johnson intersected there during at least one of those visits, and perhaps they discussed Couture.[32] Another link to Couture was surely provided by William Tilden Blodgett (d. 1875), whose family Johnson had painted in 1864 (FIG. 4).

Blodgett, a varnish manufacturer and real estate investor, was a prominent art collector and active player on New York's cultural stage. A member of both the Century and Union League clubs, he was also a founder of the magazine *The Nation* and was instrumental in organizing the Metropolitan Sanitary Fair in 1864. He served on the first executive committee of The Metropolitan Museum of Art, and with John Taylor Johnston and Alexander T. Stewart made the largest contribution to a subscription fund to buy paintings for the museum.[33] His own collection combined European paintings with American: his purchase in 1859 of Frederic Church's *Heart of the Andes* (1859, The Metropolitan Museum of Art, New York) for $10,000.00 made headlines as the largest amount ever paid for an American painting. But Blodgett was a special patron of Thomas Couture: he corresponded directly with the artist; visited him in his home at Villiers-le-Bel; and commissioned several works from him.[34] When Frederic Church made his first trip to Europe in 1867, Blodgett wrote him a letter of introduction to Couture.[35] Around 1867, along with two Couture pupils, Elizabeth Boott (1846–1888) and William Marshall (1837–1906), Blodgett attempted (unsuccessfully) to purchase Couture's *The Enrollment of the Volunteers of 1792.*[36] By 1875 his collection included at least one drawing, *Idle Student,* and three paintings, *Pierrot and Harlequin, The Police Court,* and *Liberty in Chains, (France),* by Couture;[37] it also contained "numerous fine specimens from Eastman Johnson."[38] Johnson—not only as the painter of Blodgett's family portrait but as a fellow member of the Century and Union League clubs, a fellow worker on the Metropolitan Sanitary Fair,[39] and a fellow founding trustee of The Metropolitan Museum of Art—had several opportunities to visit with Blodgett and view his collection. It seems likely that their conversations about art would have included mention of Thomas Couture.

If Couture's influence on Johnson was rarely acknowledged during his own lifetime, it was noted by several critics after the turn of the twentieth century.[40] Sadakichi Hartmann suggested that while Couture's subjects were of no interest to Johnson, "it was the Frenchman's technique, so superb in breadth, so simple and dignified, which fascinated the young American painter."[41]

And so when it came time for Johnson to apply his eclectic European training toward work on a "more *pretentious*" picture, the French influence would prevail. The influence of Couture had been percolating, expressed tentatively and never publicly in the sketches for a sugaring-off picture, finally becoming more evident as Johnson's fame and exposure increased in the 1870s. But it is in *The Cranberry Harvest* and its related works—even more than in the 1876 *Husking Bee, Island of Nantucket,* for which there are only a limited number of preliminary studies and sketches—that the method Johnson learned in France comes to fruition. In examining the development of this one painting, one not only learns the depth of Johnson's technical expertise and the extent of his debt to Couture but also watches the development of Johnson's fullest, most mature expression of joy in rural life and communal labor.

THE CREATION OF *THE CRANBERRY HARVEST, ISLAND OF NANTUCKET*

Although we have no records or accounts that enable us to document with certainty the sequence of Johnson's drawings and oil sketches for *The Cranberry Harvest,* we can assume that his efforts began with pencil sketches. Several drawings on the backs of oil sketches, for instance those on the verso of *Cranberry Pickers—Study* (no. 6), testify that Johnson's pencil was active throughout his long spells of "cranberry fever," working to capture a fleeting moment, particular posture, or picturesque grouping. Although we have no evidence that Johnson carried the "small album" that Couture advocated for just such a purpose, it seems that in his sketches Johnson was nonetheless following Couture's good advice to "trace beauties that strike you, startling effects, natural poses, etc. Never forget to make yourself into an ant, or a bee; pillage everywhere in order to have an abundant granary."[42] This practice was of course common to many artists, including those who had never formally studied the French method; the drawings of Hudson River School artists reveal many such studies of landscape motifs.[43] Yet Couture's admonition was to find materials for composition in one's everyday life; this is what Johnson proceeded to do as he stepped out of his studio and observed the cranberry harvests in the meadows near his house.

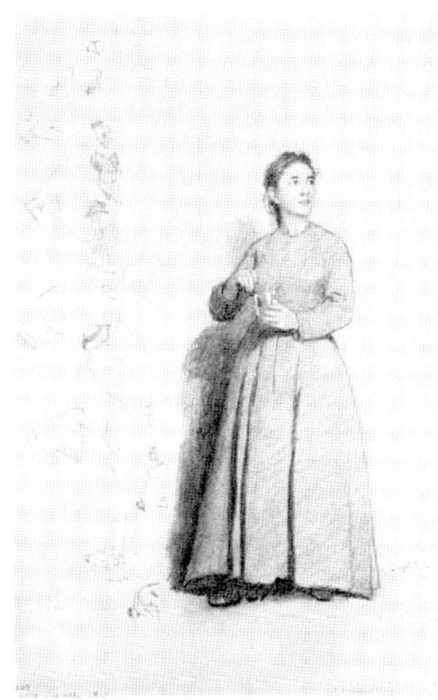

FIG. 5. Eastman Johnson, sketches of cranberry pickers, on same sheet as *Girl with Glass,* 1875. Pencil and charcoal heightened with white on brown paper, 17¼ x 11¾ inches. Private collection.

Among Johnson's earliest sketches for *The Cranberry Harvest* must have been the quick studies added to the margins of a sheet used previously for a charcoal drawing of a woman holding a glass (FIG. 5).[44] These sketches appear as hastily rendered indications of contour and shape, which give only slight attention to volume. Johnson seems most interested in the peculiar, bent-over shapes of figures half-buried in marsh grass. His observations include figures seen from both front and back and figures seated in a variety of postures. As well, a receding line of bowed heads, expressed in a bouncing rhythm of progressively smaller hat brims, seems to have been a sight that caught Johnson's fancy.

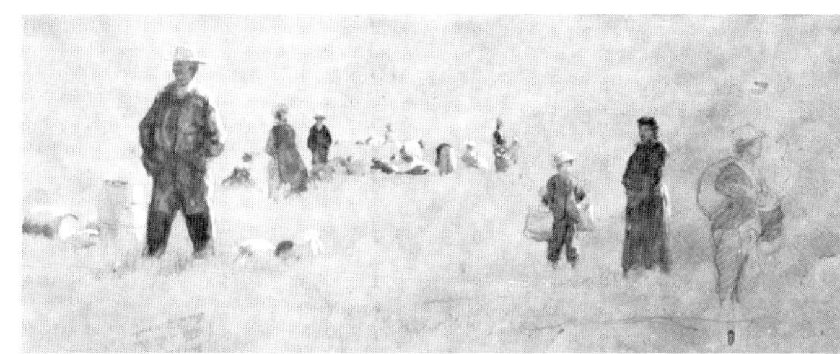

FIG. 6. Eastman Johnson, *Berry Picking,* ca. 1878–1879. Pencil, watercolor, and Chinese white on paper, 7¾ x 19⅜ inches. Addison Gallery of American Art, Phillips Academy, Andover, Mass.

In a more developed sketch—one that combines a single figure study in pencil along with a more complex grouping gone over in watercolor—Johnson broadens his interest to include standing figures that counterpoint kneeling, bending, or seated ones (FIG. 6). His cast now includes men, women, and children, particular characters rather than faceless workers. The accoutrements of berry picking—barrels, pails, and sacks—as well as the appropriate garb for such activity—high-topped boots for the older man, rolled-up pant legs for the young boy—have also been recorded. Penciled notes at the bottom edge possibly indicate subjects for further investigation: "Pails and clothes / Bottle in the tree / Fence up to [rail]." The colors are mute, but touches of white pick out the edges of forms as brilliant highlights.

The spectacle of a cranberry bog teeming with harvesters is explored in an oil sketch now known only from reproduction (FIG. 7), which appears on the verso of a more finished study, *At the Closing of the Day* (see FIG. 10). Here a veritable swarm of berry pickers covers the small panel, a faceless crowd of shapes defined primarily as masses of light and dark. The artist again uses strong highlights to define edges and create form, but he makes little attempt to relate figures

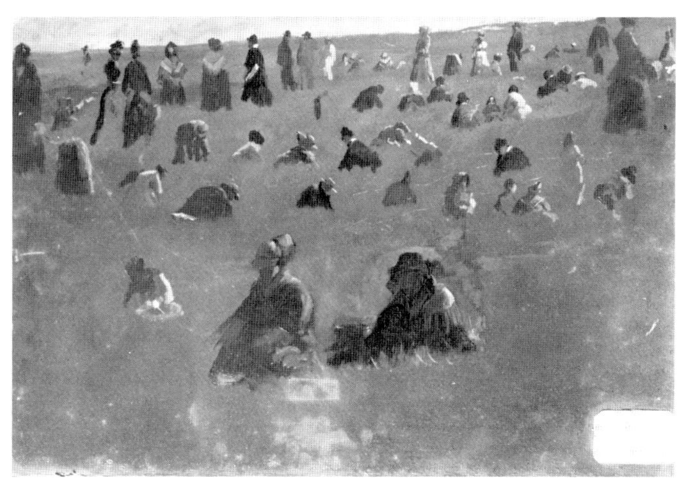

FIG. 7. Eastman Johnson, *Study for "Cranberry Pickers"* (also known as *Berry Pickers*), ca. 1878–1879. Oil on panel[?], verso of FIG. 10, 18 x 27½ inches. Unlocated. Photo courtesy of M. Knoedler & Co., Inc., New York.

one to another, either through scale or their common activity. The high horizon flattens the perspective, leaving a spectacle of individual shapes, sprouting, as it were, from the marsh itself.

In other studies Johnson continues to work in broad areas of color and generalized masses of dark and light, while considering various aspects of local color. In one he gives prominence to landscape elements (PLATE 2), in another, to distinctive costumes (FIG. 8). The horizontality of the latter sketch announces Johnson's investigation into compositional formats.[45] The measured rhythm of standing and crouching figures indicates that their placement was deliberate. Two figures in the foreground sharing a conversation provide a focal point for the composition and perhaps as well a theme to explore in further studies.

Composition is even more carefully considered in a sketch (PLATE 3) in which Johnson takes several of the bent-over, half-buried figures from *Girl with Glass* (see FIG. 5) and *Study for "Cranberry Pickers"* (see FIG. 7) and staggers them along a perspectival grid. Pencil lines plot a narrow range below the center of the board within which all activity takes place; axes drawn from the top left corner of this rectangle to its lower right edges and corner provide diagonal lines of recession. The heads of three figures in two different planes are aligned while the triangular forms of several crouching figures rise with the diagonal axis. Four standing figures, described with varying degrees of definition, provide vertical accents to the predominantly horizontal format; one of these figures is no more than the red-brown "sauce" of Johnson's first outline.[46] More clearly finished are the young boy to the right of center and a closed sack anchoring the lower right corner; these appear as primary foci of the composition.

Two larger compositional studies, closely related in size, palette, and format, take a broad perspective, pressing the landscape below a horizon line drawn approximately two-thirds of the way down the canvas and reducing the figures to tiny color accents (FIG. 9 and PLATE 4). In these two works, one sees with hindsight the inklings of features that will characterize Johnson's two most ambitious studies in this series. In both, a compositional focus is provided at the right

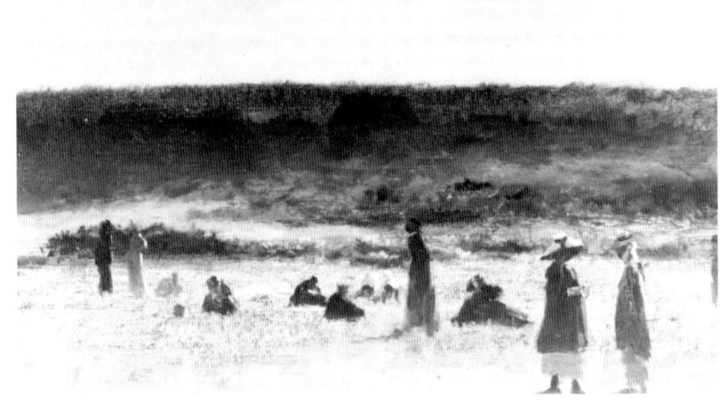

FIG. 8. Eastman Johnson, *In the Fields*, ca. 1878–1879. Oil on panel, 10 x 17 inches. Private collection.

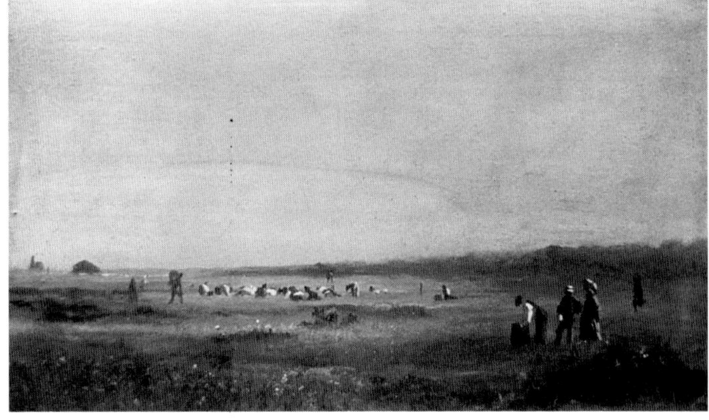

FIG. 9. Eastman Johnson, *Sketch for "Cranberry Pickers,"* ca. 1878–1880. Oil on canvas[?], 13 3/8 x 22 5/8 inches. Unlocated. Photo courtesy of Theodore E. Stebbins, Jr.

foreground: a figural group around a barrel in one, a still life of barrels, sacks, and pails in the other. In one, the horizon line lifts at the left, following a ridge rising from the sea; in the other, the horizon remains static but the foreground still life is described with hard insistence on form. In one, the foreground is speckled with the dabs of foliage and flowers; in the other, a central figure is introduced. In both, the eye is carried through the composition by a play of vertical elements—standing figures or upright barrels—against more horizontal ones—crouching pickers or rounded sacks. In these two quick studies of tone and format, one senses ideas for a picture, rather than simple observations of a scene.

The smallest of Johnson's known oil sketches for *The Cranberry Harvest* (PLATE 5) might be a plein-air sketch, or might as easily be a studio construct, executed with rapidity and brio. With brief but heavily laden strokes, Johnson sets out the barest indications of figures and landscape, as if hastily capturing a scene before him. Yet the composition is balanced and the relations between figures considered. Again, the compositional and thematic focus lies in the foreground, slightly right of center. Certain figure types and postures gain prominence: a conversational group with a taller figure bending down to address a child; a woman rising above a group of huddled workers, stretching her back; a couple in the left foreground inclining toward one another as they go about their work; a single figure standing and looking to the right; another single figure, bent at the waist and seen from the rear. Mustard yellows and heavy greens define the tonality; brighter yellows highlight the center of the landscape and white accentuates the edges of figures.

This tiny schematic rendering of format and groupings finds greater clarification in a larger sketch (PLATE 6), in which figures begin to suggest characters and activities assume a hint of narrative. The compositional focus remains to the right of center. The figure who stood and stretched at the right edge of the Ackland sketch is now brought forward and made the central character of the St. Louis composition. Her upright, arched form is contrasted to the huddled mass of a dark figure beside her; other smaller clusters of standing and crouching harvesters are scattered about her. The motif of figures grouped around barrels, possibly contributing individual work to collective bins, is introduced at the left, along with the figure of a man seated with his legs splayed, his head cast down and covered by his hat. For the first time, Johnson indicates dramatic content. His central figure, so simply and skillfully drawn with the brush, conveys the full weight not only of her body but of her tiring labor as well. With another few strokes, Johnson suggests a secondary drama enacted by three figures at the left: a child who points, a figure who rushes forward, another figure who raises his head to see what is transpiring. In this sketch one recognizes seeds of both a larger composition and a more complete narrative.

In addition to full compositional studies, Johnson also made studies of individual figural groups and dramatic vignettes in works that approach the status of finished paintings in their own right. His practice in doing this is familiar from the many studies prepared for a maple-sugaring scene. Fewer "finished studies"[47] exist for *The Cranberry Harvest* than do for the never-completed sugaring-off picture, perhaps suggesting Johnson's reduced need for preliminary study, his greater concentration on the whole, perhaps even a lessened interest in individual anecdote.[48]

Because of its unusual, higher-keyed palette, *The Conversation* (PLATE 7) may have been painted somewhat apart from the main bulk of studies for *The Cranberry Harvest*,[49] but it shares with those works an emphasis on hard, form-sculpting light. Unlike Johnson's other studies of cranberry pickers, this work includes a view to the sea and divides the composition into distinct bands of green and brown marsh, yellow sand, blue sea, pink cloud bank, and a cloudy blue sky. For the first time, we see no indication of figures at work. The setting sun falls over two broadly massed and summarily painted figures, who relax amid an assembled still life of barrels and buckets; its rays highlight their forms and cast long shadows ahead of them.

The motif of a single woman resting against a barrel dominates the painting *At the Closing of the Day* (FIG. 10); this figure is returned to the familiar focal point in the foreground right of center. Her thinly painted form is a study in lights and darks, but her posture alone manages to convey a sense of pensive repose. In the far distance stand tiny figures in rows, their work completed; some of them proceed up the hill to the left.

In a closely related study (PLATE 8) offering the same landscape setting and compositional accents, the focal motif of a single woman leaning against a barrel has been replaced by a man holding an open sack. He addresses a female companion; Johnson leaves their conversation to the viewer's imagination.[50] This study, also very thinly painted, reveals much of Johnson's technique. Strong outlines remain around the man's figure, showing how he had been drawn upon the canvas; presumably the female figure was added in this manner as well, but her form has been more heavily built up with layers of paint, and her outline is no longer so visible. The reddish brown underlayers are evident in several areas; little

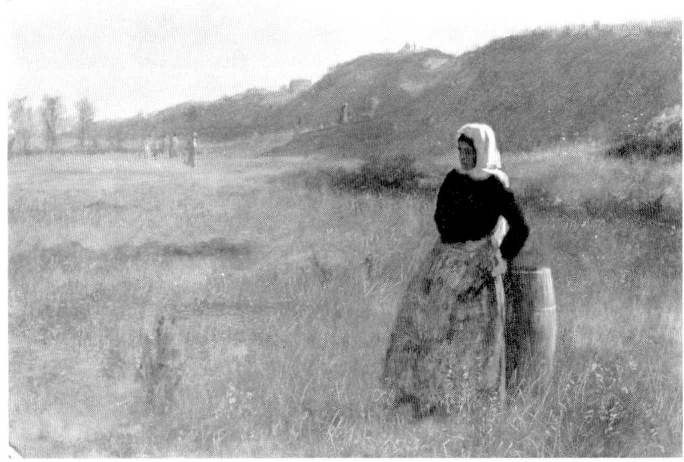

FIG. 10. Eastman Johnson, *At the Closing of the Day* (also known as *The Close of Day*), ca. 1878–1880. Oil on panel[?], 18 x 27½ inches. Unlocated. Photo courtesy of M. Knoedler & Co., Inc., New York.

more than its color defines such areas as the man's vest and pant legs, the inside of the open sack, and the bushes at the base of the hill. Although it lacks the Frenchman's grainy impasto, the sketch reveals much of Couture's legacy, not only in the obvious outlines and exposed *ébauche* but also in the small areas of bright, cool color that enliven the predominantly warm tones of the composition.[51]

The same technique is present in a more complicated figure composition (PLATE 9) that joins several ideas and familiar motifs. The man with an open sack now empties a bucket of cranberries into it; his female companion, resting against a barrel, is one half of the pair studied earlier in *The Conversation* (see PLATE 7), here shown in reverse. The other half of that pair turns to observe another conversation taking place between a man and a young girl. The man with his head cast down and his legs spread apart (see PLATE 6) has been placed at the left side of the canvas; the figure stretching her back in that study has now been transformed into a woman carrying a heavy bucket. The arched back that once connoted a heavy gesture of weary release now becomes a mundane balancing act in a figure who participates in the background narrative. Despite the attention to character and anecdote, Johnson brings very little of this sketch up to the level of finish seen in many of his maple-sugaring studies.[52] Compositional arrangement and the disposition of light and dark remain his primary concerns. However, it is interesting to note that several of the character types portrayed here, as well as the motifs of barrels and the conversational groups that surround them, were important elements of Johnson's planned maple-sugaring picture.

This sketch heralds a broad canvas (PLATE 10), a work with dimensions almost identical to the final *Cranberry Harvest, Island of Nantucket.* The existence of two works, similar in the large size of both canvas format and apparent ambition, has led to speculation that Johnson was considering two independent finished paintings.[53] But the series of oil sketches so far discussed seem all to lead to this one composition—that is, a panoramic view of a cranberry bog filled with harvesters; a compositional focus in the foreground to the right of center;

a dominant anecdote involving a conversational group assembled around barrels and baskets; scattered groups of harvesters, much smaller in scale, bent over their work; a female figure whose arched back expresses the weight of her labor; and an old man seated with his head down and legs spread apart.

Although its dimensions indicate aspirations toward a finished composition, this work is primarily an oil sketch, with figures built up from the ground layer, defined as little more than areas of light and dark, with tonal arrangements set, areas of highlight and shade determined, and selective color accents placed. One cannot know whether Johnson planned to bring this particular canvas to a higher level of finish, or whether this work was meant to serve only as an intermediary stage between the smaller studies and another finished canvas. But one can surmise that at some point during or after the composition of the Yale painting Johnson discarded the idea of a small conversational group as a focal accent. His emphasis shifted toward a more populated scene, with attention distributed among several smaller vignettes, no one of them given especial prominence. That so many features of the Yale composition appear or are transformed in the final *Cranberry Harvest* argues for its having been created before that work.[54]

In what appears to be the earliest of the studies directed toward the finished version of *The Cranberry Harvest,* a familiar landscape of field and rising hill is laid out in a somewhat more vivid, even acidic, palette of ocher and blue than has been seen before (PLATE 11). White is used to describe form as well as to indicate highlights. The composition, recalling (in reverse) the acclaimed format of Johnson's 1876 *Husking Bee, Island of Nantucket* (see FIG. 1, Simpson essay), is organized along two prominent diagonal lines of harvesters, one in the open sunlight, the other in the heavy shade of the foreground, converging at the right center edge where a wagon is positioned. The implied gaze of the standing figure in white connects with another standing figure at the left edge. At the center of the canvas, a small figure recalls the woman balancing her bucket of berries in two earlier studies (see PLATES 9 and 10). But this figure is overshadowed by the dominant form of the standing figure in white. This figure occupies that position of honor in the right center foreground; the concept of her form—a standing figure amid crouching harvesters—had appeared in earlier works (see PLATES 5 and 6). But no self-respecting, practical cranberry harvester would be dressed in white. Rather, this color distinguishes her as the central focus of the composition, the focus that will mark the final version of *The Cranberry Harvest* as well.

A much sparer compositional study (PLATE 12) explores the role of this single, central standing figure. Although one of his larger canvases, it is the emptiest of Johnson's studies for *The Cranberry Harvest*, one that demonstrates interest in only a few select features. Several pencil sketches have been transferred to (or drawn on) the canvas, but only a few have been brought up with paint. As well, the scale relations are awkward. If this painting reveals few of Johnson's ideas, it nonetheless tells much about his process.

The only work that resembles a "finished study" for the final version of *The Cranberry Harvest* is *In the Fields* (PLATE 13). Here the central standing figure holds a rectangular basket and is accompanied by a young boy. The boy stares directly out of the canvas at the viewer; his strong and forceful figure is seen nowhere else in Johnson's cranberry harvest works, even though young boys are featured prominently in other works (see FIG. 6 and PLATE 3). The other figures, familiar from other studies (see FIG. 7 for the seated woman, PLATE 12 for the man in a hat), are faceless or lost in thought. A hard, glaring light creates sharp contrasts of lights and darks; the marshy landscape is little more than daubs of paint over the red-brown ground layer.

The oil sketch (PLATE 14) that immediately precedes *The Cranberry Harvest* has most of the features of the final version in place. In addition to the broad changes seen in *Cranberry Pickers* (see PLATE 11), certain aspects of this composition appear now as reworkings of or replacements for features that were present in the Yale painting (see PLATE 10). A man in a chair, his top hat and seat recalling the Nantucket sea captains and corn huskers of Johnson's genre work of the earlier

FIG. 11. Eastman Johnson, *Woman on a Hill,* ca. 1875–1880. Oil on board, 25 1/2 x 21 1/4 inches. Addison Gallery of American Art, Phillips Academy, Andover, Mass.

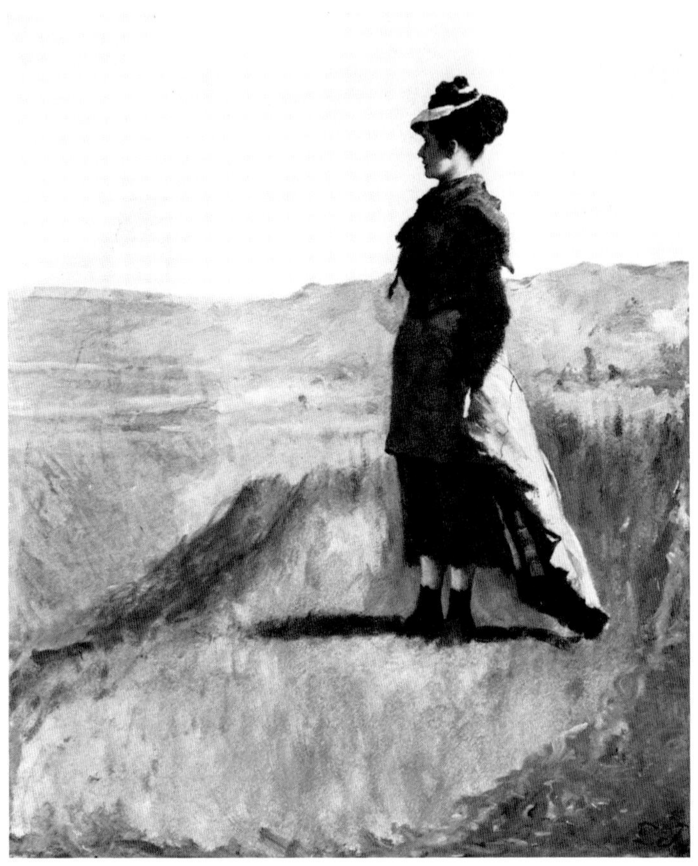

1870s, replaces the seated man with his legs spread. Many more children populate this work. There is no sleeping baby in the right corner, but a boy at the right center edge now carries a swaddled infant. The central conversation so evident in plates 8 through 10 is now diffused and distributed among several characters and figural groups.

For his final painting (see PLATE 1) Johnson chose a canvas with dimensions about ten inches larger on each side than those of *Cranberry Pickers, Nantucket* (see PLATE 14), increasing the area given to the sky and leaving room for a full townscape (and windmill) at the left side. In many cases the artist simply articulated and finished the characters and features sketched out in the earlier work, while giving breadth and spontaneity to the composition by dragging a grainy impasto of green hues into the warm tones of the fore- and middle grounds and spattering lively flecks of paint about the figures. Great clarity is given to the forms and faces of the couple in the immediate foreground, who carry both expressions and an internal relationship that have not been seen before. Not all the figures are as finished as these two; clarity naturally diminishes as the perspective recedes into the distance. This selective finish again recalls Couture, who reminded his students that

> The brill[i]ant light of the morning spreads over everything, and shows the multiplicity of form, and color; while in the evening, the great divisions are marked by beautiful masses of shadow, which cause insipid details to disappear.
>
> Why should I not do the same thing in my copying. . . . Beauty of outline, beauty of masses, as beauty of color, require an incessant sacrifice of detail.[55]

Certain compositional anchors are new, however, although some look familiar. In the lower right corner a full sack of cranberries spills over in a luxurious sign of abundance; this still life replaces the unlikely presence of an unattended sleeping baby in the Yale painting (see PLATE 10), but has roots in the Philadelphia sketch (see PLATE 3) and *The Conversation* (see PLATE 7). At the left corner a group of three urchins provides a note of sentiment familiar from Johnson's smaller domestic scenes. A new feature is the posted sign "No pass over Cranberry bog," a warning to prospective thieves and trespassers,[56] but by extension a signal that the marsh is a field of property and the harvesters on it legitimate workers.

Also new is the conception of the central standing woman, whose figure has been indicated in many previous studies. Her finished form, given prominence not only by its position but also by its exquisite description and the fall of light across it, strikes a nearly heroic stance. Her monumentality has been borrowed, in reverse, from an earlier study, *Woman on a Hill* (FIG. 11), in which a single figure surveys the landscape from a vantage point high above it.[57] Stately though the figure is, it acts as a pivot for the multiple actions that evolve in *The*

Cranberry Harvest; the woman's sideways gaze, returned by the boy carrying a child toward her but broken by the several incidents between them, encourages the viewer's tour throughout the composition. Unlike Johnson's earlier configurations, no single episode dominates his final work. The vignettes play off and amplify one another, resulting in a picture of collective labors and communal joys.

"RIGHT FEELING": EASTMAN JOHNSON AND JULES BRETON

It cannot be coincidence that Johnson painted *The Cranberry Harvest*—a celebration of bountiful land and the human labor that tends it—at the height of popularity of European peasant painting in America and Europe. Johnson's cranberry harvesters are decidedly not peasants in the European mold, but their relation to the land as it has been described by art bears some relation to contemporary European developments.

The phenomenal popularity of peasant painting was most prevalent in Boston, with the near apotheosis of Jean-François Millet (1814–1875),[58] but it was only slightly less fervent in other cities. In New York, however, Millet's popularity was eclipsed by that of Jules Breton (1827–1906), whose work had been brought to that city as early as 1857 by Goupil, Vibert, et Cie and had been actively sponsored by the art dealer Samuel P. Avery (1822–1904) as early as 1867.[59] Breton's conceptions of rural life were avidly sought by New York collectors in the 1870s and 1880s. More conservative and less controversial than Millet, his painting was admired for showing "the celebration of work in open air, with its wholesome gaiety and even its elegance";[60] his work was considered an exception to the generally "morbid" or "frivolous" character of much French art:

> It was curious at [the 1867 Universal Exposition in Paris] how far removed Jules Breton seemed from Parisian wickedness, and how completely interpenetrated by the pure and wholesome atmosphere of rural life. His works gleamed out softly and beautifully in their honest tenderness, amongst all those opera-dancers of Dubufe and Cabanel.[61]

S. G. W. Benjamin's claim that Johnson's *Husking Bee, Island of Nantucket* (see FIG. 1, Simpson essay) "loses nothing by comparison with the work of Jules Breton," may reveal more than the mere worldliness of a critic able to make the comparison. Beyond the tangible influence of Thomas Couture on Johnson's stylistic development, it seems likely that Johnson also took note of Jules Breton. Patricia Hills has observed that the motif of the central standing woman in *The Cranberry Harvest* may have been borrowed from Breton's painting *The Weeders* (*Les Sarcleuses*) (FIG. 12).[62] Although Johnson may never have seen this painting, which was in the Cincinnati collection of Henry Probasco and not known to have been in New York until its sale in 1887, it was nonetheless an acknowledged prize of Probasco's gallery: Edward Strahan described it as a "most exquisite" example of Breton's work, "a canvas in which he has garnered his treasures of light, color and grace."[63] Likewise, Johnson may or may not have seen Breton's *The Close of the Day* (FIG. 13),

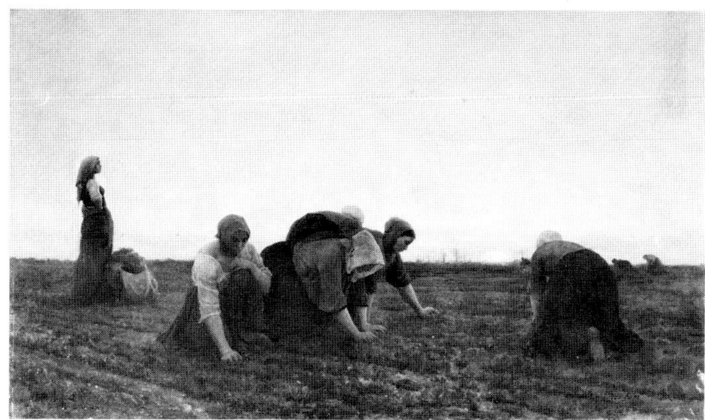

FIG. 12. Jules Breton, *The Weeders* (*Les Sarcleuses*), 1868. Oil on canvas, 28 1/2 x 50 1/4 inches. The Metropolitan Museum of Art, New York, Bequest of Collis P. Huntington.

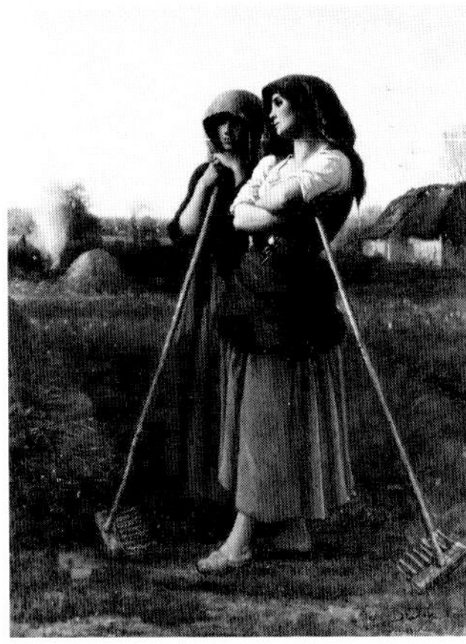

FIG. 13. Jules Breton, *The Close of the Day,* 1865. Oil on canvas, 25 3/4 x 19 inches. Walters Art Gallery, Baltimore, Md.

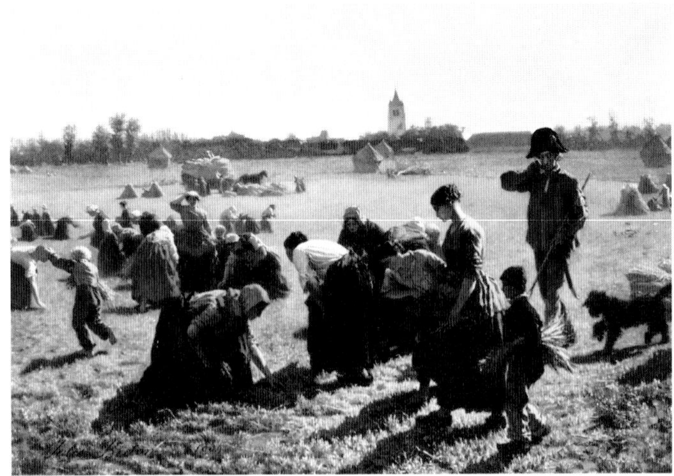

FIG. 14. Jules Breton, *The Gleaners (Les Glaneuses),* 1854. Oil on canvas, 36 1/2 x 54 inches. National Gallery of Ireland, Dublin.

which was in William T. Walter's Baltimore collection before 1878,[64] but his own *At the Closing of the Day* (see FIG. 10)[65] comes close to matching it in composition and mood.

Johnson surely became aware of Breton while he was studying in Paris in 1855. In that year Johnson studied in Paris, Breton was awarded a third-place medal on the basis of his three contributions to the Universal Exposition—the most acclaimed being *The Gleaners* (FIG. 14).[66] Several superficial parallels can be drawn between this work of 1854 and Johnson's *Cranberry Harvest* of 1880: both feature strongly realized figures in a broad landscape setting; each is a complex composition incorporating several figures and figural groups; each is a scene of workers in a field, some crouched or bent, some standing, with a wagon in the farther distance; both juxtapose the freedom of childhood with the labor of adults. And although, of course, the activities of gleaning in Courrières and cranberry harvesting in Nantucket reflect different agricultural practices and social realities,[67] each subject describes an agrarian ritual familiar to each painter's experience and memory, suited to his convivial, nonpolitical disposition, and gauged to display evolving talents and ambitions. As Johnson sought in maple-sugaring camps—and, by extension, cranberry bogs—"a picturesque & to me very interesting [subject] . . . very well adapted as I think to exhibit character & picturesque combination of form color &c," so Breton, having returned to his home in Courrières in 1854 after working in Paris and receiving acclaim for his painting of a gleaner, "thought of a composition which should contain a number of these poor women and little girls and boys who look like flocks of sparrows as they bend over the stubble."[68] The subject was both proximate and challenging to Breton, no less than maple-sugar camps and cranberry harvesters were to Johnson.

Although Johnson's brief stay in Paris may have left him little time to study Breton's work, he had many opportunities to do so back in New York. As he could have easily viewed and discussed work by Couture with fellow New Yorkers, so he could have seen and discussed work by Breton. Dealers' exhibitions and auction sales of French art had become regular events by the early 1860s,[69] and private collectors contributed examples of French art to exhibitions such as the annual Artists' Fund Society shows.[70] Works by both Breton and Couture—as well as Rosa Bonheur (1822–1899), Jean-Léon Gérôme (1824–1904), Edouard Frère (1819–1886), and many others—had found their way into New York collections as early as 1864.[71] By the 1870s Breton paintings were in the New York collections of Robert Hoe, John Taylor Johnston, George Whitney, and William P. Wright—to name only some of the more prominent collectors who also owned works by

Eastman Johnson.[72] Contemporary criticism continued to favor Breton throughout the decade of the 1870s, and the artist's popularity peaked in the mid-1880s when two of his paintings brought tremendous prices at auction. In 1885 George Seney's *Evening in the Hamlet of Finistère* (*Le Soir dans les hameaux du Finistère;* 1882, Paine Art Center and Arboretum, Oshkosh, Wisconsin) sold for $18,200; this "was deemed phenomenal until, at the [Mary J.] Morgan sale in 1886, [Breton's] painting of "The First Communion" [*Les Communiantes;* 1884, private collection, Scotland] reached the astonishing price of $45,500."[73]

Although Breton's indisputable appeal to New York collectors cannot serve to establish that any particular Breton painting had a direct influence on Eastman Johnson, it does make it seem likely that Johnson—keenly aware of social activities and exhibition opportunities in New York—knew something of the Frenchman, his art, and his popularity with collectors. In the absence of other hard evidence, one circumstance points to Johnson's knowledge, even admiration, of Breton. At some point in his career—probably in the 1860s—Johnson made a copy (FIG. 15) of Breton's *The Village Perambulator,* today known as *The Departure for the Fields* (1857, private collection, Omaha). By 1863 Breton's painting was in the collection of New York cotton broker William P. Wright (ca. 1812–1880), who, like many other civic-minded art patrons of his era, periodically opened his collection-gallery (in this case his summer home in Weehawken, N.J.) to the public.[74] In addition to Rosa Bonheur's famous *The Horse Fair* (1853, The Metropolitan Museum of Art, New York), Wright owned Johnson's *Negro Life at the South,* so it seems impossible that Johnson would not have known or visited him. In 1867 Wright's collection was auctioned, going on display in H. W. Derby's gallery one week before the sale as a benefit for the "Southern Famine Relief Commission." *The Village Perambulator* was one of only six paintings noted by the critic for *The Nation,* who called it

> probably the best picture in the collection. . . . The breadth of ripening grain, with the squat church tower rising in the distance above the golden surface, and this group in the foreground, mother and children making the baby happy with corn-flowers and scarlet poppies, are as foreign to American soil as they are near to American and all human sympathies.[75]

If we do not know when or why Johnson copied Breton's painting, it is clear that doing so gave him a chance to exercise the French technique he had studied in 1855. His copy is a thinly painted work, in which the warm layer of underpainting makes itself felt in the shadows, faces, and clothing of the figures, who have been blocked in above it and bear evident reddish brown outlines around their forms. The work is built up as a series of highlights and shadows; showing selective finish, the background is described less carefully than the figures. And the figures, especially those of the children, are types of which Johnson was especially fond.[76] Testimony to the artist's attachment to the work is the fact that it

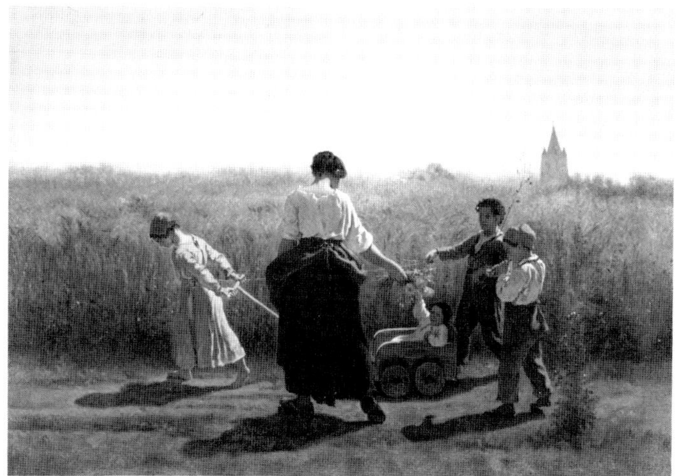

FIG. 15. Eastman Johnson, *The Baby Carriage,* ca. 1865. Copy after Jules Breton, *The Village Perambulator* (also known as *Le Départ pour les champs* [*The Departure for the Fields*]). Oil on canvas, 23 3/8 x 33 7/8 inches. Santa Barbara Museum of Art, Gift of Mrs. Sterling Morton.

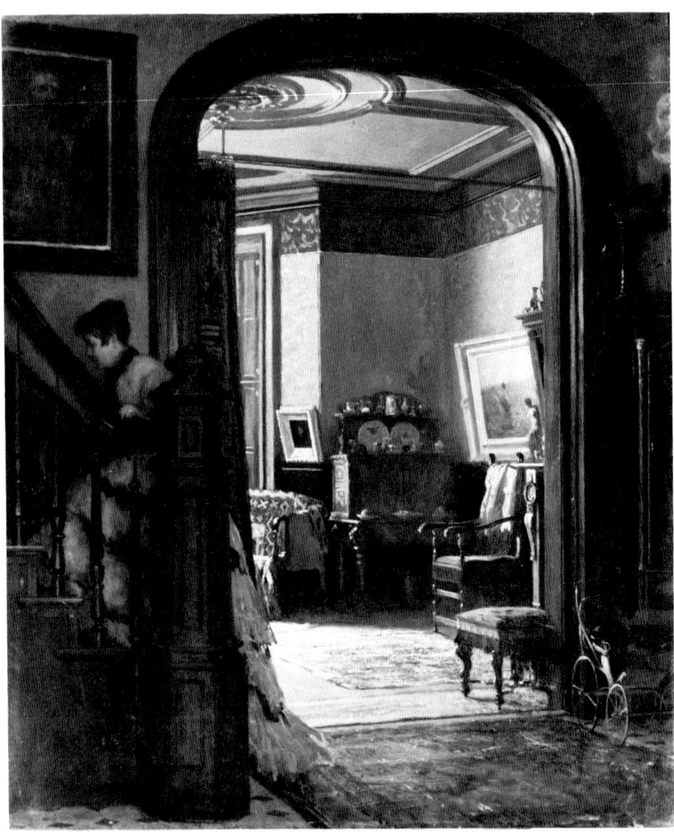

FIG. 16. Eastman Johnson, *Not at Home,* ca. 1872–1880. Oil on board, 26 1/2 x 22 1/4 inches. The Brooklyn Museum, 40.60, Gift of Miss Gwendolyn O. L. Conkling.

remained for many years in the artist's collection until he gave it to his favorite jeweler, Joseph Schwartz.[77] Interestingly, Johnson's painting *Not at Home* (FIG. 16), believed to show the interior of Johnson's own house, shows in the background a painting that may well be the artist's copy of *The Village Perambulator.* Although the young girl at the left is hardly distinct, the turn of the main figure, whose head just clears the horizon line, is the dominant characteristic of Breton's painting and replicated strongly, if generally, here.[78]

The correspondences between Johnson's work and that of Breton, as well as the instance of Johnson's outright admiration, serve not so much to prove that Breton had a direct influence on Johnson but that the two artists held in common an idealistic vision of rural labor and the painting of figures in the landscape. To recognize Johnson's regard for Breton is to understand more fully William Walton's comment of 1906, that

> [Johnson's] conception of this rendering of "the life of the poor," of "the tillers of the soil" (and the ex-toilers of the sea), preaches no ugly gospel of discontent, as does so much of the contemporary French and Flemish art of this genre; his Nantucket neighbors know nothing of the *"protestation douloureuse de la race asservie à la glèbe"*; there is no *"cri de la terre"* arising from his cranberry marshes or his hay-stuffed barns.[79]

Likewise, to recognize the components of French technique in Johnson's work—not only his method of constructing a picture, but also his ideal of creating a major composition—serves not to compromise the "American" qualities of his art, but rather to reveal the sophistication of his paintings and their appeal to connoisseurs. S. G. W. Benjamin noted that Johnson's " 'Husking' [and] his 'Cranberry-Picking' [were] suggested by the homely every-day life of the country-folk, and [are] qualified both by treatment and subject to win the applause of the connoisseur and the heart of the people."[80] Treatment and subject were the critical elements of Johnson's success, and both were informed by his knowledge of French art. The measure of that success was noted most succinctly by William Walton in 1906 when he wrote of Johnson's art that "the happy combination of right feeling and sound technique is manifest in all the details."[81]

NOTES

[1] Patricia Hills, *The Genre Painting of Eastman Johnson: The Sources and Development of His Style and Themes* (New York: Garland Publishing, 1977), 27–31. For the American Art-Union, see Mary Bartlett Cowdrey, *American Academy of Fine Arts and American Art-Union: Exhibition Record, 1816–1852* (New York: The New-York Historical Society, 1953).

[2] Hills provides insightful commentary on this search in her excellent study of Johnson, *Genre Painting of Eastman Johnson,* especially chapters 2, 4, and 8.

[3] See, for example, the review of *Fiddling His Way* and *Sunday Morning,* Johnson's contributions to the National Academy of Design Exhibition of 1866, in which one critic concluded: "How little reason we have to envy France her Edouard Frère, when we have a man like Eastman Johnson, as able to do for our rural life what Frère does for France, and with no less quiet beauty and homely truth" ("The National Academy of Design: Forty-First Annual Exhibition," *The New-York Daily Tribune,* 4 July 1866); while another noted: " 'Fiddling his Way' . . . of course, from the similarity of the subject recalls [David] Wilkie's Blind Fiddler, but Mr. Johnson's is as purely American as Wilkie's is Scotch" ("Editor's Easy Chair," *Harper's New Monthly Magazine* 33, no. 193 [June 1866]: 117).

Two years later, the artist and critic Eugene Benson commented that "As a painter of the familiar, Mr. Johnson takes his rank next to the English Wilkie. Without the vulgarity of the Dutch painters, he has their love for sensible and ordinary people. . . . As a physiognomist he is equal to [the German painter Ludwig] Knaus, though he has not the same range of subject, nor so much of the dramatic element" ("Eastman Johnson," *The Galaxy* 6, no. 1 [July 1868]: 111–12).

[4] S. G. W. Benjamin, "A Representative American," *The Magazine of Art* 5 (1882): 489.

[5] John I. H. Baur, quoting information from Henry Wadsworth Longfellow Dana, in *Eastman Johnson, 1824–1906: An American Genre Painter*, exh. cat. (Brooklyn: Brooklyn Museum, 1940), 16.

[6] These studies are discussed and reproduced in Patricia Hills, *Eastman Johnson*, exh. cat. (New York: Clarkson N. Potter in association with the Whitney Museum of American Art, 1972), 21–32. See also Patricia Condon Johnston, *Eastman Johnson's Lake Superior Indians* (Afton, Minn.: Johnston Publishing Inc., 1983).

[7] Eastman Johnson to [John F.] Coyle, New York, 13 March 1864; Archives of American Art, Smithsonian Institution, Misc. MSS: Eastman Johnson, roll D10, frames 1371–73.

[8] William Walton wrote in 1906 that Johnson "made some forty careful studies in oil" for the planned maple-sugaring picture; Hills wrote in 1972 that "there are some thirty oil studies presently known." See Walton, "Eastman Johnson, Painter," *Scribner's Magazine* 40, no. 3 (September 1906): 270; and Hills, *Genre Painting of Eastman Johnson,* 103. See also Patricia C. F. Mandel's discussion of the largest maple-sugaring study in "Selection VII: American Paintings from the Museum's Collection, c. 1800–1930," *Bulletin of Rhode Island School of Design, Museum Notes* 63, no. 5 (April 1977): 158–63.

[9] These experiments surely percolated into the rest of Johnson's work, for critics noted at later exhibitions of *Life in the South* the tremendous advance Johnson had made in his style: "Mr. Eastman Johnson's great and rapid improvement in the technical qualities of his art can best be judged by comparing his recent work, even the slightest of it, with [*Negro Life at the South*], painted only seven years ago. During those seven years the strong and dextrous painter has come into existence" ("Fine Arts: Pictures on Exhibition," *The Nation* 4, no. 84 [7 February 1867]: 114).

[10] See Hills, *Eastman Johnson,* 10–20; and a somewhat fuller account in Hills, *Genre Painting of Eastman Johnson,* 27–44.

[11] Johnson to Andrew Warner, 16 February 1851; quoted in Hills, *Eastman Johnson,* 11; and at greater length in Hills, *Genre Painting of Eastman Johnson,* 34.

[12] Henry T. Tuckerman, *Book of the Artists: American Artist Life* (1867; reprint, New York: James F. Carr, 1966), 467.

[13] Walton, "Eastman Johnson," 267–68; also Hills, *Genre Painting of Eastman Johnson,* 40–43.

[14] Walton, "Eastman Johnson," 268.

[15] See Johnson's letter to Charlotte Child, March 1851: "I am uncertain how long I shall remain here, probably leave in the summer [for] Italy, perhaps first to Paris. I am desirious [*sic*] to go somewhere where I can get something to eat for German living has taken me down dreadfully present appearances to the contrary notwithstanding" (quoted in Baur, *Eastman Johnson,* 13).

[16] Many sources follow Walton's statement that Johnson left The Hague for Paris in August 1855. Hills points out that a

drawing of *Miss Brinkley* (Elvehjem Museum of Art, Madison, Wisc.) inscribed "Paris May 1855" places Johnson in that city a few months earlier (*Genre Painting of Eastman Johnson,* 43).

[17] See Elizabeth Gilmore Holt, *The Art of All Nations, 1850–1873: The Emerging Role of Exhibitions and Critics* (Garden City, N.Y.: Anchor Books, 1981), 112, note. At this exposition, Johnson would have been able to see major displays of work by Ingres, Delacroix, and Courbet; he probably also noted the awards bestowed on Meissonier (Légion d'honneur), Jules Breton (third place), and his friend George P. A. Healy (gold medal).

[18] Albert Boime, *Thomas Couture and the Eclectic Vision* (New Haven and London: Yale University Press, 1980), 596.

[19] A discussion of Couture's American students, who in 1855 included Edward Harrison May (1824–1887), Thomas Satterwhite Noble (1835–1907), and Enoch Wood Perry (1831–1915), can be found in Marchal E. Landgren, *American Pupils of Thomas Couture,* exh. cat. (College Park: University of Maryland Art Gallery, 1970). For European and American pupils, see Boime, *Thomas Couture and the Eclectic Vision*, 495–611.

[20] My description of Couture's atelier and the components of his method depends heavily on Albert Boime's full discussion in *The Academy and French Painting in the Nineteenth Century* (London: Phaidon, 1971), 65–78.

[21] Tuckerman, *Book of the Artists,* 447–48. Tuckerman seems to have drawn portions of his description from an account published in 1855; see "A Studio in Paris," *The Crayon* 1, no. 18 (2 May 1855): 281. The earlier account also underscores the immediacy of Couture's instruction as well as its appeal to American pupils: "A favorite student, an American, with clear, bright eyes, and well-marked nose, is engaged in painting a study of the head of a beautiful little child, while Couture . . . kneels on the carpet, divested of his coat, and rapidly produces a bold sketch of the same child."

[22] Thomas Couture, *Conversations on Art Methods,* trans. S. E. Stewart (New York: G. P. Putnam's Sons, 1879), 185, 186.

[23] Albert Boime, "*The Enrollment of the Volunteers of 1792* and the Republic of 1848," in Springfield, Mass., *Enrollment of the Volunteers: Thomas Couture and the Painting of History,* exh. cat. (Museum of Fine Arts, 1980), 72; see also the American critic G.'s review, "Exhibition of Fine Arts in Paris," *The Crayon* 2, no. 19 (7 November 1855): 295.

[24] Sadakichi Hartmann, "Eastman Johnson: American *Genre* Painter," *The International Studio* 34, no. 134 (April 1908): 110.

[25] "Seven years . . . and the young master has not given us occasion to say anything new of him. His painting *Enrollment of the Volunteers* . . . is still in the studio," wrote Théophile Gautier in 1855 (quoted in Springfield, Mass., *Enrollment of the Volunteers,* xviii).

[26] Hills, *Genre Painting of Eastman Johnson,* 34–40.

[27] Walton, "Eastman Johnson," 268. Although there are no sleeping soldiers in Couture's *Enrollment of the Volunteers of 1792,* the abundance of studies for other heads of soldiers in this composition makes it likely that Johnson copied a study related to that work. Copying a head was a standard exercise of academic practice; see Boime, *Academy and French Painting,* 36.

[28] A section of Couture's 1867 *Méthode et entretiens d'atelier* describes how he decided to paint his ideas for *The Enrollment of the Volunteers* and *The Baptism of the Prince Imperial.* The conversational tone of his remarks suggests that such stories were a large part of Couture's conversations in the actual atelier as well. Mandel makes a strong case for Johnson's undertaking of the maple-sugaring subject being influenced by Couture's *Romans of the Decadence* ("Selections VII," 158–59).

[29] Walton, "Eastman Johnson," 268.

[30] Hills notes that while Johnson experimented with aspects of Couture's technique in the late 1850s and early 1860s, the appearance of the oil sketch in Johnson's work coincides with the 1867 publication of *Méthode et entretiens* (*Genre Painting of Eastman Johnson,* 130–31). Yet because Couture's volume deals rather little with *méthode,* giving much more space to *entretiens* on diverse subjects, the connection between this book and Johnson's technique is probably not so direct.

[31] George P. A. Healy, *Reminiscences of a Portrait Painter* (1894; reprint, New York: Kennedy Graphics, Inc./Da Capo Press, 1970), 84.

[32] A letter of August 1857 from Healy to a Johnson—presumably Eastman—discusses a "study of the head of General Jackson" that Healy was willing to bring with him to Washington the next spring "if it will answer your purpose

to copy the picture" (Healy to Johnson, Chicago, 2 August 1857; Archives of American Art, Smithsonian Institution, Misc. MSS: Robert Graham Collection of Autograph Letters, roll D294, frame 721). The relationship between Healy and Johnson remains unexplored. Their common roots as portrait painters, their activities in both the artistic and social realms, and the similarity of the portraits they executed in the 1880s and 1890s are issues that could benefit from further research. After Healy's death in 1894, Johnson wrote from Nantucket a note of condolence to his friend's widow: "Here in the quiet of these late October evenings I think over the long years gone by that I have known your husband—tho. to be sure with but short periods of actual contact—but how full they always are of pleasant memories, of unfailing kindness and good will out of every little act" (Johnson to Mrs. G. P. A. Healy, 29 October 1894; Archives of American Art, Smithsonian Institution, Marie de Mare Papers, roll D130, frames 76–77).

[33] Blodgett's involvement with the budding Metropolitan Museum of Art ran deeper: while in Europe in 1871 he single-handedly made the somewhat controversial purchase of 174 Dutch and Flemish pictures for the museum. See Madeleine Fidell-Beaufort and Jeanne K. Welcher, "Some Views of Art Buying in New York in the 1870s and 1880s," *The Oxford Art Journal* 5, no. 1 (1982): 50–51; also Calvin Tomkins, *Merchants and Masterpieces: The Story of The Metropolitan Museum of Art* (New York: E. P. Dutton, 1970), 36–43. For Blodgett, see "Obituary: William Tilden Blodgett," *The New-York Times*, 6 November 1875.

[34] [G. Bertauts-Couture], *Thomas Couture: Sa Vie, son oeuvre, son caractère, ses idées, sa méthode, par lui-même et par son petit-fils* (Paris: Le Garrec, 1932), 52, 68. On page 100, Bertauts-Couture publishes a list of six paintings and three drawings that Couture was working on for "un amateur (probablement M. Blodgett)." None of the titles on that list matches the three Couture paintings auctioned in 1876 after Blodgett's death. See note 37.

[35] Boime, *Thomas Couture and the Eclectic Vision*, 557.

[36] Bertauts-Couture, *Thomas Couture*, 47–48; see also Boime, *Thomas Couture and the Eclectic Vision*, 228.

[37] For *Idle Student*, see James L. Yarnall and William H. Gerdts, comps., *The National Museum of American Art's Index to American Art Exhibition Catalogues, from the Beginning Through the 1876 Centennial Year*, 6 vols. (Boston: G. K. Hall & Co., 1986), 1:852. This was probably a drawing for or related to the painting *Soap Bubbles* (1859, The Metropolitan Museum of Art, New York; first version, 1859, Walters Art Gallery, Baltimore), which was known in the nineteenth century as *Day Dreams* or *The Indolent Scholar* (Yarnall and Gerdts, *Index*, 1:852); see also Charles Sterling and Margaretta M. Salinger, *French Paintings: A Catalogue of the Collection of The Metropolitan Museum of Art*, vol. 2 (New York: The Metropolitan Museum of Art, 1966), 147–48. For Blodgett's paintings by Couture, see *Executor's Sale of the Collection of Paintings Belonging to the Estate of the Late Wm. T. Blodgett*, sale cat. (New York: Chickering Hall, 27 April 1876). No. 64, *Pierrot and Harlequin* (1857, Chrysler Museum, Norfolk, Va.), sold for $4,400 to the railroad magnate Darius O. Mills. No. 73, *The Police Court* (unlocated), exhibited in the 1870s as *Justice Asleep* or *Pierrot before the Judge*, sold for $5,800 to Mills's partner Collis P. Huntington. No. 90, *Liberty in Chains, (France)* sold for only $875 to William T. Walters of Baltimore; the Walters Art Gallery sold the work before 1887. See *The New-York Times*, 20 and 28 April 1876; Yarnall and Gerdts, *Index*, 1:852; and Edward Strahan [Earl Shinn], *The Art Treasures of America*, 3 vols. [ca. 1879–1882; reprint, New York: Garland Publishing, 1977], 1:89–90; 2:99–100, 114–15. See also Boime, *Thomas Couture and the Eclectic Vision*, 309–10, 318–19, 352–55; and William R. Johnston, *The Nineteenth-Century Paintings in the Walters Art Gallery* (Baltimore, Md.: Trustees of the Walters Art Gallery, 1982), 29.

[38] For Blodgett's collection of Johnson paintings, see "Obituary: William Tilden Blodgett." Blodgett owned at least two works by Johnson: *Christmas-Time* (see FIG. 4) and *Corn-Sheller* (probably *Corn-Shelling*, 1864, Toledo Museum of Art), both exhibited at the National Academy of Design in 1865 He seems to have supported Johnson's work from an early date: "Eastman Johnson has had an evening, and some fine works from the collection of Messrs. Blodgett and Parish have been exhibited" ("Sketchings: Domestic Art Gossip, New York," *The Crayon* 7, no. 3 [March 1860]: 84). No Johnson works were included in the Blodgett sale of 1876.

[39] Johnson and Blodgett appear together in a group photograph in a commemorative album of the New York Metropolitan Sanitary Fair, along with the

artists Worthington Whittredge, Emanuel Leutze, and William Stanley Haseltine, and the collectors Abraham M. Cozzens and Joseph H. Choate (Hills, *Genre Painting of Eastman Johnson,* 76).

[40]Carroll Beckwith reminisced that Johnson's "method of work . . . was one of the warm, transparent shadows sustaining lights and half-tones painted with vigor and *impasto.* Thomas Couture was perhaps the best exponent of this method in France," while Frank Fowler recalled that "our painter's method was, after all, a rather full-blooded one—his touch was, as opposed to that of his contemporaries, free and loose—a reminder, perhaps, of that vigorous manipulator of pigment, Couture" (Will H. Low, Carroll Beckwith, Samuel Isham, and Frank Fowler, "The Field of Art: Eastman Johnson—His Life and Works," *Scribner's Magazine* 40, no. 2 (August 1906): 254–56.

[41]Hartmann, "Eastman Johnson," 110–11.

[42]Couture, *Conversations on Art Methods,* 12.

[43]Worthington Whittredge recalled that Sanford Gifford "would frequently stop in his tracks to make slight sketches in pencil in a small book which he always carried in his pocket and then pass on, always suspicious that if he stopped too long to look in one direction the most beautiful thing of all might pass him by at his back" (*The Autobiography of Worthington Whittredge, 1820–1910,* ed. John I. H. Baur [1942; reprint, New York: Arno Press, 1969], 59). The sketching practices of American-trained landscape painters owe much to the advice of Asher B. Durand (1796–1886); see Theodore E. Stebbins, Jr., *American Master Drawings and Watercolors* (New York: Harper & Row, 1976), 121–31.

[44]The inscription "Sept. 22 75" on this drawing has provided the rationale for dating *The Cranberry Harvest* series to 1875–1880. Despite this date and the fact that the drawing was used in a painting of 1876 (*The New Bonnet* [The Metropolitan Museum of Art, New York]), there is no reason to assume that the studies of cranberry pickers necessarily date from September 1875 as well. Considering the two different media on the single sheet, and the inscription oriented to read with the figure of the woman rather than the harvesters, it seems likely that the sheet represents two different drawing sessions. That the pencil studies on the left margin stop when they approach the charcoal figure indicates that Johnson sketched them onto the edges of a sheet he had earlier set aside.

[45]This is not to say that this sketch is the first compositional study Johnson executed. It simply enters the discussion at this point because it is less closely tied to subsequent studies.

[46]After one's drawing had been transferred to canvas, Couture advocated going over the charcoal outlines with pigments bound in a "sauce" of boiled oil and spirits of turpentine: "Then you take the sable brush, dip it into your 'sauce,' then into the bistrè tint, and trace all your outline. These outlines being made, mass your shadows and you obtain a kind of sepia drawing in oil" (Couture, *Conversations on Art Methods,* 7–8).

[47]According to Baur, "finished study" is a term that Johnson himself used to describe the difference between sketches of individual incident as opposed to those of panoramic views (*Eastman Johnson,* 21).

[48]Of course, the possibility also exists that one simply does not have access to the full range of individual and compositional studies for *The Cranberry Harvest.* One can be certain, for instance, that Johnson made many more pencil drawings than the two illustrated in this catalogue. See Hills, *Genre Painting of Eastman Johnson,* 157–58.

[49]In its compositional bands and hard transitions between colors, *The Conversation* relates to such works as *Lambs, Nantucket* (1874, Collection of Mr. and Mrs. Paul Mellon, Upperville, Va.).

[50]Despite the ambiguous nature of their exchange, this conversation is the closest Johnson comes to the flirtations featured in his maple-sugaring studies, and which he seemed to enjoy as a student traveling in Germany: "They were beginning the vintage while I was on my journey [through the Rhine country]. . . . The peasantry were all at work, men and women, and it was my habit to give each party a call. Now and then a pretty girl would emerge from the vines with her tub of grapes on her head and I would help her plunge them into the great cart . . . which was an excellent commencement to a nice little rustic flirtation" (Johnson to Charlotte Child, March 1851, quoted in Baur, *Eastman Johnson,* 12).

[51]See, for example, Couture's sketch for *The Enrollment of the Volunteers of 1792* (1848, Museum of Fine Arts, Springfield, Mass.), which Boime describes

as a "combination of red browns and prismatic hues radiating a fireside warmth and intimacy" ("Current and Forthcoming Exhibitions," *The Burlington Magazine* 112, no. 810 [September 1970]: 646).

[52] See, for example, *The Story Teller of the Camp (Maple Sugar Camp)* (ca. 1861–1866, Reynolda House, Winston-Salem, N.C.) or even *A Sly Drink at the Camp* (ca. 1861–1866, The Art Institute of Chicago), two studies for a sugaring-off scene that have dimensions comparable to no. 9, but display selective areas of much greater finish.

[53] Hills, while admitting that "it is not known whether Johnson ever completed or planned to complete a painting based on the Yale study" (*Eastman Johnson,* 92), has suggested that "the works may have been intended as a pair with the Timken painting depicting the daytime picking and the Yale painting representing the evening consolidation of the day's harvest" (*Genre Painting of Eastman Johnson,* 152).

[54] It is impossible, of course, to declare with any certainty the order in which Johnson proceeded with his studies toward the final version of *The Cranberry Harvest.* There is no reason to assume he could not have worked on two very different conceptions simultaneously; yet what little correspondence we have from Johnson in 1879 reveals his increasing frustration with his progress, followed by a sudden resolution and calm. See Simpson, "Taken with a Cranberry Fit," in this volume, 38–39.

[55] Couture, *Conversations on Art Methods,* 200–201.

[56] See Simpson, "Taken with a Cranberry Fit," in this volume, 43 and n. 80, for the reasons for such a warning.

[57] Carol Troyen makes this point to conclude her catalogue entry on *The Cranberry Harvest* in Theodore E. Stebbins, Jr., Carol Troyen, and Trevor J. Fairbrother, *A New World: Masterpieces of American Painting, 1760–1910,* exh. cat. (Boston: Museum of Fine Arts, 1983), 270–71. It is worth noting that in conception and execution *Woman on a Hill* stands apart from most of the other cranberry harvest studies; like *The Conversation,* it may have been painted earlier than those works.

[58] For the popularity of Millet, see Susan Fleming, "The Boston Patrons of Jean-François Millet," in Alexandra R. Murphy, *Jean-François Millet,* exh. cat. (Boston: Museum of Fine Arts, 1984), ix–xviii; and Laura L. Meixner, "Popular Criticism of Jean-François Millet in Nineteenth-Century America," *The Art Bulletin* 65, no. 1 (March 1983): 94–105.

[59] Breton's *Cattle Crossing a Bridge, Sunset* and *The Rustic Entomologist* were on view at Goupil's gallery in New York in 1857 (Yarnall and Gerdts, *Index,* 1:432). For Avery (and several others), see Madeleine Fidell-Beaufort, "Jules Breton in America: Collecting in the Nineteenth Century," in Hollister Sturges et al., *Jules Breton and the French Rural Tradition,* exh. cat. (Omaha, Nebr.: Joslyn Art Museum in association with The Arts Publisher, Inc., New York, 1982), 51–61; also Fidell-Beaufort and Welcher, "Some Views of Art Buying," esp. 53.

[60] Théophile Thoré, remarking upon the 1867 Paris Universal Exposition, quoted in Hollister Sturges, "Jules Breton: Creator of a Noble Peasant Image," in Hollister Sturges, ed., *The Rural Vision: France and America in the Late Nineteenth Century* (Omaha, Nebr.: Joslyn Art Museum, 1987), 39. See also a review of the 1878 Paris Exposition that claimed: "It is easy to be impressive by terror. Hecatombs of Ixions could not offset the sweet impressiveness which is drawn by Jules Breton from the incidents of the commonest rural life" ("Pictures at the Exposition," *The Atlantic Monthly* 42, no. 245 [December 1878]: 713).

[61] William J. Hoppin (1873), quoted in Fidell-Beaufort, "Jules Breton in America," 51.

[62] Hills, *Eastman Johnson,* 92.

[63] Strahan, *Art Treasures of America,* 3:70.

[64] Sturges et al., *Jules Breton and the French Rural Tradition,* cat. no. 17, 76.

[65] Although most of the paintings leading up to *The Cranberry Harvest* were neither dated nor titled by Johnson, the small paper label (see FIG. 7) that identifies FIG. 10 as *At the Closing of the Day* is written in Elizabeth Johnson's hand, suggesting that the title may have been Johnson's own.

[66] For a discussion of this painting, see Jules Breton, *The Life of an Artist: An Autobiography,* trans. Mary J. Serrano (New York: D. Appleton and Company, 1890), 232–35; see also cat. entry 50 in Gabriel P. Weisberg, *The Realist Tradition: French Painting and Drawing, 1830–1900,* exh. cat. (Cleveland, Oh.: Cleveland Museum of Art in cooperation with Indiana University Press, 1980), 82–85.

[67] The literature on gleaning is extensive; a good introduction

to gleaning as a subject in French nineteenth-century art can be found in Robert L. Herbert, "City vs. Country: The Rural Image in French Painting from Millet to Gauguin," *Artforum* 8, no. 6 (February 1970): 44–55. For images of farming in American art, see Patricia Hills, "Images of Rural America in the Works of Eastman Johnson, Winslow Homer, and Their Contemporaries: A Survey and Critique," in Sturges, ed., *The Rural Vision,* 63–81; see also Sarah Burns, *Pastoral Inventions: Rural Life in Nineteenth-Century American Art and Culture* (Philadelphia: Temple University Press, 1989).

[68] Breton, *Life of an Artist,* 232.

[69] See Lois Marie Fink, "French Art in the United States, 1850–1870: Three Dealers and Collectors," *Gazette des beaux-arts,* n.s. 6, 92, no. 1316 (September 1978): 87–100; see also Alexandra R. Murphy, "French Paintings in Boston: 1800–1900," in Anne L. Poulet and Alexandra R. Murphy, *Corot to Braque: French Paintings from the Museum of Fine Arts, Boston,* exh. cat. (Boston: Museum of Fine Arts, 1979), xvii–xlvi.

[70] "The chief attractions, and in fact, the best pictures in [the current Artists' Fund Society exhibition] are from the easels of foreign painters and from private houses in this city. . . . Mr. Knoedler imports the best French pictures" ("The Artists' Fund Exhibition," *The Evening Post,* 14 November 1863).

[71] Two Breton works were displayed at the 1864 Metropolitan Sanitary Fair: *The Cabaret,* also known as *Wine Shop (Monday)* (1858, Washington University Gallery of Art, St. Louis), lent by John Hoey; and *The Harvest* (unidentified), lent by William P. Wright. Goupil's gallery showed two Breton pictures in 1857 and two more in 1860. In 1859 the Belgian dealer Ernest Gambart set up an exhibition of "Artists of the French and English Schools" at the National Academy of Design, which included two works by Breton and two by Couture, including *Decadence of Rome* (probably a study for or copy after Couture's original). See Yarnall and Gerdts, *Index,* 1:26, 431–32, 852; also "Sketchings: Domestic Art Gossip," *The Crayon* 6, no. 10 (October 1859): 320.

[72] This generalization has been made after correlating information provided by Yarnall and Gerdts's *Index* along with that contained in nineteenth-century sale catalogues, exhibition records, and sources such as *The Crayon* and Tuckerman's *Book of the Artists.*

[73] "Introduction" to Breton, *Life of an Artist,* 1; see also Fidell-Beaufort and Wechler, "Some Views of Art Buying," 53.

[74] " 'The Horse Fair' [by Rosa Bonheur] . . . now forms one of the art-treasures of Mr. Wright's beautiful gallery at Weehawken" ("Artist Biography: French," *The Crayon* 7, no. 6 [June 1860]: 168). For Wright, see "Obituary: William P. Wright," *The New-York Times,* 8 July 1880. Selections from Wright's collection—two Verboeckhovens, a Louis Gallant, a Robert Fleury, and a J.-L. Ulysse—were featured in *Lights and Shadows of New York Picture Galleries: Forty Photographs, by A. A. Turner, Selected and Described by William Young* (New York: D. Appleton and Company, 1864); his collection was catalogued ca. 1863 as an anonymous "Gallery of Paintings at Weehawken." William P. Wright, who was born and died in England, maintained a summer residence in Weehawken and should not be confused with the leather manufacturer and later senator William Wright (1794–1866) of Newark, N.J.

[75] "Fine Arts: Pictures on Exhibition," 114.

[76] After examining the painting (at the time insecurely attributed to Johnson), Hills wrote: "I recall noting to myself that the style was very similar to Eastman Johnson's. . . . (Note the similarity to the studies for *The Cranberry Harvest.*) Moreover, the general sensibility—'cute' children playing 'horse' and 'coachman' was certainly similar to Eastman Johnson's *The Old Stage Coach*" (quoted in Katherine Harper Mead, ed., *The Preston Morton Collection of American Art* [Santa Barbara: Santa Barbara Museum of Art, 1981], 264).

[77] Hills researched this painting extensively in preparation for a catalogue of the Santa Barbara Museum of Art's Preston Morton collection, but her efforts to establish a provenance were stymied when the New York galleries that co-owned the work in 1960 could offer her only incomplete records and faded memories. A librarian at the Kennedy Galleries wrote her in 1980: "Rudy Wunderlich . . . recalled that our source for the painting, Joseph Friedman, had some connection with the Johnson family, either as a descendant of Eastman Johnson or a friend of the family. The picture was acquired from Mr. Friedman together with 'The Wounded Drummer Boy,' which is now in the collection of Mrs. McCook Knox, and a third painting by Johnson, the title

of which Mr. Wunderlich was unable to recall" (Mead, ed., *Preston Morton Collection,* 264). In 1960 Norman Hirschl of Hirschl & Adler Galleries had written the Santa Barbara Museum that the painting "came from the Joseph Friedman Collection in New York. They had been a family of jewelers" (quoted in Mead, ed., *Preston Morton Collection,* 266). Records at the Frick Art Museum in Pittsburgh, Penn., to whom Mrs. McCook Knox gave *The Wounded Drummer Boy,* help set the record straight. *The Wounded Drummer Boy,* and thus *The Baby Carriage* and the third Johnson painting, came from the collection of Joseph *Feldman,* whose aunt was the daughter of Joseph Schwartz—the jeweler. *The Wounded Drummer Boy* was "acquired directly from the artist by Mr. Joseph Schwartz, who was the artist's jeweler, and who sold him many gifts for Mrs. Johnson for Christmas and birthday presents, from his jewelry store at Thirty-seventh Street and Broadway. Consistently remaining in the family of Joseph Schwartz, who was a devoted admirer of the artist, the painting remained . . . relatively unknown to the outside world" (quoted from Kennedy Galleries information sheet, curatorial files, Frick Art Museum). I am indebted to Alan Fausel, curator of the Frick Art Museum, for sharing this information with me.

[78] I am grateful to Teresa A. Carbone of The Brooklyn Museum for discussing this painting with me.

[79] Walton, "Eastman Johnson," 270–71.

[80] Benjamin, "Representative American," 489.

[81] Walton, "Eastman Johnson," 271.

Afterword/Afterwards: Eastman Johnson's Transition to Portrait Painting in the Early 1880s

Patricia Hills

One question remains: Why did Eastman Johnson leave genre painting for portrait painting just at the moment, 1880, when his career seems to have reached new heights?

Posthumous assessments have generally agreed that he *should* have continued to produce his genre paintings of national life. At the end of the nineteenth century his friend, the landscape painter Worthington Whittredge, wrote in his autobiography that "the country has reason to regret that he ever stopped painting them and went back to portraits."[1] John Baur, who organized the first major retrospective of Johnson's work in 1940, followed up on Whittredge's remarks by adding, "the regret may be echoed today."[2]

To Baur, Johnson's turn in the early 1880s "in favor of his more remunerative portrait commissions . . . was not, judging from the evidence of his art, a case of going stale, for the few genre pictures that he did do at this time show a continued development along the lines he had laid down for himself at Nantucket."[3] Baur offers the explanation that "it was probably the growing demand for his work in this field [portrait painting] together with the high prices which it brought that persuaded him to abandon genre."[4] Drawing on family documents available to him, Baur cited a letter from Johnson's nephew that recalled the artist's paintings of Grover Cleveland, John D. Rockefeller, and others, done when Johnson "used to get about $5,000 for a full length portrait and about $1,500 for a head and shoulders."[5] From these remarks we can conclude little about specific commissions or the kinds of variables that might have affected Johnson's prices in the 1880s and 1890s; nonetheless, these figures are in line with one price we know—that Johnson asked $3,500 for his double portrait *The Funding Bill* in 1881.[6] Considering the dollar's buying power in the 1880s,[7] we can rightly be impressed with the fees he could command.

But we should not ignore the fact that during this time he continued to get good prices for his genre paintings. The annual exhibitions of the Artists' Fund Society provide a useful index to prices of popular paintings, which Johnson's always were. At the society's exhibition in 1880, his *Glass with the Squire*, another Nantucket scene, sold for $1,120, and the following year his *Reading the Bible* went for $1,350, the highest price in that year's exhibition.[8] Given the fact that *The Funding Bill* was roughly five feet by six and a half feet, and *Reading the Bible* only 22 by 25 inches, we can conclude that Johnson's genre paintings then had a quite healthy market.

Thus, monetary considerations alone cannot account for Johnson's initial defection from the ranks of genre painters. With only a bit of probing into the historical circumstances, we are brought up against a host of factors that led to Johnson's taking up portraiture on a virtually full-time basis and to his moving away from his beloved genre painting—even at the moment when he was receiving high praise from a substantial number of art writers and critics, was selling his work for handsome sums, and was being showcased in the collections of prominent patrons.[9]

The primary circumstance was the pronounced change in taste and attitudes about art that occurred in the late 1870s—a change of which Johnson was fully aware and to which he attempted, in his own way, to adapt. The critics and art writers quickly picked up on the new trends, and they played a role in advancing them. S. G. W. Benjamin, writing for *The American Art Review* in 1880, sounded a consensus opinion when he observed that: "With a rapidity which hardly has an example in the history of aesthetics, the popular mind responds to the new movement of American art, and everything indicates that we are indeed passing from one era to another."[10]

Benjamin was talking about the new techniques coming over from Paris and Munich and about new subjects—more urbane, sophisticated, and international—replacing the older Americanist themes. Clearly the cultural and aesthetic hegemony of Johnson's generation—those who showed annually at the National Academy of Design exhibitions: Frederic Church, Albert Bierstadt, Jervis McEntee, and Sanford Gifford in landscape, himself and J. G. Brown in genre painting, Daniel Huntington and Thomas Hicks in portraiture—was being questioned.

Nowhere was this challenge more evident than in the exhibitions of the Society of American Artists, an organization founded in 1877 by Augustus Saint-Gaudens, Walter Shirlaw, Wyatt Eaton, and Helena de Kay Gilder, partly in response to the exclusionary tactics of the National Academy of Design old guard and partly in response to the contemporary European art then flooding the commercial galleries in the mid- to late-1870s.[11] Realizing the importance of expanding, the society's founders soon invited the more progressive academicians to participate, as well as younger American artists still working abroad, such as William Merritt Chase, J. Alden Weir, Frank Duveneck, John Singer Sargent, and Will H. Low. The first annual exhibition in 1878 and the subsequent exhibitions of 1879 and the early 1880s brought critical attention to the spontaneous brushwork, plein-air effects, and "decorative" painting characteristic of the younger artists.[12]

Mariana Griswold van Rensselaer's writings characterize the new criticism that promoted the new art. Writing on both the National Academy of Design and the Society of American Artists exhibitions held in the spring of 1880, she noted:

> In view of this year's exhibitions, it does not seem incorrect or premature to speak of an elder and a younger school in American art. A few years ago we began to hear of "new men" from Munich and Paris, who, however, diverse among themselves, united in differing by aim and method from all those whom the nation had been long accustomed to regard as its interpreters in art.[13]

Of the academicians' work in the academy show, Van Rensselaer minced no words: "When a departure was made from the dead level of commonplace and tiresome reiteration, it was usually in the direction of the strikingly bad." In contrast, she saw the pictures in the society's exhibition as being "in almost every case unconventional, novel, individual, tentative, erratic," and she continued with high praise for Sargent's portrait of *Carolus-Duran* and Chase's *General Webb*.[14]

Although no letters have come to light that explicitly document Johnson's response to the new directions, we can still infer his attitudes and sensitivities by learning something about the man and by searching for nuances in his comments on art-world events about which he held strong feelings. To begin: By the late 1870s Johnson was in his mid-fifties. He had married late and he finally had a young child, Ethel, on whom he doted.[15] It would have been a reasonable time to take stock of his career, even though, as his letters to Jervis McEntee (1828–1891) in the fall of 1879 make clear, he was moving forward (smitten with "cranberry fever") to complete a new series of pictures—with the culmination being *The Cranberry Harvest* (PLATE 1). Indeed, it was exactly because so much was at stake—his ambition to produce a grand national genre painting in the face of younger challengers—that we might expect such a reassessment.

In Johnson's letter of 17 November to McEntee we get several clues to Johnson's thoughts when he consoles McEntee, still grieving his wife's death.[16] Johnson's kindly words reveal greater self-reflection than we have come to expect from the outgoing, somewhat sentimental, club man, affectionately remembered in the memoirs of his contemporaries. But his protestations against McEntee's despondency were prompted, I believe, as much by his own situation as by McEntee's grief. Johnson writes:

> I have thought about you a good deal since this letter and while waiting to write you, and wish I could put into shape any of the thoughts and suggestions that pass vaguely thru my mind, but I beg of you on one point, not to talk or think about having "done your work" or whether you will ever paint anymore. I am sure of one thing that precisely therein, in giving more serious and if possible more ardent attention to painting and to Art generally[,] lies your best and safest refuge and of this I have no doubt you too are sufficiently conscious in your bright moments. . . .
>
> . . . It is dreadfully discouraging *to me* to hear you talk in that strain, and for my own part if I cannot fight off that idea for a good while yet I fear I shall make but a poor end.[17]

To Johnson, the notion of "having done your work" was unthinkable. He was gearing himself up to the challenges of the newer art.

In his next letter to McEntee of 13 December 1879, in which he displays a mixture of wanting both to get back to New York and to stay away, he says: "I am glad to hear that that [*sic*] there seems to be some little movement in our line. In fact I think we must certainly have our share in the revival there [than?] is generally in the commercial world, and I look for better times, unless *foreign* art swallows it *all* up."[18] This passage indicates that he shared with the Society of American Artists a concern about the dominance of foreign art[19] and offers further evidence of his resolution to push on.

The spring of 1880 saw Johnson riding a wave of success for his Nantucket scenes.[20] Typical praise came from the pen of the critic S. G. W. Benjamin when reviewing the National Academy's exhibition of 1880:

> There is no mystery and no pathos in the works of Mr. Eastman Johnson. But as a delineator of the cheerful or picturesque aspects of American genre, he not only stands near the head of our art, but continues to improve. . . . *The Cranberry Harvest in Nantucket*, representing the lasses and laddies of that seafaring isle stealing a few delightful hours from maritime and domestic pursuits to cull the scarlet berries from the moist meadow-lands, is an ambitious composition of a very meritorious character.[21]

But we wonder whether he might not have begun to feel the limitations of a praise based on nostalgia for bygone days.

Because of the overwhelming success of *The Cranberry Harvest* in particular, it is easy to overlook the other picture he sent to the National Academy of Design that year; this was *The Reprimand* (FIG. 1), a picture that reveals in images what Johnson perhaps only half-consciously wanted to say.[22] Significantly, Benjamin prefers this picture. The above-quoted remarks continue:

> *The Reprimand* is, however, a picture not only of more general attraction, but in the character of the stern old grandfather, and the haughtily imperious beauty of the high-spirited girl who turns away from him with a rebellious posture suggesting the possible dangers to which her temper is urging, we see a work offering the

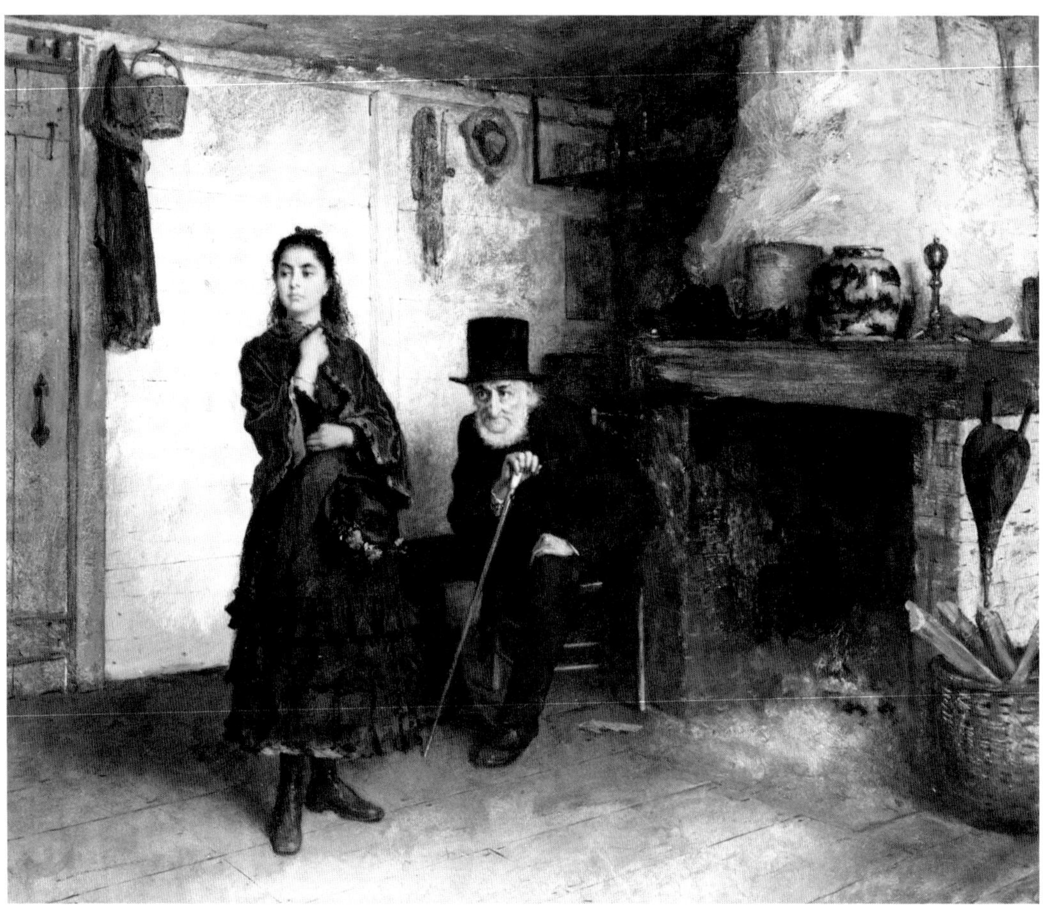

FIG. 1. Eastman Johnson, *The Reprimand,* 1880. Oil on canvas, 19 1/4 x 23 inches. Private collection. Photograph courtesy Bernard & S. Dean Levy Inc., New York.

> artist greater opportunity, of which he has availed himself with a force that he has rarely equalled before.[23]

A good part of the appeal of the picture at that time comes from its metaphoric content: The new generation rebelliously turns its back on the old—as the younger Paris- and Munich-trained artists turned from the old-guard academicians. A more feminine spirit defies the moral authority of the old patriarch—as expressive, internationalist art-for-art's sake painting was usurping the authority of the Hudson River School and nativist genre painting.[24]

Returning to *The Cranberry Harvest:* Benjamin was gentle in his remarks about Johnson, as were all critics; the expansive affability of the older artist seemed to preclude harsh criticism, and, moreover, Johnson was updating his style even when relying on distinctly "American" scenes.[25] But more and more a vigorous critical backlash arose against nativist subject matter and realist finish. Charles de Kay, the critic of *The New-York Times,* in his review of the 1880 spring annual of the Society of American Artists, provides a case in point. He summarily dismissed Johnson's contemporary John Ehninger (1827–1889) to the dustbin of history:

In spite of the date, 1879, the "Turkey Shoot" of Mr. Ehninger must belong to the ante-bellum days; it is not of the present day and generation. While it is a truthful genre picture of rural sport in Winter in the Middle States, the style of painting is far from artistic, and places the canvas rather among the Academy pictures than those of the new departure.[26]

We do not know if Johnson read this particular review or whether he might have considered the possibility that such criticism could be directed toward his own efforts (after all, Ehninger was, like Johnson, Couture-trained), but he did feel a loyalty to the generation that had come to artistic maturity with him.

Sanford Gifford (1823–1880) belonged to that generation and his death on 28 August 1880 strongly affected Johnson. Writing to McEntee on 30 August, Johnson reflected: "It makes us all feel very sad. To me it is a great break into our particular circle. It is the next one after your own dear wife, and something like it."[27]

Gifford takes center stage in Johnson's letter of 2 December, in which he encloses a newspaper article from *The World* that reviews Gifford's memorial exhibition at The Metropolitan Museum. Johnson is outraged and hopes McEntee can find someone to "horsewhip" the critic. The review itself calls the exhibition the "Gifford Chamber of Horrors," because the pictures "were photographic, they were topographic, but they never succeeded in being artistic." What must have really stung Johnson was the reviewer's condemnation of a whole generation of artists:

But it is safe to say that of all the men who were fellow-workers with Gifford and Kensett, not more than three have advanced to a point at which their pictures contain something that will live, something worth preserving. If we are to have memorial exhibitions of all of them as they pass away, and zealous friends load the Museum with specimens of their art, the walls of the two rooms devoted to modern works will be entirely occupied with pictures of no value to the exclusion of those gems which the liberality of art connoisseurs now lends for every exhibition.[28]

A cruel pronouncement: that "not more than three" artists would sustain lasting fame. No wonder Johnson wanted him horsewhipped.

In the same letter, Johnson voices his pique about an item in a subsequent issue of *The World:*

Since this there is another notice of the Philadelphia Exhibition[,] abusing the Academy for not giving the Americans abroad a fair chance at their exhibitions, all of which is a succession of lies and nearly as beastly as this I enclose. What a pity there is nobody to meet such scoundrels in a proper way.[29]

It is not surprising for Johnson to defend the National Academy of Design so rigorously. He had been on the council of the academy from 1866 to 1870 and filled the office of vice-president from 1874 to 1876. During 1880 his friend George Hall was treasurer and McEntee was on the council and exhibition committee.[30] Johnson knew the allegation was unfair because the academy had already responded by liberalizing its rules for exhibiting the work of non-academicians, and some of the academicians had even embraced the tenets of the new styles.

In spite of his fierce loyalty to his own peers, he showed a lively interest in the new generation and may have attended meetings of the Society of American Artists as early as 1879. Will Low (1853–1932) credits Johnson for prompting the younger artist's sojourn in Nantucket over the winter of 1879–1880, at a time when Low thought it important to test out the theory "that to be of one's time, to express a native sentiment in art, one should live in a characteristic native town in close touch with its life."[31] Low's recollections of Johnson, penned after the latter's death, deserve quoting at length for their thoughtful portrait of the older artist who had much to offer to a younger generation:

I had met Eastman Johnson in the meetings of the S. A. A., and perhaps the knowledge of the admirable

> work that he had done at Nantucket, in his case a true expression of his temperament, was not without its influence in the choice of a testing-ground for my theory—or rather the theory of others to which I had lent a consenting ear. . . . The bluff, hearty welcome accorded to the newcomer by the successful painter, whose pictures had long been accepted by our artists and our people, and whose portraits, if gathered together, would in themselves constitute a gallery of noted Americans, was characteristic of the man, who, lately gone from us, departed leaving none but friends. Robust, kindly petulant in manner, florid of complexion, sturdy of figure, not so far removed in type, though he was thoroughly a man of the world, from some of the retired captains that he painted so well in his "Nantucket School of Philosophy," Eastman Johnson mingled with his neighbours on terms that explain in his work the easy seizure of character, the complete fidelity of type, the essential quality of sympathetic representation rendered.[32]

Low admired him, moreover, as a master of the technical aspects of painting.

Others of Low's generation shared his fond assessment. The tribute read into the minutes of the 4 June 1906 annual meeting of the academy, following Johnson's death, stated:

> For many years in the Academy Exhibitions Johnson's compositions representing phases of American life were examples to our painters and when in 1877 the now historic Society of American Artists was formed the mature painter, without severing his loyalty to the Academy, gave hearty welcome to the newer outlook of the younger men.[33]

Like his last European teacher, Thomas Couture, he exhibited a craftsmanship that the young men admired even when they did not emulate it, a sincerity in his depiction of subject matter, and a warm welcome to new trends.

To sum up Johnson's situation in late 1880: One of his best friends, Sanford Gifford, a man his own age, had died; the artistic achievement of his own generation was being called into question; the critical reception of his Nantucket pictures was wholeheartedly warm but already tinged with nostalgia; he saw that his new, young friends, such as Will Low, were expanding art into newer realms; and he was getting to know more of them through the Society of American Artists—even planning to exhibit a picture at its 1881 spring exhibition. At this point he did not yet have a picture to send to the National Academy that would match his *Cranberry Harvest.* Instead of sending another genre painting of regional celebration like *The Cranberry Harvest,* or a genre painting that subverted the content, if not the form, of genre painting like *The Reprimand,* he tried something new. *The Funding Bill* (FIG. 2), conceived in 1880, would become the perfect solution; it would also set the course for his late painting career.

Johnson has himself documented the immediate inspiration for *The Funding Bill,* the double portrait of his wife's brother-in-law Robert W. Rutherfurd and the portrait draftsman Samuel W. Rowse.[34] In a letter to the Pennsylvania Academy of the Fine Arts in 1881, Johnson recounts the circumstances:

> I saw these two gentlemen sitting in my own house with accessories &c. as in the picture. Their conversation suggested to me the title. They are from life and in fact fair portraits. The scene struck me at the moment as the picture of a discussion and was so painted.[35]

Johnson painted a small oil sketch in 1880, at the time when the Act to Facilitate the Refunding of the National Debt, called "The Funding Bill," was being debated in financial circles.[36] Johnson's widow, writing in 1913, recalls the spontaneity of the choice of subject as well as the execution. "It happened he had no Academy exhibition picture for that year. He said in looking at them—'I see my Academy picture.' In three weeks it was finished and in the place of honor."[37] It seems likely that the sketch, dated 1880, was what inspired the decision to work up this new picture. In any event, the larger painting was finished in early 1881, in time for the academy's spring annual.

With *The Funding Bill* Johnson had moved decisively away from the generic of genre painting to the singularity of portraiture, away from the typical to the topical. And he was rewarded with instant praise when it appeared on the walls of the National Academy. The critic for *The New-York Times,* probably the same Charles de Kay who had written the devastating critique of Ehninger's *Turkey Shoot* in the previous year, now wrote on 20 March 1881. After denouncing J. G. Brown's pictures of street urchins, he turns to Johnson's portrait:

> That better exists can be seen from the large double portrait by Mr. Eastman Johnson, which holds, by the best of right, that of worth, the place of honor in the same room. In a well-subdued drawing-room, the furniture of which is handsomely painted, sit two gentlemen on a sofa. They are, if no mistake is made, Mr. Robert W. Rutherfurd and Mr. Rouse [*sic*]. The portrait of the former is a remarkable likeness, as dignified as it is alive in gesture; as clever in pose as it is well painted. It is many years since Mr. Johnson showed work equal to this. . . . If no one else has hit high-water mark this year, Mr. Johnson has.[38]

The Art Amateur said Johnson had "produced one of the best pictures of his life, filled with swift energy and decision in

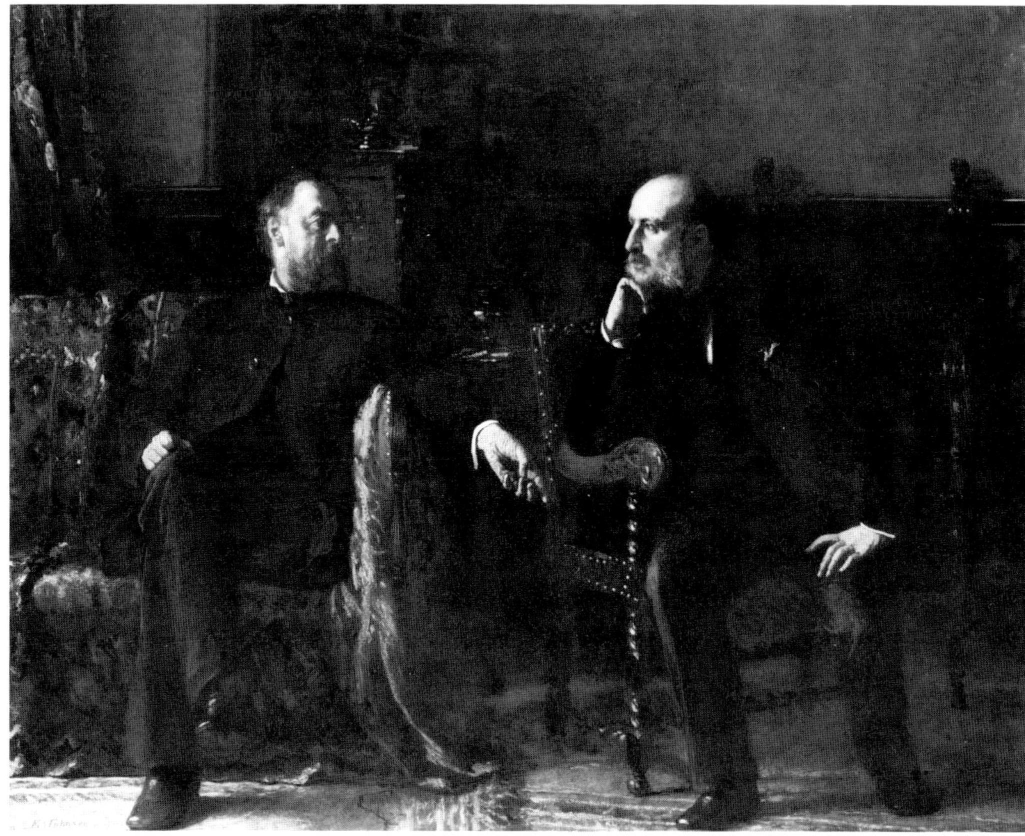

FIG. 2. Eastman Johnson, *The Funding Bill,* 1881. Oil on canvas, 60 1/2 x 78 1/4 inches. The Metropolitan Museum of Art, New York, Purchase, Robert Gordon Gift, 1898.

the painting, and treated with altogether masterly brio in a scale unusual for him."[39] One would think that *The Art Amateur* critic was talking about Sargent rather than about Johnson. And the critic for *The Nation* said:

> [T]he picture is a masterpiece; it is the perfection of that kind of painting so often urged upon unpatriotic American artists who repair to Venice and Brittany for inspiration, and neglect the possibilities with which our own life and land teem, and which are never touched without awakening a sympathetic popular echo. Artistically, too, it combines portraiture with *genre;* and whenever this is done with any success one wonders afresh why the expedient, old as it is, is not oftener resorted to.[40]

The picture was about contemporary events, it was of its time, and it pleased all groups. The critic S. G. W. Benjamin astutely remarked in 1882 about this knack of Johnson's to appease both factions:

> His work is to be seen at the exhibitions of both societies, and he is claimed by the followers of both schools. The Academicians call him theirs, because, although he studied long abroad, he has imported the style of no foreign artist, but has illustrated the principles of art in a manner entirely his own; and because, too, he has been content to look for subjects at home, thus showing himself wholly in sympathy with the attractions of his own land. These qualities have not been characteristic of the work of the new school of American artists, who, while showing ability and enterprise, have purposely imported the styles of Bonnat, Gérôme, Daubigny, Corot, or Manet, together with a selection of subjects entirely foreign, and therefore imitative. Evidences are accumulating, however, which show that some of them are endeavouring to give expression to their own individuality, and rescue their identity from the subservience in which it has been merged. They in turn lay claim to Eastman Johnson as one of their number, because his style (a quality they estimate above matter), while wholly his own, suggests the consummate technical ability of the modern Continental masters. Thus justified and applauded, he may fairly be described as a representative American.[41]

The Funding Bill was good promotion for Johnson's abilities as a portraitist. Following the academy's exhibition, the picture traveled to the Inter-State Industrial Exposition in Chicago and then to the Pennsylvania Academy of the Fine Arts as part of an exhibition called *Special Exhibition of Paintings by American Artists at Home and in Europe.* In 1882 it went to the Boston Art Club and also hung at The Metropolitan Museum in the *Loan Collection of Paintings and Sculpture.* Before the decade was out it had also been shown at the Art Gallery of the Southern Exposition, Louisville, and then, in 1889, at the Paris Universal Exposition.[42]

Commissions poured in; such contemporaneity as two men discussing financial matters would appeal to men of affairs. The exhibition of *The Funding Bill* in Chicago may have prompted the commission to paint the portrait of Mrs. George M. Pullman, a canvas Johnson worked on during the summer of 1881. A rambling, nervous letter to McEntee of 22 September 1881 reveals his all-consuming preoccupation with portrait commissions:

> My subject [unidentified] left town before yesterday, sitting to me till 5 o'clock the day before. The portrait is done, I suppose, though I have still work to do with the accessories. It has engrossed me constantly for sometime and I have done no other work at all here since I came, though I brought a number of unfinished things which I hoped and expected to work at. There was nothing to do but get through with it here and it has been reasonably successful I believe. Now besides this I have other work which I *must* do, so of course the Maine project [Johnson's annual trek with McEntee] grows dim and uncertain as to *times.* I swear I will go there, if it is midwinter and I go alone.

Johnson continues with gossip about family but returns again and again to his portrait commissions, including the

FIG. 3. Eastman Johnson. *Copy after Mihály Munkácsy, "Blind Milton Dictating 'Paradise Lost' to His Daughters,"* 1878. Oil on board, 10 x 11 inches. Unlocated.

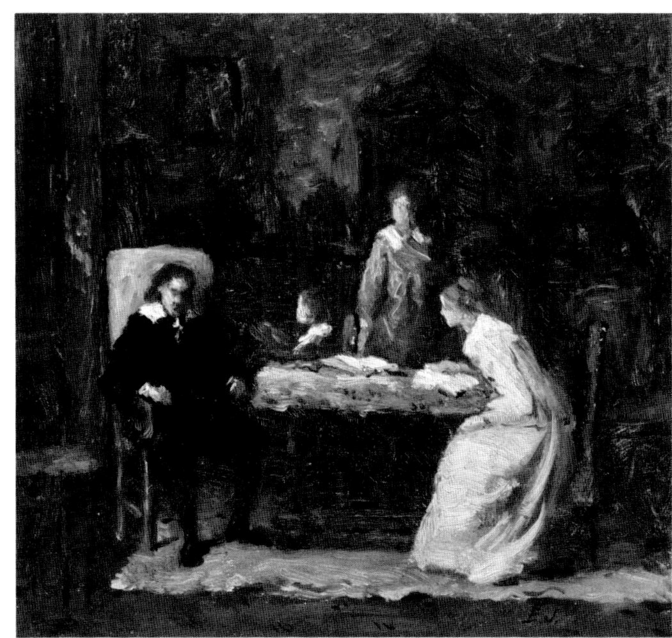

Mrs. Pullman portrait:

> I have Mrs. Pullman's portrait with me. She has just returned from England and is going back to stay a good while. She writes me that she wants this portrait finished and hung up in her house and to know if I cant do it before she goes away, in October. I think I can and may come to New York before long about it with the picture.

And again: "My portrait is full length, nearly life size, standing by the fireside four feet by six and a half." And he concludes, "Altogether we have had rather a laborious summer.—All seem alike."[43]

After 1881, with rare exceptions, he showed only portraits. He showed portraits at the Society of American Artists in 1881, the year he became a member, and in 1882, the only other year he exhibited with the society.[44] The National Academy regularly hung his recent portraits, including *Mrs. George M. Pullman* in 1882, *Bishop H. C. Potter* in 1887, and a brace of college presidents and lawyers.

True, his portrait commissions paid handsomely, but it also seems clear that he had lost enthusiasm for the old genre painting. In earlier years—as we now know—Johnson had made a copy of *The Village Perambulator* by Jules Breton (see FIG. 15, Mills essay), one of the most admired French artists on this side of the Atlantic in the 1860s.[45] In that Civil War decade (when he probably made the copy) he would have admired the subject matter of simple village life and the fact that Breton painted French national life as he, Johnson, painted the American counterpart. The copy could be stylistically faithful because Johnson shared with Breton a respect for local color, for objects in space, and for a soft finish not overly painstaking in its details.

The question of Johnson's copies has relevance here, for they help us to chart the changes in the kinds of art he esteemed, and thus a review of these copies is in order. Sometime about 1879, or shortly thereafter, Johnson made a copy (FIG. 3) after Mihály Munkácsy's (1844–1900) large painting *Blind Milton Dictating "Paradise Lost" to His Daughters,* painted in 1878, which was acquired by Robert Lenox Kennedy and given to the Lenox Library in 1879 with great fanfare.[46] In ending his letter to Jervis McEntee on 17 November 1879, Johnson writes: "What are the prospects for Art this winter? I see accounts of sales. Have you been to see Munkatey's [*sic*] picture?"[47] Johnson would have been especially interested because he had himself painted *Milton Dictating to His Daughters,* 1876, shown at the Centennial Exposition at Philadelphia that year.[48] In his copy after Munkácsy, a free sketch rather than a faithful copy like his Breton, measuring ten by eleven inches,[49] Johnson took liberties with the pose of Milton by turning the seated figure and adjusting the arms; the faces of all four figures are mere dabs of light paint. The blind Milton subject in the context of Johnson's circumstances in this 1879–1880 period also has relevance: we acknowledge the reliance of the older generation (Milton) on the younger (the three daughters) to transcribe and hence pass along to posterity the artistic legacy of that generation. Looked at this way *The Reprimand* of 1880 falls into place as a sequel—with the younger generation now rebelling against that older one, as analyzed above.[50]

Another copy contributes to this narrative. In the Archives of The Brooklyn Museum, included in the records for the 1940 Eastman Johnson exhibition, is a photograph of a version of John Singer Sargent's (1856–1925) *El Jaleo* (FIG. 4).[51] (The large Salon version, collection Isabella Stewart Gardner Museum, Boston, was shown at the Paris Salon in 1882.) Although someone might argue for an attribution to Sargent of the pictured work, we can make a strong case for Johnson's hand. Like Johnson's copy after Munkácsy, this *El Jaleo* freely copies the Gardner painting and makes changes in the poses: the fingers of the outstretched hand of the dancer are conventionally displayed, whereas in Sargent's Gardner painting the middle finger is depressed (to hold an unseen castanet), which makes the other fingers seem eccentrically posed. Also, and characteristic of a free copy, in the *El Jaleo* depicted in the Brooklyn photograph the arms of the figures in the background have also been modified and details have been eliminated.[52] More important, in the copy we do not feel that the author understood the importance of Sargent's light source—unseen footlights—and thus could not quite capture the flash of light from those footlights as it skips up to the edges of guitars and chairs and illuminates from below the billowing folds of the dancer's skirt. Informing such differences was, I believe, Johnson's different world outlook: the spectacle of the exotic, Spanish demimonde was too foreign to Johnson; Sargent's vision, based on the scrutiny of light and dark values at the expense of actual form and local color, was too radical for the older artist.[53]

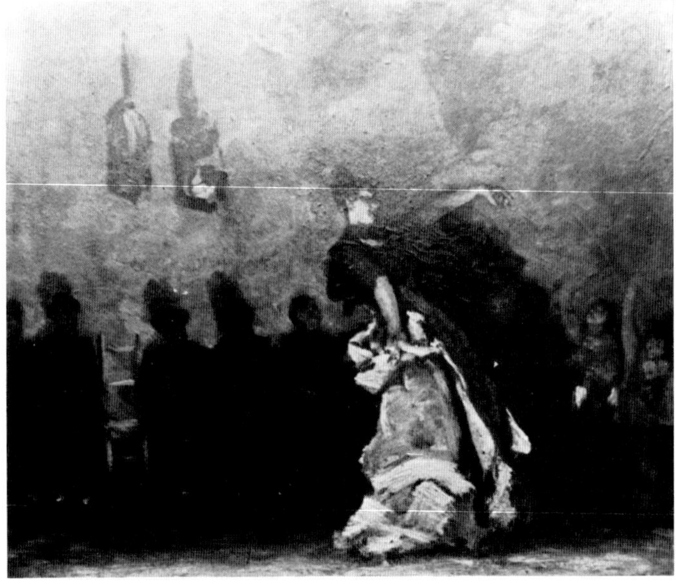

FIG. 4. Eastman Johnson, *Copy after John Singer Sargent, "El Jaleo,"* circa 1882. Unlocated. Photograph courtesy of The Brooklyn Museum Archives, Records of the Department of Painting & Sculpture, Exhibitions: "Eastman Johnson," 1940.

Johnson might try to respond to the changes of subject matter and style of the younger painters of the 1880s, but he could not master them because the content was too alien to the social and moral values he had grown up with. The sophisticated tourist's "value-free" curiosity about the spectacle of "the other"—the impulse behind such Sargent paintings as *Oyster Gatherers of Cancale* (1877, Museum of Fine Arts, Boston), shown at the 1878 Society of American Artists exhibition, and also *El Jaleo*—was replacing the patriot's ideal of community and deep attachment to the soil—Johnson's attraction to Breton and the message of *The Cranberry Harvest.* These shifts coincide with the larger issues then being debated in art circles, both here and abroad: art-for-art's sake on the one hand and, on the other, art as didactic tool to elevate the morals and patriotism of the citizenry.[54]

There is yet the even larger historical context, an understanding of which would help us make sense of these developments and of Johnson's paradigmatic career: the changing ideology of Johnson's liberal Republican patrons and contemporaries. Although it is not irrelevant to speak here of Johnson's identification with Republican party values, a fully developed analysis would exceed the bounds of this assignment for an afterword. Suffice it to say, for reasons complex and manifold, during the 1870s the Republican party retreated from the ideals of community—of a true Union, radical in its integration of ex-slaves into the body politic—and became, in the words of historian Kenneth Stampp, "the political agency of the northern middle classes and of northern business enterprise." Sometime during that process genre painting lost its moral appeal for Johnson's patrons and became, simply, nostalgia.[55] Whether fully conscious of the import of these historical shifts or not, Johnson was caught up in them. By 1880 he seems set to abandon genre painting. In contrast, the Sargents and Lows of American art, handling the changes in their own generational style, move toward modernism—toward an individually expressive art inimical to ideals of community.[56]

At this juncture portraiture—at which Johnson always excelled—offered a viable alternative that would keep him independent of the old, idealistic (national virtue, equality, etc.) way of thinking and in line with the new individualism. He, too, "could be of his times" through the delineation of the intellectual, business, and political leaders of the country: United States presidents Chester A. Arthur, Grover Cleveland, and Benjamin Harrison; financiers and industrialists Jay Gould, George M. Pullman, William and Cornelius Vanderbilt, and John D. Rockefeller; university presidents Frederick Augustus Porter Barnard of Columbia, Theodore Dwight Woolsey and Noah Porter of Yale, and The Reverend Doctor James McCosh of Princeton; and lawyer-statesman William M. Evarts. As Edgar French observed in an article published after the artist's death, "The list of portraits painted by the late Eastman Johnson reads like the rollcall of American history."[57] Johnson must have been immensely proud of this accomplishment—proud beyond the mere satisfaction of handsome fees. He knew these men, shared their values, and painted them as they wanted to be seen—solid establishment. No other American portrait painter—not even John Singer Sargent—painted such an array of distinguished American leaders in the late nineteenth century. *The Funding Bill* led the way toward this achievement at the very moment when *The Cranberry Harvest* closed a chapter of American art history.

NOTES

[1] Quoted in John I. H. Baur, *Eastman Johnson, 1824–1906: An American Genre Painter*, exh. cat. (Brooklyn: Brooklyn Museum, 1940), 24, from the unpublished autobiography of Worthington Whittredge (later published as *The Autobiography of Worthington Whittredge*, ed. John I. H. Baur, *Brooklyn Museum Journal* 2 [1942]).

In the preparation of this essay I want to thank Marc Simpson and Sally Mills for sharing with me their informative essays, in this volume. Kevin Whitfield read the manuscript with his usual scrutiny to its ideas and logic.

[2] Both Baur, in his 1940 Brooklyn Museum retrospective exhibition, and I, as curator of the Whitney Museum of American Art retrospective exhibition *Eastman Johnson* of 1972, favored the genre works. My dissertation of 1973, published as *The Genre Painting of Eastman Johnson: The Sources and Development of His Style and Themes* (New York: Garland Publishing, 1977), deals only with the genre painting; however, in the process of preparing the long-term project of Johnson's catalogue raisonné, I realize that his portraits, many of which are quite splendid, make up a considerable proportion of his total oeuvre and deserve a closer analysis.

[3] Baur, *Eastman Johnson*, 23.

[4] Baur, *Eastman Johnson*, 25.

[5] Quoted in Baur, *Eastman Johnson*, 25. The letter was written by Johnson's nephew Rear Admiral Alfred W. Johnson, U.S.N. The full quotation from Baur is as follows: "I have spent many hours in his studio in New York when I was a small boy and remember many paintings of eminent Americans that were hanging there. He sometimes made duplicate portraits, keeping one for himself. I remember meeting Grover Cleveland and General Miles in his house and once posed for John D. Rockefeller's pants and one of Vanderbilt's arms. . . . I believe his highest price for a painting was $10,000. This was a family group, but I do not recall the name. He used to get about $5,000 for a full length portrait and about $1,500 for a head and shoulders." The $10,000 referred to in the letter may have been *The Hatch Family*, collection The Metropolitan Museum of Art. I have not been able to locate this letter; in 1970 and 1971 I wrote to Miss Charlotte Wilson, who had shared this letter with Baur, about materials in her possession but she was not able to locate letters for me.

[6] Eastman Johnson to G. Corliss, 17 November 1881, Penn-

sylvania Academy of the Fine Arts, quoted in Natalie Spassky, *American Paintings in The Metropolitan Museum of Art* (New York: The Metropolitan Museum of Art in association with Princeton University Press, 1985), vol. 2, p. 234.

[7]In 1880 a skilled machinist earned $2.45 a day and the average nonfarm employee earned $1.16 a day, according to the *U.S. Department of Commerce, Historical Statistics of the United States: Colonial Times to 1970,* part 1 (Washington, D.C.: U.S. Government Printing Office, 1975), 165.

[8]I am grateful to Marc Simpson for providing me with the 1880 figure ("My Note Book," *The Art Amateur* 2, no. 4 [March 1880]: 68). The 1881 figure was published in M[ariana] G[riswold] van Rensselaer, "Pictures in New York. The Artists' Fund Society. Mr. Bridgman," *The American Architect and Building News* 9 (26 February 1881): 100. One might argue that auction prices of the Artists' Fund Society might be slightly inflated, since, after all, the money supported widows and orphans of deceased artists. In contrast, sale prices at the Society of American Artists seem to range in the low hundreds.

[9]Sally Mills, " 'Right Feeling and Sound Technique': French Art and the Development of Eastman Johnson's Outdoor Genre Paintings," in this volume, 58, documents Johnson's relationship with one such patron, William Tilden Blodgett.

[10]S. G. W. Benjamin, "Tendencies of Art in America," *The American Art Review* (1880): 105.

[11]The best discussion on the subject is Jennifer A. Martin Bienenstock, "The Formation and Early Years of the Society of American Artists: 1877–1884," Ph.D. diss., The City University of New York, 1983. See also Lois Marie Fink and Joshua C. Taylor, *Academy: The Academic Tradition in American Art,* exh. cat. (Washington, D.C.: Smithsonian Institution Press, 1975). Bienenstock, "The Formation," 13–15, discusses the European art on the market in the United States, and Fink, "American Departures: 1825–1869," in *Academy,* 47–48, discusses the measures that American artists took to combat the influx of European art.

[12]Bienenstock's dissertation charts the subtle shifts in style and content from year to year.

[13]M[ariana] G[riswold] van Rensselaer, "Spring Exhibitions and Picture-Sales in New York.—I," *The American Architect and Building News* 7, no. 227 (1 May 1880): 190.

[14]Van Rensselaer, "Spring Exhibitions," 190.

[15] This assertion is based on my knowledge of the many pictures he painted of Ethel and her cousins in the May family. Glimpses of family emerge from the few scattered letters that have survived. For example, in the early summer of 1880, because of his daughter's bout with the whooping cough, Johnson declined an invitation to the Artists' Fund Society excursion from New York to Niagara Falls. He wrote to Edward Gay: "I should take the greatest pleasure in making one of your party, especially if it could include my wife, but that could not be unless it also included the child so you see how full of difficulties the project is." Eastman Johnson to Edward Gay, 11 [June 1880]; Archives of American Art, Smithsonian Institution, Edward Gay Papers, roll D30, frame 693.

[16]Eastman Johnson to Jervis McEntee, 17 November 1879; Archives of American Art, Smithsonian Institution, Misc. MSS: Jervis McEntee, Gift of Charles E. Feinberg, roll D30, frame 455. The "cranberry fever" description of himself occurs in Johnson's letter to McEntee of 12 October 1879, quoted at length in Marc Simpson, "Taken with a Cranberry Fit: Eastman Johnson on Nantucket," in this volume, 31 and 38. McEntee's wife had died the previous year.

[17]Johnson to McEntee, 12 October 1879, AAA.

[18]Eastman Johnson to Jervis McEntee, 13 December 1879; Archives of American Art, Smithsonian Institution, Misc. MSS: Jervis McEntee, Gift of Charles E. Feinberg, roll D30, frames 460–62.

[19]One might argue that by "foreign" art he also meant the foreign-trained American artists. This might have been the outlook of the more conservative old guard such as Daniel Huntington, but unlikely for Johnson, given the evidence about his attitudes.

[20]Documented in Simpson, "Taken with a Cranberry Fit," in this volume, 39–41.

[21]S. G. W. Benjamin, "The Exhibitions. V.—National Academy of Design," *The American Art Review* 1 (1879–1880): 309.

[22]I want to thank Dean Levy for bringing my attention to the *Study for "The Reprimand,"* not dated, oil on board, 17½ x 11 inches, collection Bernard & S. Dean Levy Inc., New York.

[23]Benjamin, "The Exhibitions," 309.

[24]We could pursue this line of interpretation: Johnson's *Embers,* also painted about 1880,

shows the old gent of *The Reprimand* (the model was Captain Charles Myrick) staring into the dying embers of a New England hearth. The obvious reading would postulate that he is reflecting on days gone by (his youth, his seafaring days), but we could also read him as Johnson's surrogate for his own generation, left to his own memories after the young woman has flounced off. (I give another, but by no means antithetical, reading of this picture in Patricia Hills, *The Genre Painting of Eastman Johnson: The Sources and Development of His Style and Themes* [New York: Garland Publishing, 1977], 173.)

[25] Mills, " 'Right Feeling and Sound Technique,' " in this volume, reviews those aspects of his style relevant here.

[26] "One Day in the Gallery—Society of American Artists," *The New-York Times,* 26 March 1880, 5. The writer, according to Jennifer Bienenstock, was Charles de Kay, brother of Helena de Kay, one of the founders of the Society of American Artists. He and Clarence Cook, who had been invited to the founding meeting of the society, were supporters of the younger generation. I am grateful to Bienenstock's dissertation for citing the sources for the various reviews of the society's exhibitions.

[27] Eastman Johnson to Jervis McEntee, 30 August 1880; Archives of American Art, Smithsonian Institution, Misc. MSS: Jervis McEntee, Gift of Charles E. Feinberg, roll D30, frames 463–67.

[28] Eastman Johnson to Jervis McEntee, 2 December 1880; Archives of American Art, Smithsonian Institution, Misc. MSS: Jervis McEntee, Gift of Charles E. Feinberg, roll D30, frames 468–70. The clipping, undated, is frame 471. Johnson painted three portraits of Gifford (collections The Metropolitan Museum of Art, National Academy of Design, both New York, Pennsylvania Academy of the Fine Arts), all of which were probably posthumous; the Metropolitan version is dated 1880.

[29] Johnson to McEntee, 2 December 1880, AAA.

[30] Johnson was part of an inner network of artists—who not only ran the affairs of the National Academy but also were members of the Century Club and on the board of the Artists' Fund Society. In April 1883 they (Daniel P. Huntington, Thomas W. Wood, E. Wood Perry, Frederick Dielman, Jervis McEntee, John B. Bristol, Aaron Draper Shattuck, Albert Bierstadt, and Johnson) formed the American Art-Union in an effort to bolster flagging sales. See Fink and Taylor, *Academy,* 70–72. The SAA and the NAD eventually merged in 1906.

[31] Will H. Low, *A Chronicle of Friendships, 1873–1900* (New York: Charles Scribner's Sons, 1908), 266.

[32] Low, *Chronicle of Friendships,* 266–67. Low produced a nativist subject, *Skipper Ireson,* shown at the Society of American Artists exhibition in 1881, which he concluded was an artistic disaster. In *Chronicle,* 266, he summed up the problem: "Nantucket was not Barbizon."

[33] Cited in the exhibition catalogue by Abigail Booth Gerdts, *An American Collection: Paintings and Sculpture from the National Academy of Design* (New York: National Academy of Design, 1989), 34. My thanks to Gerdts for providing me with this citation.

[34] For information on Rowse, see Patricia Hills, "Gentle Portraits of the Longfellow Era: The Drawings of Samuel Worcester Rowse," *Drawing* 2 (March–April 1981): 121–26.

[35] Eastman Johnson to G. Corliss, 17 November 1881, fully cited in note 6 above.

[36] Although passed by Congress, President Rutherford B. Hayes vetoed it. See Spassky, *American Paintings,* 233. The sketch is *Two Men (Study for "The Funding Bill"),* 1880, oil on canvas, 22 1/4 x 27 inches, private collection; illustrated in Spassky, *American Paintings,* 235 and Patricia Hills, *Eastman Johnson,* exh. cat. (New York: Clarkson N. Potter in association with the Whitney Museum of American Art, 1972), 114.

[37] Mrs. Johnson's letter, dated 28 January 1913, Archives of The Metropolitan Museum of Art, is quoted more fully in Spassky, *American Paintings,* 233. Because of the dating of the sketch, I maintain that the sketch inspired the decision. That was the purpose of the sketch—to work out new approaches and ideas as well as solutions to compositional problems, placement of lights and darks, etc.

[38] *The New-York Times,* 20 March 1881, 2; quoted in part in Spassky, *American Paintings,* 234.

[39] *The Art Amateur* 4 (May 1881): 116, quoted in Spassky, *American Paintings,* 233.

[40] *The Nation* 32 (31 March 1881): 229, quoted in Spassky, *American Paintings,* 234.

[41] *The Magazine of Art* 5 (1882): 490, quoted in Spassky, *American Paintings,* 222. Johnson's first major picture, *Negro Life at the South,* 1859, also pleased all groups when shown that year

at the National Academy of Design annual exhibition; see Hills, *Eastman Johnson*, 32–34.

[42] See Spassky, *American Paintings,* 235–36, for the list of exhibitions.

[43] Eastman Johnson to Jervis McEntee, 22 September 1881; Archives of American Art, Smithsonian Institution, Misc. MSS: Jervis McEntee, Gift of Charles E. Feinberg, roll D30, frames 475–77. With such work, no wonder it was "laborious."

[44] Both for 1881 and 1882 the paintings were called simply *Portrait;* the owner for the 1882 work was Mr. Einstein. The 1881 submission is *Girl with Skates,* 1880, Museum of Fine Art, Springfield, Massachusetts. The 1882 portrait is of the daughter of Mr. and Mrs. David Einstein, later Lady Walston, mentioned in Spassky, *American Paintings,* 236 (and New York art market, 1984).

[45] Because of the research of Sally Mills (see Mills, " 'Right Feeling and Sound Technique,' " in this volume, 67–68), we can now make a firm attribution of this picture to Johnson. I did not have such evidence and hence hedged on the attribution when I wrote "Copy after Jules Breton, *Le Départ pour les champs*, unknown artist, Catalogue No. 50," in Katherine Harper Mead, ed., *The Preston Morton Collection of American Art* (Santa Barbara: Santa Barbara Museum of Art, 1981), 263–66.

[46] I want to thank Robert Rainwater of the New York Public Library for providing me with information about this picture, now housed in the New York Public Library. Johnson also made a copy after a head of a woman by Munkácsy (art market, 1987). D. Dodge Thompson has recently written about American paintings inspired by, or copies after, Hals's paintings in "Frans Hals and American Art," *Antiques* 136 (November 1989): 1170–83. He correctly observes correspondences between Johnson's *Funding Bill* and *The Meager Company* by Hals and Pieter Codde. Earlier in his career Johnson had made copies after Rembrandt when he lived in The Hague; his professional career really began when he painted a copy of Leutze's *Washington Crossing the Delaware* in 1851 for the engraver.

[47] Eastman Johnson to Jervis McEntee, 17 November 1879; Archives of American Art, Smithsonian Institution, Misc. MSS: Jervis McEntee, Gift of Charles E. Feinberg, roll D30, frame 455.

[48] Johnson's painting, measuring 23 1/2 x 29 inches, is now at the Blanden Memorial Art Gallery, Fort Dodge, Iowa. Another version (whereabouts unknown) was reproduced in William Walton, "Eastman Johnson, Painter," *Scribner's Magazine* 40, no. 3 (September 1906): 270.

[49] The work was at one time at the Newhouse Gallery, New York. See Eastman Johnson file at the Frick Art Reference Library, photo number 114-2/b.

[50] Themes of the generations in harmony (at work and at leisure) were prevalent throughout the history of American genre painting; Johnson mined these themes throughout his career.

[51] No information attaches itself to the current Brooklyn Museum archival photograph, and John Baur did not include any such painting in his list of Johnson paintings appended to his 1940 catalogue. In my opinion the work photographed (FIG. 4) is the same painting, attributed by some to Sargent, oil on board, measuring 21 5/8 x 26 3/8 inches, private collection; to my understanding, from information passed to me by the present owner, the painting was purchased in Rotterdam in 1961 from a dealer claiming it came from the estate of the daughter of Eastman Johnson.

Johnson would have had ample opportunity to study Sargent's large *El Jaleo* at first hand. Following its 1882 exhibition at the Paris Salon and July exhibition in London, it traveled to New York, where it was shown from 7 to 17 October at the William Schaus Gallery, then to Williams and Everett's gallery in Boston from 22 to 29 October 1882, and finally to Thomas Jefferson Coolidge, the Boston collector who had purchased it.

[52] Including the "Olè Olè" reputedly on the original version.

[53] As revealed by the drawings for *El Jaleo* (Isabella Stewart Gardner Museum, Boston), Sargent's primary concern was to draw light and shadow, not form. See my essay, "The Formation of a Style and Sensibility," in Patricia Hills, *John Singer Sargent,* exh. cat. (New York: Whitney Museum of American Art in association with Harry N. Abrams, Inc., 1986).

[54] I develop my views about this in *Eastman Johnson,* 92, 101, and "The Formation of a Style and Sensibility."

[55] Kenneth M. Stampp, *The Era of Reconstruction, 1865–1877* (New York: Vintage Books, 1965), 95.

Johnson bragged in his letter to McEntee, dated 2 December 1880, that he had contributed money to the Garfield election campaign (Archives of American Art, Smithsonian Institution, Misc. MSS: Jervis McEntee, Gift of Charles E. Feinberg, roll D30, frames 468–70). Years before, in 1867, he had joined the Union League Club, an organization formed in the early years of the Civil War to rally support for the Union. Club members, like the Republican party at the time, identified themselves with patriotism and nationalism, and they were the very men who supported Johnson's work. At one point, in the late 1860s, the far-reaching reforms proposed by some radical Republicans, if indeed they had been enacted, would have changed the course of race relations in this country. But the Republicans retreated. The coup de grâce to radical reconstruction came in 1877 with the pullout of federal troops from the South; the Republican party no longer needed the black vote (protected by federal troops) because the votes coming in from the Northwestern territories assured their political hegemony. In Stampp's words: "Thus, with the Old Northwest made safe for the Republican party, the political motive for radical reconstruction vanished, and practical Republicans could afford to abandon the southern Negro. With the decline of the idealism and the disappearance of the realistic political and economic considerations that had supported it, radical reconstruction came to an end" (212–13).

The most recent reassessment of reconstruction is Eric Foner, *Reconstruction: America's Unfinished Revolution, 1863–1877* (New York: Harper & Row, 1988); Foner refers to the 30 December 1874 issue of the *New York Times,* which, "in noting the passing of abolitionist Gerrit Smith, [commented that] the 'era of moral politics' had come to a definitive end" (527).

In other words, sometime in the mid-1870s the ideal of community (which inevitably portends a classless and racially integrated society) and moral politics gave way to the realpolitik of capitalist individualism, moving, as it was, onto the international stage.

[56] Johnson did only a very few genre paintings after 1880, including *Nantucket School of Philosophy* (1887, The Walters Art Gallery, Baltimore), which is explicitly nostalgic. About 1882 he and Jervis McEntee collaborated on *Babes in the Woods,* oil on canvas, 30½ x 24 inches, signed lower left *E. Johnson* and lower right *JMcEntee* (art market, January 1987). It is a double portrait of two small children, Percival and Madeleine Baxter, standing in a clearing in the woods and clinging together as if in anticipation of danger. Another version, with less woods, is in the Bowdoin College Museum of Art and signed solely by Johnson. Both are attempts to blend landscape, genre, and portraiture; I know of no other such efforts by Johnson.

[57] Edgar French, "An American Portrait Painter of Three Historical Epochs," *World's Work* 13 (1906): 8307.

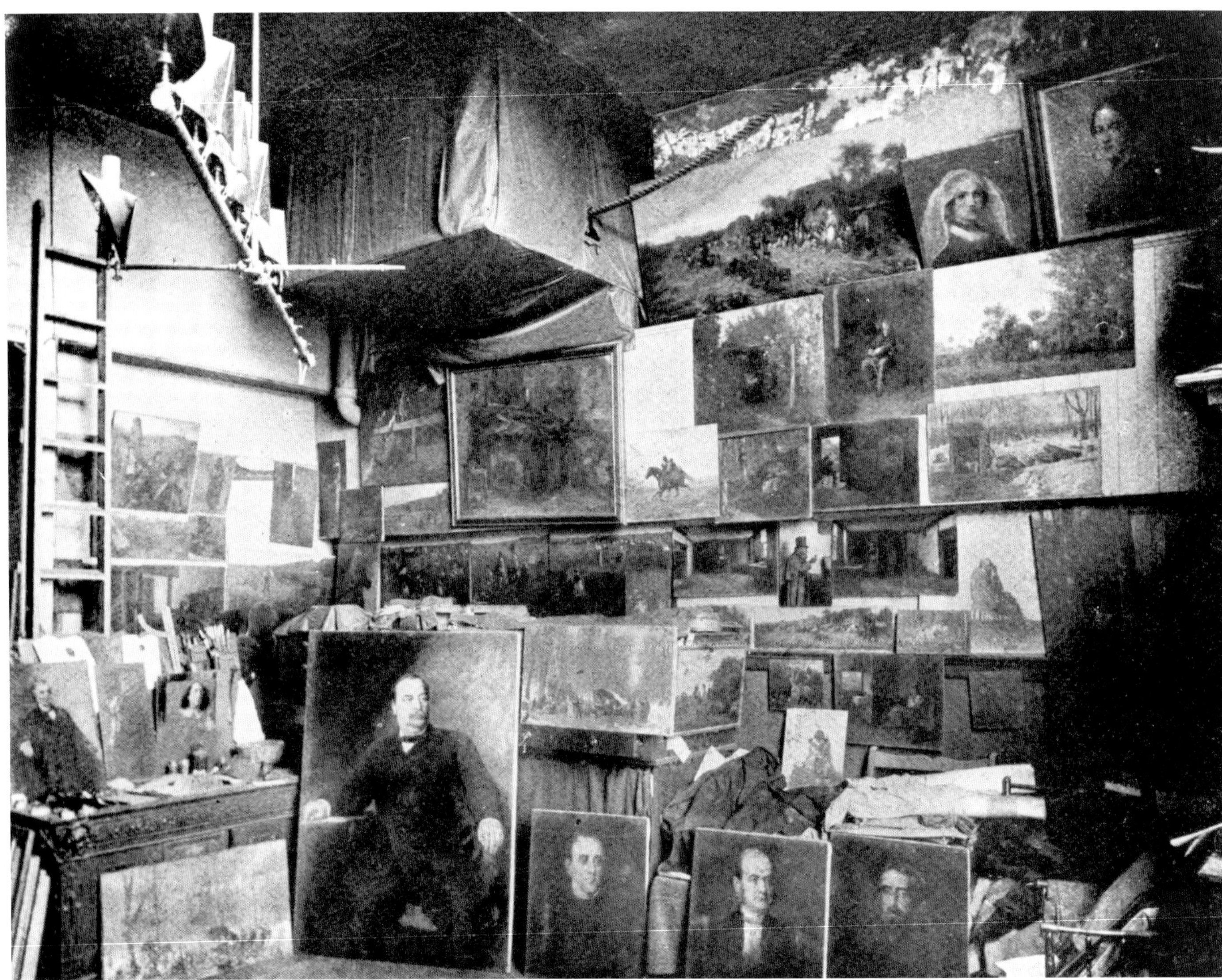

FIG. 1. "A Glimpse of Mr. Johnson's Studio." Photograph in Edgar French, "An American Portrait Painter of Three Historical Epochs," *The World's Work* 13, no. 2 (December 1906): 3817. Note the studies of *The Cranberry Harvest* in the middle row.

Chronology

1824
Born 29 July in Lovell, Maine. In 1827–1828 moved with family to Fryeburg, Maine, and in the winter of 1834–1835 to Augusta, Maine, where his father held various positions in the state government

1839
Moved to Boston. During the next five years spent some time in a lithography shop in Boston (possibly Bufford's). Began a career as a portrait draftsman

1844–1845
In winter or early spring moved with family to Washington, D.C., and continued his portrait practice

1846–1849
Worked in Cambridge, Massachusetts

1849
Sailed for Antwerp 14 August with George H. Hall; by November in Düsseldorf; studied at the Royal Academy

1850
In fall sent two genre paintings to the American Art-Union in New York

1851
In January began study with Emanuel Leutze; left Düsseldorf in July, stopping to visit Amsterdam and London

1851–1855
By fall 1851 was living in The Hague

1855
In Paris by May; enrolled in studio of Thomas Couture; left Paris in late October; settled in Washington, D.C.

1856
In late summer visited his sister in Superior, Wisconsin

1857
Back in Washington, D.C., by spring. By July had returned to Superior. In November moved to Cincinnati, where he took a studio and painted portraits

1858
Took a studio in the University Building, New York

1859
With acclaimed exhibition of *Negro Life at the South* (The New-York Historical Society), elected an associate of the National Academy of Design

1860
Elected a full member of the National Academy of Design

1861–1865
Followed Union troops of George McClellan in early years of the Civil War. By 1864 had taken four trips in the late winter–early springs to sketch

the maple-sugaring camps near Fryeburg, Maine

1862
Elected to the Century Club, New York

1868
Elected to the Union League Club, New York. Taught at the National Academy of Design

1869
Married Elizabeth Williams Buckley of Troy, New York, on 29 June; honeymooned in Murray Bay, Canada, during July. May have made his first visit to Nantucket, Massachusetts

1870
In January, elected to a committee of the Union League Club charged with founding New York's Metropolitan Museum of Art. Only child, Ethel, born in May. The family resided in Nantucket over the summer

1871
Bought first property in Nantucket in April

1872
Moved to 65 West 55th Street, which served as both home and winter studio

1872–1880
Spent summers, and increasingly, falls on Nantucket. In 1877 and 1878 visited his sister in Kennebunkport, Maine; in 1879 began concentrated work on *The Cranberry Harvest*

1880
After the exhibition of *The Cranberry Harvest* in March, began to paint fewer genre scenes, returning to portraiture as primary artistic expression. By end of career, had painted many of the country's leading politicians, industrialists, and financiers

1881
Elected a member of the Society of American Artists. Begins speculative purchases of land on Nantucket (see Appendix 3 for a full account of these purchases)

1887
Painted his last dated genre work, *The Nantucket School of Philosophy* (The Walters Art Gallery, Baltimore)

1906
Died 5 April in New York City

Appendix 1: Eastman Johnson on Nantucket

Included in this section are transcripts of selected nineteenth-century notices, ordered chronologically, concerning Eastman Johnson and his stays on the island of Nantucket. Since scholars know of few primary sources pertaining to Johnson—letters, diaries, and accountbooks are apparently lost—these references, particularly those from Nantucket's own newspapers, should be useful for establishing a chronology of his visits. Also included are selected notices of the cranberry harvest taken from both the national and island press.

There is this to be said in favor of Nantucket as a resort for strangers, that those who have one season's experience of its attractions, are very apt to come again. Among the familiar and welcome faces now to be seen on our streets are . . . Eastman Johnson, the artist forever famous as the author of Abraham Lincoln, the log cabin boy. William S. Tiffany, of Binghamton, N.Y. and E. W. Perry, M. Morse, and Virgil Williams, of New York, are also here on their second visit, in search of subject, inspiration and life for new contributions to American art.
"Visitors at Nantucket," *Inquirer and Mirror,* 13 August 1870.

Among the noted visitors to be met here every Summer is the clever artist, Eastman Johnson. His spirited, and really fine painting, so much admired at one of the Brooklyn Art Receptions in the Winter of '70 and '71, "The Old Stage Coach," was finished here. He told me that the boys' faces and forms in and around the old coach are from life—Nantucket life. The boys were captured and imprisoned in his studio on the "Bluffs" here long enough to paint them. Mr. Johnson's best work is done here.
Liberal Christian, quoted in *Inquirer and Mirror,* 31 August 1872.

The distinguished artist, Eastman Johnson, with his family, left us this week for New York, having prolonged his stay with us through all the summer and fall. We have not had the pleasure of visiting Mr. Johnson's studio, but we learn that he has executed some very fine paintings which will doubtless be heard from in due time.
Inquirer and Mirror, 23 November 1872.

In fact, the high ground just above this beach, and commanding a magnificent sweep of the ocean, is the spot which ought to be occupied by cottages and hotels. The artist, Eastman Johnson, has shown his usual fine taste in taking up his summer residence here, and has transformed two or three old houses that stood on the site into a home, a convenient studio, etc.
Henry M. Baird, "Nantucket," *Scribner's Monthly* 6, no. 4 (August 1873): 390.

At the top of the cliff an artist from New York, Eastman Johnson, has converted an old dwelling into a studio and taken up his summer residence.
"Nantucket. The Cliff," *Inquirer and Mirror,* 20 September 1873.

Our cranberry growers have now commenced gathering in their crop, which we have heard was generally good, although it received much injury from the frost of two or three weeks ago.
"Cranberries," *Inquirer and Mirror,* 26 September 1874.

As for the Cape girls, it's a pretty sight to see them picking cranberries. With rosy cheeks and rippling laughter and bursts of song; with a shout for the baby girl who proudly carries up her tiny cupful to be measured and written down to her credit; with pleasant jokes over the sorting and barreling; with kindly emulation and neighborly helpfulness—the picking goes on. I wonder if it will ever be discovered by womankind that a sun-bonnet and a calico dress are as dangerous to the male heart as the costliest satin and diamonds?

The cranberry is one of the most important products of the Cape. It is grown, as

every body knows, on bogs that have been drained and redeemed; and thus the cranberry patch lies usually in a kind of bowl, and you look down upon it from the road. The crimson fruit is concealed beneath a tangled mass of russet vine; and the "patch" looks sufficiently commonplace until it is enlivened by the gay colors of a little army of pickers. Harwich is the principal seat of the cranberry culture on the Cape, and the importance of this industry may be seen from the fact that this little town, of about three thousand inhabitants, exported in 1873 over eighty thousand dollars' worth of cranberries—nearly twenty-seven dollars a head for every man, woman, and child in the town. This is the product of brains applied to agriculture. The Cape has a great many fresh-water ponds, and much swamp and bog land. Twenty-five years ago these bogs were worthless; now they form the most valuable land on the Cape. Patient labor, intelligently directed, makes a redeemed swamp bear from two to four hundred dollars per acre per annum; and the cranberry culture has done much to enrich the people of Cape Cod, and to afford pleasant and profitable employment to women and girls during the picking season.
Charles Nordhoff, "Cape Cod, Nantucket, and the Vineyard," *Harper's New Monthly Magazine* 51, no. 301 (June 1875): 59–60.

Boating, fishing, and comfortable living among a pleasant population and in a very pleasant old town are the amusements of Nantucket. . . . Of late auctions have furnished recreation also to summer visitors, where they purchased curious old furniture, old china, old table gear; and I was even offered a magnificent brass warming-pan. There is also a public library, an interesting museum, and very pleasant, intelligent society. Eastman Johnson, the artist, has a studio here.
Charles Nordhoff, "Cape Cod, Nantucket, and the Vineyard," *Harper's New Monthly Magazine* 51, no. 301 (June 1875): 65.

Eastman Johnson, the celebrated New York artist, arrived in town last Friday, to occupy for the season his quaint cottage at the North Cliff, and now all the summer houses at that part of the town are open. Mr. Johnson has a fine studio on his grounds that he works in incessantly. This gentleman is always doing some queer thing, or carrying out some quaint conceit, and now he is going to erect a miniature water mill, and build a tank of toward an hundred barrels capacity, that he may have little fountains and also irrigate his land by wind. It will look novel, but pretty, to see such things in operation.
"Personal," *The Island Review,* 29 July 1875.

Eastman Johnson, the well-known artist, arrived in town last Friday. He will spend the remainder of the season here.
"Personals," *Inquirer and Mirror,* 31 July 1875.

Eastman Johnson, the artist, has opened his cottage at the Cliff for the summer.
"Personal," *Inquirer and Mirror,* 15 July 1876.

The cranberry pickers are getting out their camphire antidotes for running ivy poison.
"Review Scraps," *Island Review,* 16 September 1876.

Cranberry thieves are now making raids. Folger & Bunker, who own around Cupaam Pond and Trots Hills have had a barrel or more of the tart berries stolen within a few days. The thieves can expect no leniency if they are detected in their predatory visits.
"Review Scraps," *Island Review,* 27 September 1876.

Eastman Johnson yesterday took several views in the west part of the town, to be embodied in one of his canvasses.
"Review Scraps," *Island Review,* 30 September 1876.

Eastman Johnson is still at his summer home here. He will not return to his studio in New York till late in November.
"Personal," *Inquirer and Mirror,* 30 September 1876.

Eastman Johnson and family arrived here Tuesday, and opened their cottage at the Cliff.
"Personal," *Inquirer and Mirror,* 30 June 1877.

A short time ago Mr. Eastman Johnson painted a very pretty picture of some children seated on a beam in a barn, a little baby-girl, if we remember rightly, between two baby-boys, and the charming idyl—a parody on the love-making of the butterflies and sparrows—was so successful that the artist has repeated the experiment, leaving the love-making and infantile element out, and substituting for the cherubs in pinafores and bits of trousers a row of prosaic girls and boys, doing nothing but sit for their pictures, on the same beam in the same barn. The original picture was so pretty, and so entirely in Mr. Johnson's best vein, that we wonder some enterprising publisher didn't buy it for reproducing; but this pic-

ture is a tame performance, though, all the same, no one among us but Mr. Johnson could have painted it.
The New-York Daily Tribune, quoted in "Art Notes," *Inquirer and Mirror,* 1 June 1878.

Eastman Johnson, the artist, has opened his studio here, and will remain several months.
"Personal," *Inquirer and Mirror,* 14 September 1878.

The cranberry crop this season is reported as exceedingly slim.
Nantucket Journal, 26 September 1878.

A portrait of Mr. F. C. Sanford, President of the Pacific National Bank, has been hung in the banking room by the painter, Eastman Johnson, as a specimen of his artistic skill. The portrait is an excellent one.
"Fine Arts," *Inquirer and Mirror,* 16 November 1878.

There hangs in the Pacific National Bank, a large oil painting from the easel of Eastman Johnson. It is a life-like portrait of F. C. Sanford Esq., President of the Bank, and has been much admired for its fidelity to the subject.
"Oil Painting," *Nantucket Journal,* 20 November 1878.

Eastman Johnson, the artist, arrived in town last week, accompanied by his family.
"Personal," *Inquirer and Mirror,* 13 September 1879.

Cranberry pickers are busy and the crop is a good one.
"Local Items," *Nantucket Journal,* 15 October 1879.

The cranberry crop the entire length of the Cape is very large, Provincetown being the only exception, where the crop is fully one-third short of last year. Abijah Doane, of Harwich, gathered ninety-eight and one-half barrels of cranberries from half an acre, selling them at $7.50 per barrel.
Inquirer and Mirror, 18 October 1879.

On our drive to town again [from the Cliff], we passed the fine large cottage of the artist, Eastman Johnson, who doubtless was then painting his picture, "The Nantucket Sea-Captain." . . .

Another day in comes, like a breeze from the mountains, with a hearty greeting, another friend, bringing with him, as he says in his introduction, "the King of Nantucket, Mr. Sanford!" and the artist, Eastman Johnson. We show them the simple wonders of our mansion, but modestly assure them that while our cottage is small, yet the boundless ocean, just back of the cottage, is ours!
A. Judd Northrup, *'Sconset Cottage Life: A Summer on Nantucket Island* (New York: Baker, Pratt & Co., 1881), 92, 150.

I have pleasing thoughts of the famous artist of the old north cliff. I refer to Eastman Johnson, whose studio stands on a breezy hill, almost Italian in its soft summer garniture; our somewhat classic cliff luminous with sunlight; our harbor to the right; the cool bath-houses along the ocean border; the distant fleet of snowy sails; all so dreamy and tremulous,—strangers tell us it is a poem; and so it is. In this queer studio the 'Old Stage-Coach' and the 'Tramp' were painted.
Dr. A. E. Jenks, quoted in Edward K. Godfrey, *The Island of Nantucket, what it was and what it is; being a complete index and guide to this noted resort* (Boston: Lee and Shepard, 1882), 17.

Professions. Artists.
Eastman Johnson (summer resident). Studio, Centre St.
Edward K. Godfrey, *The Island of Nantucket, what it was and what it is; being a complete index and guide to this noted resort* (Boston: Lee and Shepard, 1882), 262.

Eastman Johnson, the painter of "Cranberry-Picking" and the "Confab," was born in the village of Friburg [*sic*], in the State of Maine, about fifty-five years ago. . . .

"Cranberry-Picking," which we engrave below, is a reminiscence of Nantucket. This island is largely settled by three families, a circumstance that often occurs with slight variation in New England districts near the coast. . . . At Nantucket the leading clans or families are Macys, Folgers, and Coffins, these last the descendants of Admiral Tristam Coffin. For many years one of the three great whaling ports of the United States, it was rich in wealth and traditions of the sea. The traditions remain, but the wealth has gone, together with those who accumulated it. Now the once thriving port is a waste of decaying wharves and crumbling mansions. But Nantucket is gradually becoming a sanitary resort on account of the mildness of the climate, while the sentiment of its scenery and traditions and the quaint seafaring character of its people offer unusual attractions to the artist. Mr. Johnson was one of the first to discover its advantages. He purchased a cottage near the town, and there he passes the summer and autumn. The ocean is only a little way from his house, and his studio, once an old barn, is close at hand.
S. G. W. Benjamin, "A Representative American," *The Magazine of Art* 5 (1882): 485–89.

While Miss Ray was thus struggling with the ocean, and Bessie, and Tom were sporting like two fish—for both were at home in the water—Mr. Gordon was looking around the Cliff with his business eye wide open. As he walked along the road back from the shore, and saw the fine views which it afforded him, he admired the judgment of Eastman Johnson, the artist, in building his summer house and studio there. . . . So the value of the Cliff or Bluffs was jotted down in his note-book for future use.
"Ten Days in Nantucket," *The Granite Monthly* 8, nos. 7, 8 (July–August 1885): 217.

Sailing across Buzzard's Bay and skirting the shores of the Vineyard, we reach Nantucket, one of the rare spots which preserve the flavor and atmosphere of the olden time. The island, with its types of old men and women that are fading out elsewhere, even in other remote nooks of Massachusetts, its queer houses and windmills, its antique furniture and costume—has long been the artistic "property" of Mr. Eastman Johnson. The man and the place have a natural sympathy for each other. He is a chronicler of a phase of our national life which is fast passing away, and which cannot be made up with old fashion-plates and the lay figure of the studio. He lives in a fascinating "house of seven gables," filled with curiosities brought to Nantucket by seafaring men,—keepsake pitchers inscribed with amatory poetry, and made in England a century ago as gifts for sailors' sweethearts, and many another treasure in willow-ware or other china. Mr. Johnson's studio is stored with antique furniture, spinning-wheels, and costumes. A row of battered hats suggest the antiquated squires, Quakers, and gentlemen of the olden time that have made their bow to us in his pictures.
Lizzie W. Champney, "The Summer Haunts of American Artists," *The Century Magazine* 30, no. 6 (October 1885): 854.

The [cranberry] picking is a picturesque sight, the common costume for the women being a calico dress and a sun-bonnet (in shape the same as the Shakers wear). They pick with their backs to the sun, in rows divided by strings, to insure "clean picking," each one being kept in the prescribed place till the vines are well picked. A cranberry barrel is smaller than ordinary, 100 quarts to the barrel being the rule, but they are tightly pressed and forced in, so that after shipping they are found to be solid in the barrel. A dealer will have nothing to do with a barrel in which the berries shake. A good price is $10 per barrel. Sometimes it is $16, $17, or more. It "pays" at $4 per barrel, but good berries never sell as low as that.
"Making a Cranberry Bog," *Harper's Weekly* 29, no. 1503 (10 October 1885): 670.

Mr. Eastman Johnson's "A Glass with the Squire," etched by Mr. Jas. D. Smillie, from the original in the possession of Mr. George N. Curtis, of New York, has a thoroughly American flavor, slightly biased only by the teamster, who might possibly be an Irishman. But, if I may be permitted the perpetration of an Irish bull, how could a picture be thoroughly American that had not an Irishman in it? Among the older American artists, Mr. Johnson, as Mr. Smedley among the younger, is the most successful and the most thoroughly artistic,—in point of color, indeed, often more so than his younger colleague,—of those who have had faith enough in their native land to look about in it for themes for their brush. The picture here reproduced, with its unmistakable New England interior,—the bare white walls, the old-fashioned mirror and mahogany sideboard, the chest of flasks, the Chinese porcelains on the top of the corner closet, telling of former days of prosperity in the East India trade, and sufficient to turn to a livid green the envious visage of the bric-à-brac hunter,—is one of several which Mr. Johnson painted about the same time, in the same locality, and partly even from the same models. To another class belong the "Stagecoach," the "Cranberry Harvest," and, most important of all, the admirable "Corn Husking," while still a third class, and of an earlier period, is formed by the pictures which deal with negro life, with "The Old Kentucky Home" as its best known type.
S. R. Koehler, *American Art* (New York: Cassell & Company, 1887), 54–55.

The absence of affectation, the utter truthfulness, in the pictures of Nantucket life, are very impressive. The painter has made you see the scenes as they are. In the "Husking Bee" how easy to have composed a group which should tell a sentimental story in connection with his rustic island-gathering of industrious folk! Yet that would have been to intrude the theatre upon a thing as remote from it, as foreign to it, as are the Egyptian Pyramids. The picture is like one of George Sand's descriptions, with a wealth of detail which challenges admiration and testifies to consummate skill as well as to a prodigious faculty of observation. No story is lugged in. We are allowed to look in upon real beings, untouched by self-consciousness.
Edward King, "The Value of Nationalism in Art," *The Monthly Illustrator* 4, no. 14 (June 1895): 267–68.

Appendix 2: Critical Responses to *The Cranberry Harvest, Island of Nantucket*

Included in this section are transcripts of selected nineteenth-century critical reviews of The Cranberry Harvest, Island of Nantucket. *The vast majority of the reviews were occasioned by the first public exhibition of the work during the National Academy of Design Spring Annual, 30 March through 29 May 1880. The reviews are in chronological order, and within that alphabetical by periodical title.*

Enter the south room from the corridor and you are confronted by a large Eastman Johnson "Picking Cranberries." There are many pickers in a broad field. . . . The exhibition is unusually bright and interesting.
"The Academy Exhibition," *The Evening Post,* 26 March 1880.

The principal picture in the whole collection is unquestionably Eastman Johnson's "Cranberry Pickers;" fifty persons, men and women, are in the foreground and middle distance, busily engaged in picking cranberries in a rather uninviting swamp.
"National Academy of Design," *New York Commercial Advertiser,* 27 March 1880.

Among the over seven hundred works hung one of the very best and most creditable to American art is Eastman Johnson's scene on a cranberry patch, which has deservedly been given the position of honor in the centre of the southern wall of the south gallery. A fine effect of sunlight strikes on about fifty remarkably well posed, painted and individualized figures hard at work in a cranberry field, on the stretch between a low cliff line and the seashore by which are seen the buildings of a quiet little town. It is an excellent work and a credit to American art.
"Fifty-Fifth Annual Exhibition of the National Academy of Design—Private View Day—First Article," *New York Herald,* 27 March 1880.

The cranberry-field of Mr. Eastman Johnson will be found, perhaps, the most agreeable picture by any one of the older band of artists. More than 50 human figures are introduced, and the picture is, therefore, to be considered of the highest importance by all people who count importance by the number of figures. Without going so far as to rank this scene with Mr. Johnson's corn-shucking picture, exhibited several years ago, it may be admired for its unusualness, as well as for the natural grouping of the workers. All ages and conditions are represented among the male and female gatherers of the cranberry crop.
"The Academy Exhibition," *The New-York Times,* 27 March 1880.

It needed no "bill," however, to inform the most casual visitor that the fifty-fifth exhibition is a remarkably large and brilliant one. The five rooms and the interior hall fairly glow with color. It was naturally to the long south room that the visitor first paid his attention. One hundred and thirty pictures hang upon its walls, and all too soon for a proper inspection of the pictures in the other rooms fled the moments between 2 and 5 o'clock. Directly opposite the door, filling up a good space of the valuable wall, is a picture by Eastman Johnson containing from thirty to fifty figures scattered over a rather uninviting patch of swamp land and engaged in the occupation of cranberry picking.
"The Academy Exhibition," *The World,* 27 March 1880.

Passing into the large southern gallery on our second visit . . . we stop once more before [one of] our favorites, Eastman Johnson's "The Cranberry Harvest, Island of Nantucket."
"Fifty-Fifth Annual Exhibition of the National Academy—Opening Reception—in the South Gallery—Second Notice," *New York Herald,* 30 March 1880.

The South Room is, as usual, the most interesting, and the most noteworthy pictures among the one hundred and thirty it con-

tains are as follows . . . Eastman Johnson's really superb work, one of the best in the Exhibition, "Cranberry Pickers at Nantucket," the grouping of figures in the foreground, the play of light and shade, and the far-off glimpse of sea, making up a canvas worthy of all praise.
"National Academy of Design Exhibition. First Notice," *The Art Interchange* 4, no. 7 (31 March 1880): 54–55.

There is no mystery and no pathos in the works of Mr. Eastman Johnson. But as a delineator of the cheerful or picturesque aspects of American genre, he not only stands near the head of our art, but continues to improve in his later works both in genre and portraiture. *The Cranberry Harvest in Nantucket,* representing the lasses and laddies of that seafaring isle stealing a few delightful hours from maritime and domestic pursuits to cull the scarlet berries from the moist meadow-lands, is an ambitious composition of a very meritorious character. The grouping is cleverly arranged, interestingly suggestive, and harmoniously introduced into the well-painted landscape.
S. G. W. Benjamin, "The Exhibitions. V.—National Academy of Design," *The American Art Review* 1 (1879–1880): 309.

A large class of pictures in the Academy are *genre* subjects, many of which nearly approach the character of landscapes. Foremost among them are Eastman Johnson's two of 'The Cranberry-Harvest' and 'The Reprimand.' In the former, which is on a large scale, country people, men in their homely blue trousers and straw hats, and the women in sunbonnets, are diligently hunting about in a low meadow for cranberries. The out-door look of this picture is very agreeable, while the low-toned landscape is lighted by the artist's consideration of "values," by the real sunshine in the sky, and its bright touches on the clothes of the cranberry-pickers.
"The New York Spring Exhibitions. I. The National Academy Exhibition," *The Art Journal* 6, no. 5 (1880): 154.

Mr. Eastman Johnson's "Cranberry Harvest—Island of Nantucket" is a cheerful companion piece to his "Corn Husking," now in the Art Gallery of the Metropolitan Museum, and shows the same qualities. There is here abundance of incident, much sparkling play of sunshine, and real people working in a real scene. As a picture it is, however, ineffective seen a few feet off; nor, indeed, was there any room here for the art of composition. The landscape is too monotonous and the groups too scattered for any possibility of pictorial effect, and we must content ourselves with a picture to be seen at close hand on a drawing-room wall. Mr. Johnson has a curious inability to maintain a quiet chord of color, or of tone, we must rather say, for colorist he is none. Here he refuses to let the eye rest anywhere, much less does he compel it by strong or gentle means, to rest in one spot: he scatters his colors, as he does his glints of sunlight, all over the canvas, and as we can make out nothing at a distance, so when we come near we enjoy most the imaginary parcelling out of the picture into a number of smaller ones, each a clever study in its way.
"National Academy of Design. Fifty-Fifth Annual Exhibition. (Third Article)," *The New-York Daily Tribune,* 18 April 1880.

Mr. Eastman Johnson's "Cranberry Harvest—Island of Nantucket" is on exhibition at the National Academy of Design New York. The *Tribune* says, it is a cheerful companion piece to his "Corn Husking," now in the Art Gallery of the Metropolitan Museum, and shows the same qualities. There is here abundance of incident, much sparkling play of sunshine, and real people working in a real scene.
Inquirer and Mirror, 24 April 1880.

Eastman Johnson sends the "Cranberry Gatherers," a landscape speckled with groups in full sunshine, and in some respects a worthy successor to the noble "Corn Huskers," owned by Mr. Sarony; but it lacks the unity of arrangement seen in that work, and the glitter of full daylight has been less of an opportunity to the painter than was the tempered cloud-shadow of the former painting.
"Exhibition of the Academy of Design," *The Art Amateur* 2, no. 6 (May 1880): 112.

There were but few interesting figure or *genre* subjects in the exhibition apart from portraits properly so called. . . . Mr. Eastman Johnson's Cranberry Harvest was to be praised for everything except composition.
M[ariana] G[riswold] van Rensselaer, "Spring Exhibitions and Picture-Sales in New York.—II," *The American Architect and Building News* 7, no. 228 (8 May 1880): 201.

"Cranberry-Picking," which we engrave below, is a reminiscence of Nantucket. . . . Among the many subjects which he has painted at Nantucket none is more characteristic or agreeable than his "Cranberry-Picking." The cranberry of the United States is nearly the size of a cherry; it grows in marshes and peat-lands, and is allied to the *Oxycoccus palustris* of Europe. It is greatly valued in America as a sauce, having a pleasant tartness; the time of gathering it is in autumn, and, like hop-picking in En-

gland, the business is made the occasion of much mirth and love-making. In his picture the artist has admirably represented this familiar scene. The colour is rich and harmonious, and the landscape is suffused by the mild glow of an autumnal afternoon.
S. G. W. Benjamin, "A Representative American," *The Magazine of Art* 5 (1882): 489.

Mr. Johnson has also painted several subjects drawn from rural life in his native Maine and at Nantucket, where for several years past he has had a summer home. His "Sugar Camp—Boiling-day" and "The Husking-bee" were subjects found in Maine, while "The Cranberry-pickers" . . . is a page of life at Nantucket.
Clarence Cook, *Art and Artists of Our Time,* 3 vols. (1888; New York: Garland Publishing, 1978), 3:263.

"The Cranberry Harvest," "The Peddler," "Fiddling his Way," "The Old Stage-Coach," "What the Shell Says," "Two Men," and "The Pension Agent," are some of the pictures that have made his [Johnson's] fame as a painter, and have given him popularity.
William A. Coffin, " 'The Century's' American Artist Series. Eastman Johnson," *The Century Magazine* 48, no. 6 (October 1894): 958.

Appendix 3: The Johnsons as Property Owners on Nantucket

Included in this section are summaries of the real estate transactions involving Eastman and Elizabeth Williams Johnson from 1871 to Eastman Johnson's death in 1906, arranged chronologically by transaction date. All information comes from the record books maintained by the Nantucket Registry of Deeds. The entries' format is: date of transaction; seller/purchaser; price; acquisition. Date recorded by Nantucket registrar of deeds. Book, page [Nantucket Registry of Deeds].

14 April 1871; William C. and Susan C. Dorman/Eastman Johnson; $450.00; for land with dwelling house bounded on North Street. Recorded 20 April 1871. 61, 248.

17 April 1871; Henry Coleman/Eastman Johnson; $250.00; land with buildings, adjacent to above, including the premises formerly known as the "Jethro Coffin estate." Recorded 21 April 1871. 61, 252.

31 May 1871; Eastman Johnson/Frederick C. Sanford; $1.00; land with buildings on North Street (as above total), in trust to convey same to Elizabeth Williams Johnson. Recorded 6 June 1871. 61, 292.

31 May 1871; Frederick C. Sanford/Elizabeth Williams Johnson; $1.00; land with buildings on North Street (as above). Recorded 6 June 1871. 61, 293.

18 November 1872; Henry Coleman/Elizabeth Williams Johnson; $50.00; for land (40 rods) adjacent to above. Recorded 18 November 1872. 62, 160.

28 October 1880; Henry Coleman/Elizabeth Williams Johnson; $10.00; for land (strip 4 to 7 feet wide) adjacent to Johnson property. Recorded 28 October 1880. 66, 200.

26 October 1881; Charles H. Robinson/Elizabeth Williams Johnson; $700.00; for land (Clifton Springs, lots 25, 26) bounded and described as corner of Lincoln and Indian Avenue, 280′ north to corner along Indian Ave., 100′ SE, 267′ S to Lincoln Ave., 100′ W along Lincoln Ave. to point of beginning. Recorded 21 November 1881. 66, 539.

26 October 1881; Alfred Swain/Elizabeth Williams Johnson; $30.00; for land (Clifton Springs) between lots 25, 26 and the sea. Recorded 21 November 1881. 66, 540.

12 November 1881; Josiah C. Gardner/Eastman Johnson; $600.00; land (26 acres in Wannacomet, including Reed Pond lot and land from there to sea) north of the highway. Recorded 16 December 1881. 66, 561.

17 November 1881; George W. Macy/Eastman Johnson; $10.00; 2 sheep commons. Recorded 18 November 1881. 66, 536.

28 November 1881; Henry Coleman/Elizabeth Williams Johnson; $12.00; four sheep commons. Recorded 28 November 1881. 66, 546.

30 November 1881; George W. Macy/Elizabeth Williams Johnson; $50.00; 10 sheep commons. Recorded 10 December 1881. 66, 556.

16 December 1881; Common land equivalent to 6 sheep commons set off for Eastman Johnson. Recorded 16 December 1881. 66, 562.

16 December 1881; Andrew M. Myrick/Elizabeth Williams Johnson; $40.00; 8 sheep commons. Recorded 19 December 1881. 66, 567.

19 December 1881; George W. Macy/Elizabeth Williams Johnson; $1.00 and other valuable considerations; 70 sheep commons. Recorded 20 December 1881. 66, 573.

21 December 1881; Mary Rawson, Sarah A. Coffin, Charlotte Luce, Eliza C. Bates, Phebe Bunker, George Rawson, and Charles W. Rawson/Elizabeth Williams Johnson; $28.33; $5\frac{2}{3}$ sheep commons. Recorded 4 February 1882. 67, 35.

22 December 1881; George R. Coffin, Charles H. Gardner, Grafton Gardner, and Ann Coffin/Elizabeth Williams Johnson; $10.00 and other considerations; $5\frac{2}{3}$ sheep commons. Recorded 6 January 1882. 67, 8.

22 December 1881; Mary C. Stickney and Lydia C. Folger/Elizabeth Williams Johnson; $10.00 and other valuable considerations; $5\frac{2}{3}$ sheep commons. Recorded 6 January 1882. 67, 9.

17 January 1882; Andrew M. Myrick/Eastman Johnson; $120.00; 24 sheep commons. Recorded 25 January 1882. 67, 22.

27 February 1882; Andrew M. Myrick/Eastman Johnson; $50.00; 10 sheep commons. Recorded 27 February 1882. 67, 58.

1 April 1882; Amelia M. Coffin, Peter M. Coffin, and George W. Coffin/Eastman Johnson; $75.00 and other considerations; $15\frac{1}{4}$ sheep commons. Recorded 10 May 1882. 67, 142.

4 September 1882; Henry Coleman/Eastman Johnson; $125.00; land (Wannacomet, 9 acres) bounded on north and west by Coleman heirs, south by highway, east by Eben McHinckley. Recorded 6 September 1882. 67, 322.

4 September 1882; Henry Coleman, Ann Abbott, and Sarah Ellis/Eastman Johnson; $600.00; land (Wannacomet, 30 acres) bounded on east by Eben Hinckley and Coleman, south Coleman and highway to Wannacomet waterworks, west Eastman Johnson, north the sea. Recorded 6 September 1882. 67, 323.

4 September 1882; George W. Macy/Eastman Johnson; $1.00 and other considerations; 40 sheep commons. Recorded 26 September 1882. 67, 384.

23 September 1882; Henry Coffin, Alfred Swain, Matthew Barney, Charles H. Robinson, Jane C. Perry, Frederick G. Coffin, Charles H. Coffin, Abbott Coffin, and Mary C. Greene/Elizabeth Williams Johnson; $1.00 and other considerations; land (Sherburne Bluffs, blocks M, N, Q, P, and AA). Recorded 23 December 1882. 67, 536.

25 September 1882; Elizabeth Williams Johnson/Caroline McGuffy and Laurence Laughlin; $1.00; right of way through Sherburne Bluffs. Recorded 22 August 1883. 68, 305.

9 October 1882; Proprietors set off tract of common land for Elizabeth Williams Johnson (Wannacomet, 30 acres, 42.95 rods surrounding Capaum Pond) in exchange for 30 sheep commons. Recorded 10 October 1882. 67, 426.

9 October 1882; Charles H. Robinson/Elizabeth Williams Johnson; $1.00 and other considerations; land (Clifton Springs, No. 2, lots 22, 23, 24). Recorded 25 December 1882 and 31 July 1883. 68, 267.

16 October 1882; Charles C. Mooers/Eastman Johnson; $500.00 and other considerations; land (2 tracts at North Shore near the Cliff); 1, beginning at east corner of Johnson's land northeast 370′ to North Beach St, NW 660′ to land of Gibbs, SW 350′ along Gibbs's border, SE 609′ to beginning; 2, 60′ x 359′ along Cliff Avenue. Recorded 14 December 1882. 67, 519.

31 October 1882; Proprietors set off tract of common land for Elizabeth Williams Johnson (Wannacomet, 3 acres, 146.17 rods) in exchange for 4 sheep commons. Recorded 31 October 1882. 67, 473.

October 1882; Proprietors of Sherburne Bluffs have agreed to sell land between Central Avenue and Hamblin's, from Indian to Atlantic Avenue, to Elizabeth Williams Johnson. She agrees to provide roads in lieu of Central Avenue for allowing others access to land between Central Ave. and the sea. Recorded 16 December 1882. 67, 525.

14 November 1882; Henry Gardner Bridges and Mary Ann Bridges/Eastman Johnson; $2100.00; two parcels of land near the Cliffs ($985\frac{28}{100}$ rods and $181\frac{28}{100}$ rods). Recorded 13 July 1885. 70, 20.

20 November 1882; Proprietors set off tract of common land for Elizabeth Williams Johnson (Wannacomet, 1 acre, 25 rods) in exchange for 1 sheep common. Recorded 21 November 1882. 67, 482.

20 November 1882; Franklin H. Delano/Eastman Johnson; $1.00 and other considerations; land (2 tracts at North Shore near the Cliff): 1 (ca. $\frac{1}{2}$ acre), bound to west by North Street, north by Congdon, east by Delano, south by Delano, Folger, and Elizabeth Williams Johnson; 2, 403′ x 100′ on North Street. Recorded 14 December 1882. 67, 520.

18 December 1882; Charles H. Robinson/Elizabeth Williams Johnson; $1.00 and other considerations; a tract of land (Clifton Springs #2, lots 16 [+ dwelling house], 17 18); starting Lincoln and Beach, SW along Beach 202′ to Clifton, NW 210′, NE 200′ to Lincoln, SE 191′. Recorded 22 December 1882. 67, 534.

22 January 1883; Sherburne Bluffs Company/Eastman Johnson; $1.00 and other good and valuable considerations; a tract of land along the Cliff known as Sherburne Bluffs (approximately 32 acres and 49 rods, minus land already sold from parcel). Recorded 16 February 1883. 68, 32.

7 February 1883; Proprietors/Elizabeth Williams Johnson; 34 sheep commons; 34 acres and 34 rods land (Trott's Hills). Recorded 5 January 1884. 68, 522.

16 March 1883; Eastman Johnson/R. Gardner Chase; $1.00 and other valuable considerations; land from Delano and Mooers. Recorded 16 April 1883. 68, 125.

23 July 1883; Elizabeth Williams Johnson and Eastman Johnson/Isabella Connolly Chalfin; $1.00 and other good considerations; land (Clifton Springs, No. 2, lot 16). Recorded 6 October 1883. 68, 424.

1 October 1883; Henry Coffin, Alfred Swain, Matthew Barney, Charles H. Robinson, Jane C. Perry, Frederick G. Coffin, Charles H. Coffin, Abbot Coffin, and Mary C. Greene/Eastman Johnson; $1.00 and other good and valuable consideration; land near the Cliff (279′ x 214½′ x 279′ x 214½′). Recorded 24 October 1883. 68, 462.

10 October 1883; Elizabeth Williams Johnson/Charles O'Conor; $1.00 and divers other considerations; land (Clifton Springs, between lots 25 and 26 and the sea). Recorded 19 November 1883. 68, 485.

10 October 1883; Eastman Johnson/Charles O'Conor; $1.00 and other divers consideration; land near the Cliff (32 acres and 49 rods). Recorded 19 November 1883. 68, 489.

26 November 1883; Charles O'Conor/Elizabeth Williams Johnson; $1.00; land (Sherburne Bluff, lots 7 and 11). Recorded 26 November 1883. 68, 496.

25 February 1886; Eastman Johnson and Elizabeth Williams Johnson/Fanny B. Workman; $1.00; land near the Cliff (3.941 acres). Recorded 13 March 1886. 70, 402.

24 September 1887; Elizabeth Williams Johnson/Henry Coleman; $1.00 and other considerations; 4 sheep commons. Recorded 1 October 1887. 71, 572.

4 October 1887; Eastman Johnson/William H. Workman; $1.00 and other considerations; land near the Cliff (Sherburne Bluffs). Recorded 5 October 1887. 71, 572.

4 January 1888; Maria T. Swain/Eastman Johnson; $1.00 and other considerations; land near the Cliff. Recorded 1 January 1889. 73, 27.

4 and 12 January 1888; Eastman Johnson and Maria T. Swain exchange tracts of land. Recorded 13 February and 3 May 1888. 72, 170; 72, 254.

3 July 1888; Eastman Johnson/Elvira H. Bullock; $1.00 and other valuable considerations; land near the Cliff. Recorded 7 July 1888. 72, 326.

4 October 1888; Nathaniel W. Jenkins/Eastman Johnson; $1.00 and other valuable considerations; land, dwelling house and buildings on North Street. Recorded 15 May 1889. 73, 182.

6 March 1890; Judith C. Folger/Eastman Johnson; $1.00 and other considerations; land, dwelling house, and buildings on North Street. Recorded 23 April 1890. 74, 74.

21 April 1890; Eastman Johnson/Judith C. Folger; $1,000.00; land, dwelling house, and other buildings on North Street. Recorded 23 April 1890. 74, 75. See also 74, 337.

1 July 1890; Eastman Johnson/Frederick Hopkins; $1.00 and other valuable considerations; 80 sheep commons. Recorded 11 July 1890. 74, 251.

1 July 1890; Eastman Johnson and Elizabeth Williams Johnson/Frederick S. Hopkins; $1.00 and other valuable considerations; 32 sheep commons. Recorded 25 July 1890. 74, 280.

10 July 1890; Eastman Johnson/William H. Macy; $1.00 and other considerations; 8 sheep commons. Recorded 10 July 1890. 74, 248.

10 July 1890; William H. Macy/Elizabeth Williams Johnson; $1.00 and other consid-

erations; 8 sheep commons. Recorded 10 July 1890. 74, 248.

19 October 1894; Elizabeth Williams Johnson and Eastman Johnson/Ellenwood B. Coleman; $1.00 and other considerations; land north of Trott's Hills. Recorded 12 December 1906. 87, 449.

15 November 1897; George O. Wales/ Elizabeth Williams Johnson; $300.00; land on North Beach Street. Recorded 20 November 1897. 80, 403.

17 October 1898; Maria T. Swain/Eastman Johnson; $1.00 and other considerations; a small piece of land near the west end of North Beach Street. Recorded 20 December 1898. 81, 278.

4 August 1903; Elizabeth Williams Johnson/ Charles P. Howland; $100.00 and other valuable considerations; land on North Beach Street. Recorded 11 August 1903. 85, 220.

4 August 1903; Charles P. Howland/ Eastman Johnson; $100.00 and other valuable considerations; land on North Beach Street. Recorded 11 August 1903. 85, 221.

15 August 1903; Eastman Johnson and Elizabeth Williams Johnson/Franklin Folger; $1.00 and other consideration; 9 1/4 sheep commons. Recorded 15 August 1903. 85, 225.

2 November 1903; Elizabeth Williams Johnson and Eastman Johnson/Allan B. Fay; $1.00 and other valuable considerations; land (2 tracts "Sherburne Bluffs," lots 7 and 11). Recorded 10 November 1903. 85, 350.

Bibliography

Eastman Johnson was one of the principal American artists of the nineteenth century, recognized and successful in his day. Despite the fact that he has a place in nearly every written history of American art, the monographic literature on him is extremely limited. A handful of articles from the turn of the century, obituary notices, and the catalogue of the studio sale in 1907 are the major sources of information. Every student of Johnson is, therefore, obligated to the groundbreaking work on the artist of the late John I. H. Baur (1940) and the more recent explorations of Patricia Hills (1972, 1977). Their writings set forth the outline of the career, establish the major works, and pose the questions that today still seem most relevant. Professor Hills is currently at work on a catalogue raisonné of Johnson's works.

BOOKS AND PERIODICALS

Adams, G. E., and L. H. Bailey. "Turkeys and Cranberries." *Country Life in America* 3 (November 1902): 7–10.

"Artist Biography: French." *The Crayon* 7, no. 6 (June 1860): 168

"The Artists' Fund Exhibition." *The Evening Post,* 14 November 1863.

Asterisk. "The Cranberry and Its Allies." *Once a Week* 9 (22 August 1863): 232–34.

Austin, Jane G. *Nantucket Scraps.* Boston: James R. Osgood, 1883.

Baird, Henry M. "Nantucket." *Scribner's Monthly* 6, no. 4 (August 1873). 385–99.

Baur, John I. H. *Eastman Johnson, 1824–1906: An American Genre Painter.* Exh. cat. Brooklyn: Brooklyn Museum, 1940.

Benjamin, S. G. W. "A Representative American." *The Magazine of Art* 5 (1882): 485–90.

Benson, Eugene. "Eastman Johnson." *The Galaxy* 6, no. 1 (July 1868): 111–12.

[Bertauts-Couture, G.]. *Thomas Couture: Sa Vie, son oeuvre, son caractère, ses idées, sa méthode, par lui-même et par son petit-fils.* Paris: Le Garrec, 1932.

Bliss, William Root. *September Days on Nantucket.* Boston: Houghton, Mifflin and Company, 1902.

"The Blodgett Paintings." *The New-York Times,* 20 April 1876.

Boime, Albert. *The Academy and French Painting in the Nineteenth Century.* London: Phaidon, 1971.

———. "Current and Forthcoming Exhibitions." *The Burlington Magazine* 112, no. 810 (September 1970): 646–51.

———. *Thomas Couture and the Eclectic Vision.* New Haven and London: Yale University Press, 1980.

Breton, Jules. *The Life of an Artist: An Autobiography.* Translated by Mary J. Serrano. New York: D. Appleton and Company, 1890.

Burns, Sarah. *Pastoral Inventions: Rural Life in Nineteenth-Century American Art and Culture.* Philadelphia: Temple University Press, 1989.

Byers, Edward. *The Nation of Nantucket: Society and Politics in an Early American Commercial*

Center, 1660–1820. Boston: Northeastern University Press, 1987.

Catalogue . . . of Oil Paintings, Formerly the Private Collection of W. P. Wright, Esq., of New Jersey. Sale cat. New York: Henry H. Leeds & Miner, 18 March 1867.

Champney, Lizzie W. "The Summer Haunts of American Artists." *The Century Magazine* 30, no. 6 (October 1885): 845–60.

Coffin, Marie M. *The History of Nantucket Island: A Bibliography of Source Material.* Nantucket, Mass.: Nantucket Historical Trust, 1970.

Coffin, William A. "Eastman Johnson: The Century's American Artist Series." *The Century Magazine* 48, no. 6 (October 1894): 958.

Cook, Clarence. *Art and Artists of Our Time.* Vol. 3. New York: Selmar Hess, 1888.

Cook, R. H. *Historical Notes of the Island of Nantucket and Tourist's Guide.* Nantucket, Mass.: Privately printed, 1871.

Couture, Thomas. *Conversations on Art Methods.* Translated by S. E. Stewart. New York: G. P. Putnam's Sons, 1879.

Cowdrey, Mary Bartlett. *American Academy of Fine Arts and American Art-Union: Exhibition Record, 1816–1852.* New York: The New-York Historical Society, 1953.

[______]. *National Academy of Design Exhibition Record, 1826–1860.* 2 vols. New York: Printed for The New-York Historical Society, 1943.

"Cranberry Culture." *The Land We Love* 4, no. 2 (December 1867): 156–58.

de Crèvecoeur, J. Hector St. John. *Letters from an American Farmer and Sketches of Eighteenth-Century America.* Edited by Albert E. Stone. New York: Penguin Books, 1981.

Crosby, Everett U. *Eastman Johnson at Nantucket.* Nantucket, Mass.: Privately printed, 1944.

Denison, Rev. Frederic. *Illustrated New Bedford, Martha's Vineyard, and Nantucket.* Providence, R.I.: J. A. and R. A. Reid, 1879.

diCurcio, Robert A. *Art on Nantucket: The History of Painting on Nantucket Island.* Nantucket, Mass.: Nantucket Historical Association in cooperation with the Nantucket Historical Trust, 1982.

Douglas-Lithgow, R. A. *Nantucket: A History.* New York: G. P. Putnam's Sons, 1914.

Drake, W. B. "Nantucket." *Lippincott's Magazine* 2, no. 15 (September 1868): 283–92.

"Editor's Easy Chair." *Harper's New Monthly Magazine* 33, no. 193 (June 1866): 117.

Executor's Sale of the Collection of Paintings Belonging to the Estate of the Late Wm. T. Blodgett. Sale cat. New York: Chickering Hall, 27 April 1876.

"A Feast for Art Lovers." *The New-York Times,* 28 April 1876.

Fidell-Beaufort, Madeleine, and Jeanne K. Welcher. "Some Views of Art Buying in New York in the 1870s and 1880s." *Oxford Art Journal* 5, no. 1 (1982): 48–55.

"Fine Arts: Pictures on Exhibition." *The Nation* 4, no. 84 (7 February 1867): 114.

Fink, Lois Marie. "French Art in the United States, 1850–1870: Three Dealers and Collectors." *Gazette des beaux-arts,* n.s. 6, 92, no. 1316 (September 1978): 87–100.

[Folger, Isaac H.]. *Handbook of Nantucket, containing a Brief Historical sketch of the Island, with Notes of Interest to summer visitors.* Nantucket, Mass.: Island Review, 1875.

French, Edgar. "An American Portrait Painter of Three Historical Epochs." *The World's Work* 13, no. 2 (December 1906): 8307–23.

G. "Exhibition of Fine Arts in Paris." *The Crayon* 2, no. 19 (7 November 1855): 295.

Garland, Catherine A. *Nantucket Journeys.* Camden, Me.: Down East Books, 1988.

Gemming, Elizabeth. *The Cranberry Book.* New York: Coward-McCann, 1983.

Gibbons, Marianna. "Old Nantucket." *Lippincott's Magazine* 28 (September 1881): 303–10.

Godfrey, Edward K. *The Island of Nantucket, what it was and what it is; being a complete index and guide to this noted resort.* Boston: Lee and Shepard, 1882.

Hartmann, Sadakichi. "Eastman Johnson: American *Genre* Painter." *The International Studio* 34, no. 134 (April 1908): 106–11.

Healy, George P. A. *Reminiscences of a Portrait Painter.* 1894. Reprint. New York: Kennedy Graphics, Inc./Da Capo Press, 1970.

Herbert, Robert L. "City vs. Country: The Rural Image in French Painting from Millet to Gauguin." *Artforum* 8, no. 6 (February 1970): 44–55.

Hills, Patricia. *Eastman Johnson.* Exh. cat. New York: Clarkson N. Potter in association with the Whitney Museum of American Art, 1972.

———. *The Genre Painting of Eastman Johnson: The Sources and Development of His Style and Themes.* New York: Garland Publishing, 1977.

Holt, Elizabeth Gilmore. *The Art of All Nations, 1850–1873: The Emerging Role of Exhibitions and Critics.* Garden City, N.Y.: Anchor Books, 1981.

Hoyt, Edwin P. *Nantucket: The Life of an Island.* Brattleboro, Vt.: Stephen Greene Press, 1978.

Johnston, Patricia Condon. *Eastman Johnson's Lake Superior Indians.* Afton, Minn.: Johnston Publishing Inc., 1983.

Johnston, William R. *The Nineteenth-Century Paintings in the Walters Art Gallery.* Baltimore, Md.: Trustees of the Walters Art Gallery, 1982.

Keck, Sheldon. "The Technical Examination of Paintings: Its Uses and Limitations in Art Criticism." *Brooklyn Museum Journal* 1 (1942): 71–82.

King, Edward. "The Value of Nationalism in Art." *The Monthly Illustrator* 4, no. 14 (June 1895): 265–68.

Koehler, S. R. *American Art.* New York: Cassell & Company, 1887.

Lancaster, Clay. *Nantucket in the Nineteenth Century.* New York: Dover, 1979.

Landgren, Marchal E. *American Pupils of Thomas Couture.* Exh. cat. College Park: University of Maryland Art Gallery, 1970.

Lights and Shadows of New York Picture Galleries: Forty Photographs, by A. A. Turner, Selected and Described by William Young. New York: D. Appleton and Company, 1864.

Low, Will H. *A Chronicle of Friendships, 1873–1900.* New York: Charles Scribner's Sons, 1908.

Low, Will H., Carroll Beckwith, Samuel Isham, and Frank Fowler. "The Field of Art: Eastman Johnson—His Life and Works." *Scribner's Magazine* 40, no. 2 (August 1906): 253–56.

Ludlum, Stuart D., ed. *Exploring Cape Cod/Exploring Nantucket.* Utica, N.Y.: Brodock & Ludlum, 1973.

McCalley, John W. *Nantucket: Yesterday and Today.* New York: Dover, 1981.

Macmillan, Rev. Hugh. "The Cranberry." *Good Words* 43 (September 1902): 661–66.

Macy, Obed. *The History of Nantucket with a Concise Statement of Prominent Events from 1835 to 1880, by William C. Macy.* 2d ed., 1880. Reprint. Ellinwood, Kans.: Macys of Ellinwood, 1985.

Macy, William F. *The Nantucket Scrap Basket: Being a Collection of Characteristic Stories and Sayings of the People of the Town and Island of Nantucket, Massachusetts.* 2d ed., 1930. Reprint. Ellinwood, Kans.: Marshall S. Macy, 1984.

———. *The Story of Old Nantucket: A Brief History of the Island and its People from its Discovery down to the Present Day.* 2d ed., 1928. Reprint. Ellinwood, Kans.: Macys of Ellinwood, 1983.

"Making a Cranberry Bog." *Harper's Weekly* 29, no. 1503 (10 October 1885): 670.

Mandel, Patricia C. F. "Selection VII: American Paintings from the Museum's Collection, c. 1800–1930," *Bulletin of Rhode Island School of Design, Museum Notes* 63, no. 5 (April 1977): 158–63.

Mead, Katherine Harper, ed. *The Preston Morton Collection of American Art.* Santa Barbara: Santa Barbara Museum of Art, 1981.

Meixner, Laura L. "Popular Criticism of Jean-François Millet in Nineteenth-Century America." *The Art Bulletin* 65, no. 1 (March 1983): 94–105.

Minturn, R. R. "Nantucket." *The Lakeside Monthly* 10, no. 56 (August 1873): 140–44.

Murphy, Alexandra R. *Jean-François Millet.* Exh. cat. Boston: Museum of Fine Arts, 1984.

Nantucket Guide 1989. Nantucket, Mass.: Deborah M. Anderson, 1989.

"The National Academy of Design: Forty-First Annual Exhibition." *The New-York Daily Tribune,* 4 July 1866.

Naylor, Maria K., comp. and ed. *The National Academy of Design Exhibition Record, 1861–1900.* 2 vols. New York: Kennedy Galleries, Inc., 1973.

Nordhoff, Charles. "Cape Cod, Nantucket, and the Vineyard." *Harper's New Monthly Magazine* 51, no. 301 (June 1875): 52–66.

Northrup, A. Judd. *'Sconset Cottage Life: A Summer on Nantucket Island.* New York: Baker, Pratt & Co., 1881.

"Obituary: William Tilden Blodgett." *The New-York Times,* 6 November 1875.

"Obituary: William P. Wright." *The New-York Times*, 8 July 1880.

Overton, Frank. "Three Hundred Dollars an Acre from Cranberries." *Country Life in America* 11 (November 1906): 71–72.

P. "Country Correspondence." *The Crayon* 5, no. 9 (September 1858): 269–70.

"Pictures at the Exposition." *The Atlantic Monthly* 42, no. 245 (December 1878): 707–17.

Poulet, Anne L., and Alexandra R. Murphy. *Corot to Braque: French Paintings from the Museum of Fine Arts, Boston*. Exh. cat. Boston: Museum of Fine Arts, 1979.

Robinson, N. "The Islands of the Bay State." In *Exploring Cape Cod/Exploring Nantucket*. Edited by Stuart D. Ludlum. Utica, N.Y.: Brodock & Ludlum, 1973.

Selby, Mark. "An American Painter: Eastman Johnson." *Putnam's Monthly* 2, no. 5 (August 1907): 533–42.

Sheldon, G. W. *American Painters*. 1881. Reprint. New York: Benjamin Blom, 1972.

———. *Hours with Art and Artists*. New York: D. Appleton, 1882.

———. *Recent Ideals of American Art*. New York: D. Appleton and Co., 1888.

"Sketchings: Domestic Art Gossip." *The Crayon* 6, no. 10 (October 1859): 320.

"Sketchings: Domestic Art Gossip, New York." *The Crayon* 7, no. 3 (March 1860): 84.

Spassky, Natalie. *American Paintings in The Metropolitan Museum of Art*. Vol. 2. New York: The Metropolitan Museum of Art in association with Princeton University Press, 1985.

Springfield, Mass. *Enrollment of the Volunteers: Thomas Couture and the Painting of History*. Exh. cat. Museum of Fine Arts. 1980.

Starbuck, Alexander. *The History of Nantucket, County, Island, and Town*. 1924. Reprint. Rutland, Vt.: Charles E. Tuttle, 1969.

Stark, Louise. "Early Nantucket Artists." *Historic Nantucket* 6, nos. 1 (July 1958): 12–24; 2 (October 1958): 28–39; and 4 (April 1959): 8–17.

Stebbins, Theodore E., Jr. *American Master Drawings and Watercolors*. New York: Harper & Row, 1976.

Stebbins, Theodore E., Jr., Carol Troyen, and Trevor J. Fairbrother. *A New World: Masterpieces of American Painting, 1760–1910*. Exh. cat. Boston: Museum of Fine Arts, 1983.

Sterling, Charles, and Margaretta M. Salinger. *French Paintings: A Catalogue of the Collection of The Metropolitan Museum of Art*. Vol. 2. New York: The Metropolitan Museum of Art, 1966.

Strahan, Edward [Earl Shinn]. *The Art Treasures of America*. 3 vols. Ca. 1879–1882. Reprint. New York: Garland Publishing, Inc., 1977.

Strother, D. H. "A Summer in New England [Third Paper]." *Harper's New Monthly Magazine* 21, no. 126 (November 1860): 745–63.

"A Studio in Paris." *The Crayon* 1, no. 18 (2 May 1855): 281.

Sturges, Hollister, et al. *Jules Breton and the French Rural Tradition*. Exh. cat. Omaha, Nebr.: Joslyn Art Museum in association with The Arts Publisher, Inc., New York, 1982.

Sturges, Hollister, ed. *The Rural Vision: France and America in the Late Nineteenth Century*. Omaha, Nebr.: Joslyn Art Museum, 1987.

"Ten Days in Nantucket." *The Granite Monthly* 8, nos. 7 and 8 (July–August 1885): 215–25.

Tomkins, Calvin. *Merchants and Masterpieces: The Story of The Metropolitan Museum of Art*. New York: E. P. Dutton, 1970.

Tuckerman, Henry T. *Book of the Artists: American Artist Life*. 1867. Reprint. New York: James F. Carr, 1966.

Walton, William. "Eastman Johnson, Painter." *Scribner's Magazine* 40, no. 3 (September 1906): 263–74.

"Warning to City Visitors." *Harper's Weekly* 21, no. 1079 (1 September 1877): 685, 690.

Weisberg, Gabriel P. *The Realist Tradition: French Painting and Drawing, 1830–1900*. Exh. cat. Cleveland, Oh.: Cleveland Museum of Art in cooperation with Indiana University Press, 1980.

Whittredge, Worthington. *The Autobiography of Worthington Whittredge, 1820–1910*. Edited by John I. H. Baur. 1942. Reprint. New York: Arno Press, 1969.

The Works of the Late Eastman Johnson, N.A. Sale cat. New York: American Art Galleries, 1907.

Worth, Henry Barnard. *Nantucket Lands and Land Owners*.

Nantucket, Mass.: Nantucket Historical Association, 1906.

Yarnall, James L., and William H. Gerdts, comps. *The National Museum of American Art's Index to American Art Exhibition Catalogues, from the Beginning through the 1876 Centennial Year.* 6 vols. Boston: G. K. Hall & Co., 1986.

MANUSCRIPT AND UNPUBLISHED SOURCES

Archives of American Art, Smithsonian Institution. Jervis McEntee diary, 1872–1890. Roll D180.

Archives of American Art, Smithsonian Institution. Marie de Mare Papers. Roll D130.

Archives of American Art, Smithsonian Institution. Misc. MSS: Eastman Johnson. Roll D10.

Archives of American Art, Smithsonian Institution. Misc. MSS: Jervis McEntee, Gift of Charles E. Feinberg. Roll D30.

Archives of American Art, Smithsonian Institution. Misc. MSS: Robert Graham Collection of Autograph Letters. Roll D294.

Curatorial records. Eastman Johnson, *The Wounded Drummer Boy.* Frick Art Museum, Pittsburgh, Penn.

Hirschl, Norman. "Eastman Johnson: Forerunner of Homer and Eakins." Typescript exh. cat. New York: Frederic Frazier, Inc., [1937].

Nantucket Registry of Deeds. 1865–1912. Nantucket Town Building, Nantucket, Mass.

NEWSPAPERS AND SELECTED PERIODICALS, WITH DATES CONSULTED

The Academy. New York. 1880.
The American Architect and Building News. New York. 1880.
American Art Journal (Watsons Weekly). New York. 1880.
The American Art Review. Boston. 1880.
The Art Amateur. New York. 1880.
The Art Interchange. New York. 1880.
The Art Journal. New York. 1880.
Boston Evening Transcript. Boston. 1880.
The Evening Post. New York. 1880.
Inquirer and Mirror. Nantucket, Mass. 1870–1880.
Island Review. Nantucket, Mass. 1874–1878.
Nantucket Journal. Nantucket, Mass. 1878–1879.
New York Commercial Advertiser. New York. 1880.
New-York Daily Tribune. New York. 1880.
New York Herald. New York. 1880.
The New-York Times. New York. 1880.
The Sun. New York. 1880.
The World. New York. 1880.

Checklist of the Exhibition

Note: *Titles listed are those given by the current owners of the objects. As far as we know, with the exception of* The Cranberry Harvest, Island of Nantucket *itself, Johnson himself did not title these works. Although none but the Timken Art Gallery's painting is dated, it seems that the remaining works can safely be assigned to ca. 1879.*

1. *The Cranberry Harvest, Island of Nantucket,* 1880
Oil on canvas
27 3/8 x 54 1/2 inches
(69.5 x 138.4 cm)
Signed and dated lower right: *E. Johnson 1880.*
Timken Art Gallery, Putnam Foundation Collection

2. *Cranberry Harvest*
Oil on board
9 1/4 x 8 1/4 inches (sight)
(23.5 x 21 cm)
Initialed lower left: *E. J.*
Kenneth Lux Gallery, New York

3. *The Cranberry Pickers*
Oil on board
13 1/2 x 17 1/4 inches
(34.3 x 43.8 cm)
Not signed
Philadelphia Museum of Art, Gift of Mr. and Mrs. Arthur U. Crosby

4. *Study for "Cranberry Pickers"*
Oil on board
12 1/2 x 22 inches (31.7 x 55.9 cm)
Initialed lower left: *E. J.*
Childs Gallery, New York & Boston

5. *Cranberry Pickers*
Oil on board
3 13/16 x 7 3/4 inches (9.7 x 19.7 cm)
Initialed lower right: *E J*
The Ackland Art Museum, The University of North Carolina at Chapel Hill, Gift of Mr. and Mrs. Norman Hirschl, NYC

6. *Cranberry Pickers—Study*
Oil on board, with pencil sketches of cranberry harvesters on verso
11 3/8 x 22 inches (28.9 x 55.9 cm)
Initialed lower right: *E J*
Washington University Gallery of Art, St. Louis, University purchase, Parsons Fund, 1963

7. *The Conversation*
Oil on board
22 1/2 x 26 1/2 inches
(57.1 x 67.3 cm)
Initialed lower right: *E. J.*
Addison Gallery of American Art, Phillips Academy, Andover, Massachusetts

8. *Cranberry Pickers*
Oil on board
19 x 29 inches (48.3 x 73.7 cm)
Initialed lower right: *E. J.*
Private collection

9. *Cranberry Pickers*
Oil on board
22 1/2 x 26 3/4 inches
(57.1 x 67.9 cm)
Initialed lower right: *E. J.*
Private collection

10. *Cranberry Pickers*
Oil on canvas
27 x 54 1/8 inches
(68.6 x 137.5 cm)
Not signed
Yale University Art Gallery, Bequest of Christian A. Zabriskie

11. *Cranberry Pickers*
Oil on board
$19\frac{3}{4}$ x 30 inches (50.2 x 76.2 cm)
Initialed lower right: *E. J.*
Private collection

12. *Cranberry Pickers in Nantucket*
Oil on canvas

27 x $43\frac{1}{2}$ inches
(68.6 x 110.5 cm)
Not signed
Art Museum, Arizona State University, Tempe, Gift of Oliver B. James

13. *In the Fields*
Oil on board
$17\frac{3}{4}$ x $27\frac{1}{2}$ inches
(45.1 x 69.9 cm)
Initialed lower right: *E. J.*
Detroit Institute of Arts, Founders Society Purchase, Dexter M. Ferry Fund

14. *Cranberry Pickers, Nantucket*
Oil on canvas
19 x $43\frac{1}{4}$ inches
(48.3 x 109.9 cm)
Initialed lower right: *E. J.*
Manoogian Collection